" # Economic Adjustment and Political Transformation in Small States

# Economic Adjustment and Political Transformation in Small States

Erik Jones

OXFORD
UNIVERSITY PRESS

**OXFORD**
UNIVERSITY PRESS

Great Clarendon Street, Oxford OX2 6DP

Oxford University Press is a department of the University of Oxford.
It furthers the University's objective of excellence in research, scholarship,
and education by publishing worldwide in

Oxford New York

Auckland Cape Town Dar es Salaam Hong Kong Karachi
Kuala Lumpur Madrid Melbourne Mexico City Nairobi
New Delhi Shanghai Taipei Toronto

With offices in

Argentina Austria Brazil Chile Czech Republic France Greece
Guatemala Hungary Italy Japan Poland Portugal Singapore
South Korea Switzerland Thailand Turkey Ukraine Vietnam

Oxford is a registered trade mark of Oxford University Press
in the UK and in certain other countries

Published in the United States
by Oxford University Press Inc., New York

© Erik Jones 2008

The moral rights of the author have been asserted
Database right Oxford University Press (maker)

First published 2008

All rights reserved. No part of this publication may be reproduced,
stored in a retrieval system, or transmitted, in any form or by any means,
without the prior permission in writing of Oxford University Press,
or as expressly permitted by law, or under terms agreed with the appropriate
reprographics rights organization. Enquiries concerning reproduction
outside the scope of the above should be sent to the Rights Department,
Oxford University Press, at the address above

You must not circulate this book in any other binding or cover
and you must impose the same condition on any acquirer

British Library Cataloguing in Publication Data
Data available

Library of Congress Cataloging in Publication Data
Data available

Typeset by SPI Publisher Services, Pondicherry, India
Printed in Great Britain
on acid-free paper by
Biddles Ltd., King's Lynn, Norfolk

ISBN 978–0–19–920833–3

1 3 5 7 9 10 8 6 4 2

For Una, Isak, Jakob, and Sara

# Contents

*List of Figures* viii
*List of Tables* ix
*List of Abbreviations* x
*Preface* xiii
*Acknowledgments* xvi

Introduction 1

1. The Politics of Economic Adjustment 27

2. Consensual Adjustment in Consociational Democracy 81

3. The Implications of Change 139

4. "Consensual" Adjustment in Post-Consociational Democracy 165

Conclusion 207

*Notes* 225
*References* 250
*Index* 273

# List of Figures

| | |
|---|---|
| 4.1. Primary fiscal balances | 177 |
| 4.2. Adjusted wage share in manufacturing | 178 |
| 4.3. Belgian real Deutschemark exchange rates | 179 |
| 4.4. Dutch real Deutschemark exchange rates | 180 |
| 4.5. Belgian real guilder exchange rates | 182 |
| 4.6. Satisfaction with democracy | 200 |
| C.1. Relative real unit labor costs versus EU 15 | 212 |
| C.2. Net exports | 213 |
| C.3. Gross public debt | 214 |
| C.4. Primary fiscal balances | 215 |
| C.5. Long-term interest rate differentials with Germany | 217 |

# List of Tables

| | |
|---|---|
| 2.1. The regional structure of Belgium (1947–9) | 116 |
| 3.1. Various indicators of fiscal stance | 151 |
| 4.1. Average annual productivity growth (percent) | 183 |
| 4.2. Medium-term exchange rate variability (1961–89) | 192 |
| 4.3. Inflation performance (1972–89) | 194 |
| 4.4. Deutschemark exchange rate variability (1975–93) | 195 |
| 4.5. The regional structure of Belgium (1993–5) | 203 |

# List of Abbreviations

## General

| | |
|---|---|
| EC | European Community |
| ECOFIN | Council of Economics and Finance Ministers |
| ECSC | European Coal and Steel Community |
| ECU | European Currency Unit |
| EDC | European Defence Community |
| EEA | European Economic Area |
| EEC | European Economic Community |
| EFTA | European Free Trade Association |
| EMS | European Monetary System |
| EPC | European Political Community |
| ERM | Exchange Rate Mechanism |
| EU | European Union |
| EU 15 | fifteen member states of the European Union (post 1994) |
| GATT | General Agreement on Tariffs and Trade |
| GDP | Gross Domestic Product |
| GNP | Gross National Product |
| IMF | International Monetary Fund |
| NAFTA | North American Free Trade Association |
| OECD | Organisation for Economic Co-operation and Development |
| OUP | Oxford University Press |
| UK | United Kingdom |
| US | United States |

# List of Abbreviations

# Belgium

| | |
|---|---|
| ABVV | Algemeen Belgisch Vakverbond |
| ACV | Algemeen Christelijk Vakverbond |
| ACW | Algemeen Christelijk Werknemersverbond |
| CCI | Comité Central Industriel |
| CD&V | Christen-Democratisch en Vlaams |
| CDH | Centre Démocrate Humaniste |
| CRB | Centrale Raad voor het Bedrijfsleven |
| CSC | Confédération des Syndicates Chretiens |
| CVP | Christelijke Volkspartij |
| FDF | Front Démocratique des Bruxellois Francophones |
| FGTB | Fédération Générale du Travail de Belgique |
| FIB | Fédération des Industries de Belgique |
| JET | Jeugd, Ekonomie, Toekomst |
| MOC | Mouvement Ouvrier Chrétien |
| PLP | Parti de la Liberté et du Progrès |
| PRL | Parti Réformateur Libéral |
| PSC | Parti Social-Chrétien |
| PVV | Partij voor Vrijheid en Vooruitgang (Belgium) |
| RW | Rassemblement Wallon |
| VB | Vlaams Blok, later Vlaams Belang |
| VBN | Verbond der Belgische Nijverheid |
| VLD | Vlaams Liberalen en Democraten |
| VU | Volksunie |

# Netherlands

| | |
|---|---|
| ARP | Anti-Revolutionaire Partij |
| CDA | Christen Democratisch Appel |
| CHU | Christelijke Historische Unie |
| CNV | Christelijk Nationaal Vakverbond |

## List of Abbreviations

| | |
|---|---|
| CSWV | Centraal Sociaal Werkgeversverbond |
| D66 | Democraten '66 |
| EVC | Eenheidsvakcentrale |
| FNV | Federatie Nederlandse Vakbeweging |
| KAB | Katholieke Arbeidersbeweging |
| KVP | Katholieke Volkspartij |
| NVV | Nederlands Verbond van Vereniging |
| PvdA | Partij van de Arbeid |
| PVV | Partij voor de Vrijheid (Netherlands) |
| SP | Socialistische Partij |
| VNO | Verbond van Nederlandse Ondernemingen |
| VVD | Volkspartij voor Vrijheid en Democratie |
| WAO | Wet op de Arbeidsongeschiktheidsverzekering |

# Preface

When I first went to Belgium and the Netherlands in the late 1980s, what struck me most was how conservative both countries were. Everyone I knew who had been there always described them as liberal in the relaxed and tolerant sense. That was not what I saw. The people were unbelievably charming, cultured, and polite. But their tolerance was for foreigners and they never appeared too relaxed among themselves. Of course it may be that I saw only what I wanted to see. Having grown up in the American South and Southwest—at a time when adults did not have first names and when parents were known affectionately as Sir and Ma'am—I was well tuned to look for social rules. Certainly, it was not hard to find them. Along the way, I also began to note the subtle distinctions between West and East, North and South, Catholic and Protestant, oui (ooay) and oui (hwee), and hard "g" and soft. These discoveries made the two countries much more attractive. They were not blandly tolerant; they were complicated and diverse.

Almost as soon as I started to become familiar with the formal complexity of the Belgian and Dutch societies, I began to see how things were fraying at the edges as well. Older generations were more tightly wedded to tradition while younger generations were more open to change. There was nothing unique in this pattern and it was not exactly uniform either. The generation gap was a cliché that never fit anywhere well. Belgium and the Netherlands were no exception. I knew young people in Flanders who grew up speaking French and others who were passionately *flamingante*. And I ran into plenty of Dutch people in the Randstad who were

## Preface

eager to point out to me which of my friends—by surname—must be Catholics from the South.

Even so, the process of value change from one generation to the next seemed unusually disruptive. That was when I learned about the literature on consociational democracy and depillarization. It did not take me long to realize that I was witnessing the passage from one system to another. The traces of the old consociational framework remained while the forces for a new and more pluralist order spread ever more widely.

Every school child in Belgium and the Netherlands learns about the demise of consociational democracy. You can even find words like *verzuiling* and *ontzuiling*—pillarization and depillarization—printed in the daily newspaper. The implications are less well understood. You can see them in relations between one generation and another, but they are elsewhere as well. The changing structure of society is weakening the bonds between politicians and voters, it is changing attitudes toward trade unions and employers' associations, it is diluting the "message" in the media, and it is fostering more diversity in the schools. Moreover, the change in society is both cause and effect. As traditional attitudes give way, the pace of social change in Belgium and the Netherlands accelerates. If he were alive today, the Nobel prize-winning economist and sociologist Gunnar Myrdal would probably describe the process as cumulatively causal. The point is not that the more things change, the more they stay the same; it is that change begets change.

This book starts from just one of the possible implications. My question is: How does the change in social organization in Belgium and the Netherlands affect the possibilities for economic policymaking? The question is important because both countries are so small, so densely populated, and so open to world market forces. When things go wrong and economic policymaking breaks down, there is literally nowhere to run. So far the record for both countries is mixed. They have done well, but they have also done badly. Even when they did badly, however, they came out of it pretty well. You can find some weak spots in the data and some dodgy neighborhoods in the big cities, but by and large they are nice places to live.

It took me a short time to answer my question and a long time to develop the argument. The answer is that the political transformation of the two countries is constraining the possibilities for economic adjustment. The Belgians and the Dutch could do things in the past that they can no longer do today. Both countries are more vulnerable economically as a result. The argument explains why that should be the case. That is what the rest of this book is about.

EJ

# Acknowledgments

The research presented here was possible because of the generous financial support of two organizations: the Tri-lateral Commission for Educational Exchange (Fulbright Commission) between the United States, Belgium, and Luxembourg, and the Belgian-American Educational Foundation. Institutional support was provided by the Centre for European Policy Studies, the University of Nottingham, and the SAIS Bologna Center of the Johns Hopkins University. At different times and in different ways, I benefited greatly from the advice and guidance of David Calleo, Georges Delcoigne, Daniel Gros, Paul Heywood, and Patrick McCarthy. My research assistants over the years have been another source of invaluable support. Particular thanks go to Kimberly De'Liguori Carino for helping me to complete and copy-edit the initial draft.

A number of colleagues read the manuscript in whole or in part. They all deserve thanks and recognition. Some, however, went well beyond the call of community. In particular, I should thank Peter Katzenstein, Paulette Kurzer, Jonathon Moses, Jurg Steiner, and Steven Wolinetz for their patience and generosity over the years. I also thank Dominic Byatt and the referees commissioned by Oxford University Press (OUP) for their constructive and meticulous work. They urged me to bring a greater coherence to the manuscript, and so if my argument makes sense they deserve the lion's share of the credit.

## Acknowledgments

This book is dedicated to my wife Una and our children Isak, Jakob, and Sara. As is so often the case, I could not have written it without their support. But perhaps a better way of putting it is that they will be happier than anyone to see it finally in print.

EJ

# Introduction

National responses to economic change depend to a great extent upon the characteristic features of national politics. For example, Belgium and the Netherlands used to be described as consociational democracies. This means that while Belgian and Dutch societies were deeply fragmented across ideological or religious cleavages, political elites in both countries strove to form broad consensual governments. As a result, Belgium and the Netherlands typically responded to economic change through negotiated solutions that share the burdens of adjustment (lost incomes, unemployment, bankruptcy, and so on) across society. Two examples of such consensual adjustment are the Dutch price–incomes policies of the 1950s and the Belgian modernization program of the 1960s. In these cases, broad coalition governments headed by confessional and socialist elites had employers and unemployed workers accept income losses in order to put the unemployed back to work and, ultimately, to raise the purchasing power of labor income.[1]

As a more pluralist democracy, the United States has tended toward a different pattern of adjustment. Americans are no less diverse in their interests than the Belgians or the Dutch, but American society does not possess the same deep cleavages found in the Low Countries. Americans typically engage in a wide variety of interest groups, which are generally without a fixed or comprehensive ideological framework. Political elites compete for followers and are challenged to find solutions suitable to a majority of the electorate. Therefore, a pluralist democracy like the United States responds to economic change in the interests of an aggregated majority, and often forces the burdens of adjustment on political minorities. Here an example might be the Reaganomics of the early 1980s, where tax cuts and increased defense spending brought the US economy out of recession while at the same time increasing income disparities across socioeconomic groups.

Generalizations about the relationship between national politics and economic adjustments offer a sense of orderliness in a world that has witnessed bewildering economic change over the past decades. In spite of oil price shocks, fluctuations in the dollar, third world competition, or what have you, different types of democracies will tend to offer particular types of solutions. The Swedes will continue to adhere to an extreme form of social democracy, the Americans will rely on a combination of labor mobility and entrepreneurial spirit, and so on. Perhaps the balance between labor and capital, wages and profits, social protection and deregulation will change, but the characteristic attitudes and actions of different countries will remain just that—characteristic.

Unfortunately for those who appreciate an orderly world, however, countries are beginning to depart from their characteristic adjustment patterns.[2] They may not be becoming more like one another. But they are becoming different from what they used to be. Belgium and the Netherlands were textbook examples of consociational democracy in the 1950s and 1960s, but while they may be divided, they are no longer so stable. Instead, political volatility has risen to unprecedented levels in both countries. The Dutch populist Pim Fortuyn based much of his electoral platform on the rejection of consensus, both in economics and elsewhere. At the same time, right-wing Flemish extremists promote a chauvinistic view of the state's role in managing the economy.[3]

Of course, the problem is to assess how important are current phenomena as indicators of change. Fortuyn's political movement imploded soon after the assassination of its leader and virtually the whole of the Belgian political spectrum rejects the Flemish Interest. Nevertheless, the evidence for changing patterns of economic and political performance runs deep. The economic adjustment strategies adopted at the start of the 1980s in both Belgium and the Netherlands were sponsored by narrow center-right coalition governments that appeared to be more interested in shoring up corporate profits than in sharing the burdens of adjustment across societal cleavages or socioeconomic groups.[4] It was only in the mid-1990s that analysts reinterpreted the Dutch model as being a consensual one. Even then, moreover, the effectiveness of the "polder" model as a consensual adjustment strategy remained controversial.[5] There was no such confusion in Belgium—and particularly not in Flanders. If anything, Belgian political elites sought to distance themselves from both the rhetoric and the practice of consensus in favor of a more vaguely defined notion of "political renewal."[6]

How can we explain this change from the consensual adjustment strategies of the 1950s and 1960s to the more majoritarian strategies of the 1980s and afterwards? One possible answer is that political institutions in Belgium and the Netherlands have changed during the postwar period. Students of comparative politics often refer to institutional factors—electoral systems, constitutional frameworks, party systems, and the like—as the primary determinants of consensual or majoritarian behavior. According to Arend Lijphart, proportional representation, separation of powers, federalism, and multiparty systems give rise to consensual behavior, while plurality elections, concentration of powers, centralism, and two-party systems tend to support majoritarian behavior. Therefore, it may be possible that changes in the political institutions of Belgium and the Netherlands resulted in a change in their adjustment strategies. The problem is that the pattern of institutional development is the opposite of what we should expect. Political institutions in the two countries should show more majoritarian features over time. Instead, Lijphart argues that successive rounds of constitutional decentralization have made Belgium more consensual in character rather than less since the end of World War II. Lijphart's analysis is confirmed by Peter Mair, who adds that Dutch political institutions have become less

# Introduction

consensual only in comparison with other countries and not in comparison with their own past.[7] Thus institutions may explain why Belgium and the Netherlands behaved differently than other countries during the 1980s—a position argued forcefully by Paulette Kurzer—but they cannot explain why Belgian and Dutch adjustment strategies have changed over time.[8]

A second explanation for the change in economic adjustment strategy lies in the change in economic circumstances. It is possible that a particular economic challenge such as rising unemployment denies a characteristically national solution. Belgium and the Netherlands could not repeat their consensual adjustment strategies during the 1980s because sharing the burdens of adjustment was not economically viable. Here the empirical record is only partly supportive. A difference in economic situation between the 1950s and 1960s on the one hand, and the 1980s on the other hand, should explain the nature of an economic adjustment, but not its political character. In fact, the opposite seems to be true. In the 1950s and 1960s, broad center-left coalitions in the Netherlands and Belgium relied on a combination of price–incomes policies and trade liberalization for their macroeconomic adjustment. In the 1980s, narrow center-right coalitions in Belgium and the Netherlands relied on price–incomes policies and exchange rate stabilization for macroeconomic adjustment. The change in economic circumstances across the postwar period can explain the changeover from trade liberalization to exchange rate stabilization. It is harder to believe, however, that changed economic circumstances can explain either the shift to the center-right or the reliance on narrow-majority coalitions.

If we are to explain the change in Belgian and Dutch economic adjustment strategy, we need to seek causality in some transformation of national politics in the two countries. Here there are two complementary lines of inquiry—one focusing on ideas, the other on behavior. The argument about ideas has gained considerable traction in the literature.[9] In essence, the claim is that political entrepreneurs have been able to take advantage of the unexpected

## Introduction

turmoil of the 1970s to promote a new way of understanding the possibilities for economic policymaking. Within this new approach, the only reasonable choices for policymakers are those that favor the interests of capital as opposed to labor. Hence, the center-right dominates the management of economic policy through the force of neoliberal economic ideology even though center-right politicians represent the interests of at best a small majority (and most likely a minority) of the population.[10]

The possibility that neoliberal ideas were the key to changing economic adjustment strategies in the Low Countries is intriguing but unconvincing. Mainstream economics changed a lot as a social science during the 1970s and early 1980s, and with important implications for policymaking. Yet the political significance of that change was less in some countries than in others. Margaret Thatcher and Ronald Reagan may indeed have ushered in a conservative revolution in Britain and the United States during the early 1980s. But there was little that was revolutionary in the economic ideas that were put forward in Belgium and the Netherlands during that same period. Policymakers in both countries and from all parts of the political spectrum have long held the economic views that are today considered neoliberal. Hence, there was no room for ideological conversion. By the same token, it is hard to see how changing economic ideas can explain a shift from left to right or from broad consensus to a narrower majority.[11]

Emphasis on the role of economic ideas is not only unconvincing but also unnecessary. The changeover from consensual to majoritarian economic adjustment strategies can be explained as a result of changes in elite behavior and national political cultures. Consociational democracy nurtured one pattern of economic adjustment. The end of consociational democracy gave rise to another. As elites became more competitive and political cultures less fragmented, Belgian and Dutch adjustment strategies took on more majoritarian than consensual attributes. Ironically, the forces at work owed much more to the end of ideology than to its reinvigoration by the center-right. Once ideological bonds weakened within political parties, the prospects for managing

# Introduction

consensus between them weakened as well. Politicians faced the unenviable challenge of holding onto the support of their core constituencies while at the same time competing for a growing and amorphous electoral center. In this way, politics polarized between right and left.[12] Both a rise in electoral volatility and a more majoritarian approach to economic adjustment strategies were the result.

## So What?

This argument about the changeover from more consensual to more majoritarian adjustment strategies in Belgium and the Netherlands is important because it underscores the limits of small country success in world markets. The claim is not that Belgium and the Netherlands have abandoned consensus altogether. Rather my concern is that their capacity for consensus-building is deteriorating over time.

To understand the significance of this point, it is necessary to make a short digression starting with three seminal contributions to the literature about small states. The first is by Arend Lijphart.[13] Lijphart wanted to explain the anomalous stability of deeply fragmented societies in small advanced industrial states. He sketches a solution in his work on consociational democracy and *The Politics of Accommodation*. Essentially, he describes how elites can cooperate across vertically integrated subnational political cultures existing within the same national space. Hence, although the countries are socially fragmented, they are politically consensual. The constant pursuit of elite consensus in turn explains the stability of the country as a whole. The model is somewhat complicated and it will be presented in greater detail later on in this introduction. Here it is only necessary to consider three aspects. Such "consociational" democracies are at the same time fragmented and inclusive. They can operate only where subnational political cultures are tight and coherent. And they succeed only so long as no particular group is left out.

# Introduction

The second contribution is by David Cameron.[14] Cameron explains how small open economies respond to the challenges posed by the internationalization of economic activity through the development of redistributive mechanisms in the welfare state (or public economy). Such mechanisms work to stabilize economic performance in the face of external, stochastic shocks. In this way, small states are able to sustain political support for extensive interaction between the national economy and the outside world. Cameron hypothesizes that the growth of the public economy is due in part to the strength of subnational functional actors—such as employer associations or trade union confederations—each of whom is eager to secure insulation from the influence of the global market economy. Since such functional interest groups tend to be better organized in smaller countries, the public economies of smaller countries tend to be larger as well.

These two arguments—by Lijphart and Cameron—are not necessarily interdependent. Consociational democracies can exist without extensive welfare states and the reverse. Nevertheless, there is a clear potential for complementarity between the two different patterns of small state development. Inclusive and yet fragmented consociational democracies could encourage the formation of industrial concentrations and powerful national trade union federations. They could also foster the development of generous welfare-state institutions. Similarly, big welfare states could be useful mechanisms for maintaining peace between different groups in consociational democracies.

The third aspect of this literature is from Peter Katzenstein.[15] Katzenstein focuses on the juxtaposition of the contributions made by Lijphart and Cameron. Katzenstein's argument is that small states are consensual because they are exposed to world market forces and because politicians in small countries are aware of the vulnerability that such exposure implies.[16] Hence, consensual politics is a rational act of national self-preservation. This sense of vulnerability also explains the heavy participation in policymaking by representatives of organized capital and labor. In other words, small states are not only consensual but also corporatist. Moreover,

7

## Introduction

these small, consensual, and corporatist states have well-developed public economies as a result of successive reactions to world market forces. Small states are also welfare states. Finally, these small, consensual, and corporatist welfare states actively engage in the process of international economic liberalization and international integration through institution-building. Hence, they are not only small because they are exposed, they are exposed because they are small.

The contributions by Lijphart, Cameron, and Katzenstein have had very different fates. As mentioned, Lijphart's original consociational democracy, the Netherlands, ceased to function along consociational lines. Indeed, the breakdown can be traced back to the same time period in which Lijphart formulated his original argument. Hence, while scholars—including, but not limited to, Lijphart himself—have sought to expand the application of consociational democracy as a model to cases such as Northern Ireland, Bosnia, or even India, analysis of consociationalism in Europe has become predominantly an exercise in political history.

Cameron's work on small welfare states has also been challenged by subsequent events. The spread of economic interdependence and particularly the liberalization of capital flows undermined the complementarities between economic performance and welfare-state development. Whether through higher taxes or more rigid labor markets, the fear is that more generous welfare states will lower investment by giving domestic capital an incentive to flee and foreign investors a reason to look elsewhere. Much of this analysis has focused on a different conclusion made by Cameron in his original article. Cameron noted that social democratic governments tend to have larger public economies than right-leaning governments in the larger European countries. Analysts now consider what room for maneuver is left for the political left.[17] This debate about international restrictions on "social democracy" has clear implications for the smaller countries as well.

Meanwhile, Katzenstein's thesis about small states and world markets remains relatively unchallenged.[18] Writers like Anton Hemerijck and Herman Schwartz have explored episodes in which

## Introduction

small states have run into big trouble.[19] And yet most analysts remain comfortable with the core propositions of the Katzenstein thesis:

- small states are more consensual because they are more vulnerable to world market forces (and because they are aware of that vulnerability);
- small states shore up consensus through the elaboration of corporatist practices and welfare-state institutions;
- small states use these corporatist practices and welfare-state institutions to help extend their exposure to world markets through multilateral liberalization and international institution-building; and
- greater exposure not only encourages greater consensus but also provides the resources for greater redistribution.

The experience of the Dutch polder model in the mid-to-late 1990s seems to bear out the wisdom of this "small states in world markets" perspective. Not only did the Dutch succeed in preserving consensus well beyond the formal practice of consociational democracy, but they also managed to use that consensus to facilitate welfare-state reform, enhance international competitiveness, support further integration in world markets and European institutions, and engineer an economic miracle.

Events since the 1990s point in a different direction. The recent record of political turmoil gives reason to doubt the underlying stability of consensus politics in the Netherlands. The advent of Pim Fortuyn and the aftershocks of the May 2002 elections make it possible to believe that Dutch politics has somehow changed fundamentally. The simultaneous and sudden deterioration of Dutch economic performance is at least suggestive of the possibility that political instability might have important economic effects. However, all of this leaves open the prospect that the Dutch are simply the odd man out among the smaller welfare states of Europe—and that given enough time the logic of small states and world market will reassert itself. In this scenario, Pim Fortuyn is an unfortunate exogenous shock disturbing an otherwise happy equilibrium. And once (or even if) things settle down a bit in the political arena, it will be back to business as usual in the Netherlands.

A similar point can be made about Belgium. Political instability has been on the rise in that country as well. However, while much of the conflict in Belgium centers on economic concerns, it plays out between rival linguistic groups. Such linguistic diversity is not a common feature in small countries and so, in this sense at least, Belgium may be just another exception to the rule.

## The Argument

The more dangerous possibility is that political instability and economic conflict are somehow endogenous to the practice of consensual adjustment. National responses to economic change do depend on the characteristic features of national politics. But national economic adjustment strategies can contribute to forces that threaten to alter the characteristic features of national politics as well. More simply: economic adjustment encourages political transformation. Katzenstein suggests that such transformation is supportive, and self-consciously so. Small states learn from experience to trust in the virtues of consensual adjustment.[20] Fortuyn's anti-consensus rhetoric suggests otherwise, as does the similar experience of Belgium.

My argument in this book is that consensual adjustment strategies are self-destructive even when they succeed in fostering economic adjustment. The causal mechanism I focus on runs from consensual adjustment to political instability. Small states react to international vulnerability by forging consensus. But over time, the citizens of small states begin to chafe under the discipline that such consensual politics implies. Once they throw off the discipline of consensus at home, their vulnerability to world markets reveals itself in force. Politicians used to promoting adjustment with broad-based popular support are unable to act effectively without it. Moreover, economic and political actors are not alone

## Introduction

in this exposure. Welfare-state institutions are affected as well. An institution that plays an important redistributive function in one context may emerge as a powerful constraint on competitiveness in another. Rather than serving as bulwarks for political consensus, welfare-state institutions become focal points for political conflict.

This mechanism rests on two observations. The first is that when the political culture of a society changes, relations between political elites will adapt to reflect the new political culture. By the late 1960s, the traditional cleavages in the Netherlands had given way to a more homogenous political culture. The process was no different from the "end of ideology" and the "transformation of West European party systems" that had been experienced elsewhere.[21] But the implications were nevertheless important. Dutch elites became less concerned with forming broad national coalitions, and more active in competing for the support of the majority of voters. The softening of traditional cleavages occurred in Belgium as well, although it was obscured by the intensification of linguistic conflict between the Dutch-speaking Flemings and French-speaking Walloons. This linguistic conflict divided Dutch-speaking and French-speaking elites, who attempted to recreate consociational systems within their respective language communities. Such decentralization only changed the venue for political transformation from the national to the regional level. As traditional political cleavages softened, the Flemish and Walloon societies became more homogenous. In turn, Belgian political elites became more competitive within the confines of their language groups.

The second observation concerns the willingness of elites to cooperate with one another. When relations between political elites break down due to a change in the structure of political competition, national governments may not be able to respond to economic change. Economic adjustment strategies are difficult to design and implement even in a stable political environment. When elites no longer agree on the rules for decision-making, forging an effective adjustment strategy is nearly impossible. Belgium

# Introduction

and the Netherlands went through a period of elite conflict during the 1970s and early 1980s. Consequently, both countries had difficulty adapting to the collapse of the Bretton Woods system, the twin oil price shocks, and the many other factors of economic change that rocked the world economy.

At the start of the 1980s, however, political elites in both Belgium and the Netherlands engineered complex strategies for economic reform. So, was this a restoration of consensus or a last gasp of the small state model? Here we need to go through the mechanisms in somewhat greater detail. Specifically, the goal is to unpack different processes of change and to link them back together.

## The Need for Adjustment

The principal challenge facing policymakers in Belgium and the Netherlands at the end of the 1970s was unemployment. Therefore, the first step is to examine why so many people were out of work, and why the numbers grew so sharply. The most common explanation is that European unemployment in the late 1970s and early 1980s stemmed from a decline in employment opportunities. Jobs disappeared because workers became too expensive. Consequently, either there were no jobs or there were no jobs that people were willing to accept—given any possible level of consumer demand for production. As workers became more expensive than machines, producers bought more machines and hired fewer workers.

Nevertheless, the rise in unemployment did not spark a fall in the relative cost of labor. Powerful trade unions and welfare-state legislation protected real (price-deflated) wage levels and sometimes even accelerated real wage growth. Inevitably, producers were forced to respond to rising wage claims by raising prices where it was possible to do so and cutting costs where it was not. When nonlabor costs could not be cut—as often was the case in the traded-goods sector—the result was bankruptcy. In this way, price rises in the service sector nurtured inflation while bankruptcies in the traded-goods sector fed unemployment. Whether indirectly via wage costs or directly via business failure, the problem of unemployment worsened.[22]

In outline form, this explanation is accepted by a majority of economists in both Belgium and the Netherlands.[23] Wage explosions in the 1960s and early 1970s started the accelerating rise in labor costs that resulted in an explosion of unemployment in the early 1980s. The difficulty for policymakers, however, is that the effects of high real wages describe only the process that created unemployment. It is a mechanism without being a cause.[24] Going any deeper into the roots of the unemployment dilemma uncovers an explosive political debate between professional economists.[25] Thus, while it is possible to offer a synthesis of many different hypotheses regarding the emergence of unemployment, it is necessary to concede that such a synthesis might not find support from a majority of economists in either country.

The first point to consider is why workers began making wage claims that were "too high." In the Netherlands, workers in the early 1960s claimed higher wages because trade unions argued that Dutch pay scales were low internationally and out of proportion with respect to labor productively across sectors. Union leaders claimed that too long a reliance on price–incomes policies had resulted in substantial distortions of the labor market. These claims were supported by both government and industry, which saw rising wages as a means to encourage productivity increases and to loosen excessively tight labor market conditions. This so-called wage "explosion" of the early 1960s was originally intended as a labor market corrective, by redistributing scarce labor resources to where they could be most productive.[26]

The Belgian situation during the early 1960s was slightly different. Belgian wages were internationally high and labor productivity was generally low. Belgian elites competed across the Church–state divide during the 1950s and consequently had been unable to generate nationwide cooperation in economic policymaking. Thus Belgium had not enjoyed effective control over wage

## Introduction

growth during the first decades of the postwar period. In the early 1960s, government and industry asked trade unions to make wage claims in the context of a larger program for industrial modernization. Their objective was not only to increase productivity but also to provide more jobs. Belgian trade unions ultimately accepted the need for wage restraint, but soon struggled to recapture forgone incomes. Wage explosions in Belgium occurred in the late 1960s and early 1970s and followed the longest period of productivity growth in that country's postwar history.

The second consideration is why industry began substituting machines for labor. Here again subtle differences emerge between the Dutch and Belgian cases. Dutch manufacturers turned to capital-intensive production in order to escape reliance on labor inputs which—because of the distortions introduced by the price–incomes policies of the 1950s—were at the same time cheap and scarce. Belgian manufacturers looked to machines as the building blocks for modernization. Since Belgian workers were already expensive internationally, export manufacturers needed to increase labor productivity in order to compete abroad. Trade unions in both countries accepted that better machines were the essential counterpart to higher wages in the medium and long term. Given historically tight labor market conditions, the problem of unemployment received little or only periodic consideration.

The third consideration is why workers continued to make excessive wage claims even as economic performance deteriorated. Unemployment became a politically important problem in Belgium and the Netherlands by the start of the 1970s. Nevertheless, wages continued to rise in international terms as well as in relation to the cost of machinery. Although the Belgian and Dutch economies were in different positions during the 1960s, they converged on the common dilemma of accelerating labor costs and burgeoning unemployment by the early 1970s.

Part of the explanation for excessive wage claims during the 1970s is a gradual change in the politics of trade unions. Specifically, trade unions became increasingly concerned with the needs of the employed rather than the needs of the working population as a whole. Union representatives were willing to fight for real wage increases even if it meant a marginal increase in the rate of unemployment.[27]

Another part of the explanation for continuing wage increases lies in the functioning of the welfare state. Social welfare legislation supported trade unions in their efforts to secure real wage increases: price-indexed minimum wages set a minimum standard for collective bargaining, while income maintenance programs established a basic wage below which employment was financially less attractive than government support—at least until a better-paying job could be found.[28]

The increasing complexity of productive machinery also, ironically, increased the power of trade unions to secure real wage raises. Companies using complicated machines had to rely on highly skilled employees and therefore required costly training programs. Few such companies could afford to fire workers who had already received expensive training, nor could they afford to train workers whom they did not need. Companies could not lower wages because workers might accept a better-paying job elsewhere or else they might lose enthusiasm for their jobs and work less productively with their very expensive machines. Therefore, management was more willing to accept wage increases rather than face worker defection or discouragement.

Capital modernization also exacerbated the growth of unemployment. Unemployed workers found the increasing use and complexity of machines to be a growing impediment to finding a job: not only were the jobless less and less qualified to work with successively more complicated machinery, but they had to accept starting salaries low enough to compensate for the cost of their training. As training became more expensive, starting salaries declined.[29]

Already by the early 1970s a curious dynamic was at work in Belgium and the Netherlands as they converged on the mutual dilemma of accelerating wage growth and rising unemployment. Unemployed workers were willing to look longer for better

15

## Introduction

employment and industries made openings less interesting by lowering starting wages in order to compensate for the cost of training. Job aspirants became more choosy and starting positions less attractive. The result was an increase in both the number of unemployed and the number of unfilled employment vacancies.[30] Meanwhile, the trade unions continued to battle for higher wages on behalf of members who already had jobs, and employers preferred to pay for wage rises rather than assume the burden of hiring someone new. By this line of reasoning, the reversal of price–wage restraint practiced in the Netherlands during the 1950s and in Belgium during the 1960s had set in motion a chain of events which, for a variety of reasons already described, drove up unemployment levels even under the best of circumstances.[31]

The circumstances were hardly the best. The collapse of the Bretton Woods system and the first oil price shock simultaneously accelerated domestic inflation, flattened foreign demand for exports, and squeezed corporate profitability. Although unemployment already threatened the Belgian and Dutch economies, the oil shock made a threefold contribution to the problem. First, the increase in energy prices fuelled the further growth of labor costs. Second, it sapped the market for manufacturing output while straining the financial ability of corporations to keep the labor force at work. Third, and most important, the oil price rise shattered whatever consensus remained in either country about the link between rising labor productivity and increasing real wages. Industry focused on energy efficiency as the primary concern for investment, and labor looked to rising wages as only fair compensation for the higher price of heating and transport fuel.[32]

Developments similar to these occurred throughout most of the Organisation for Economic Co-operation and Development (OECD) countries, albeit to varying degrees. And it soon became clear that the standard instruments of fiscal, monetary, and exchange rate policy were insufficient to stabilize economic performance. By the early 1970s, government attempts to sustain employment levels through fiscal stimulus, throughout the

## Introduction

OECD but particularly in the United States, resulted in a general increase in the trend level of world inflation. Even countries that refrained from the counter-cyclical use of fiscal policy, like Germany, Belgium, and the Netherlands, faced the prospect of transmitted inflation via movements of international trade and capital. This transmitted inflation fed the growth of Belgian and Dutch labor costs through wage-indexation and collective bargaining.

During the mid-1970s, both Belgium and the Netherlands tried to stem "imported" inflation through the selective use of capital controls and by pegging their exchange rates to the Deutschemark. However, Belgian and Dutch hard-currency policies played an ambiguous role in the drama following the oil price shock. The monetary authorities of both countries did succeed in mitigating some of the inflationary impact of the oil price rise by holding to their Deutschemark pegs as the German currency appreciated in the period to 1976. Nevertheless, appreciating exchange rates exacerbated the problem of export competitiveness in the face of declining world markets. Hard-currency policies also drove a pricing wedge between industries that relied on foreign exports or competed with foreign imports and those that had little interaction with producers abroad. Traded-goods industries that were already suffering from the loss of price competitiveness could not pass the increase in energy prices or the increase in labor costs on to consumers. Industries that operated solely in domestic markets and with domestic competitors could and did. Price inflation within the service and non-traded-goods sectors of the Belgian and Dutch economies accelerated and, in doing so, exacerbated the upward pressure on wages.

These developments inevitably resulted in rising unemployment. Yet by the mid-1970s, unemployment was no longer linked to increasing labor productivity. Welfare-state outlays increased but government tax revenues did not. The governments of both Belgium and the Netherlands resorted to moderate fiscal stimulus in the aftermath of the 1975 global recession, but this did more to worsen government accounts than to stabilize output or

## Introduction

employment performance. As a consequence, government deficits and, in the case of Belgium, foreign borrowing began to have an adverse effect on domestic interest rates. When interest rates were low relative to Germany, they undermined the stability of the hard-currency policies. And, when real (price-deflated) interest rates were high, they increased the pressure on corporate and even government balances. The problem of low interest rates relative to Germany arose during the middle of the 1970s, and prevented either country from following the German revaluations after 1976. The problem of high and increasing real interest rates started in the late 1970s and early 1980s, and resulted in a wave of corporate bankruptcies as well as a self-propelled growth of public debt.

Yet in spite of the manifest problems in both economies, wage costs remained high and trade unions retained considerable power in collective bargaining. The trade unions continued to act in the interests of the employed rather than those of the working class more generally, both because the employed constituted the dues-paying membership and because faith remained in the soundness of the two welfare states. By the end of the 1970s, however, the downward pressure of unemployment on general wage levels began to take its toll. Real labor costs relative to other European countries declined marginally, starting in Belgium in 1977 and in the Netherlands in 1979. The second oil price shock temporarily reversed the downward trend in wages, and initiated a new upward price–wage spiral, but less so than in other countries. Even so, progress in real wage reduction was too slow to sustain corporate profits, and the renewed growth of energy prices, in combination with a variety of other factors (rising interest rates and payroll taxes, declining export demand and market shares), sparked a massive burst of corporate bankruptcies and so-called "technical" unemployment. By the early 1980s, the unemployment situation in Belgium and the Netherlands reached crisis proportions.

The main focus for economic adjustment in Belgium and the Netherlands was the high level of unemployment. But unemployment was not the only problem. The two countries also had to contend with high government deficits, mounting public debts, and weakened control over domestic inflation. Economic analysis makes clear the corrections that were needed to restore the two economies to sound footing. First, Belgian and Dutch workers had to become less expensive in relation to foreign competitors. Second, Belgian and Dutch corporations had to return to profitability as a means both to sustain existing levels of employment and to invest in labor productivity and employment opportunities for the future. Third, the governments of Belgium and the Netherlands had to stabilize their own financial balances in order to alleviate the upward pressure on interest rates, to mitigate the tax burden on workers and employers alike, and to provide support for monetary and exchange rate policy.

These corrections took place by increments during the 1980s. Real labor costs plummeted at the start of the decade, corporate profitability improved, investment increased, the two governments marshaled control over their finances, although they scarcely began retiring outstanding public debt, and ultimately unemployment began to decline. Progress was slow but occurred similarly in the two countries: both Belgium and the Netherlands exhibited many of the classic symptoms of export-led growth.

The politics behind the adjustment process was less clear cut. Even under ideal circumstances, the economic crisis in Belgium and the Netherlands implied a political agenda of inordinate complexity. Building a consensus around real wage reductions, higher corporate profits, budgetary austerity, and disinflation is a tall order. At best, that order was only partly met in the early 1980s.

A transformation in the political organization for Belgium and the Netherlands paralleled and reinforced the problems facing their economies. The late 1970s and early 1980s were a period of indecision as well as dislocation. However, before there was recovery in economic performance there was an increase in political stability. Center-right coalitions led by Ruud Lubbers and Wilfried Martens generated narrow but effective majorities for rigorous austerity measures. While social scientists expressed concern

## Introduction

about authoritarian politicians manning an interventionist state, voters re-elected center-right coalitions that promised to continue austerity.[33]

## The Role of Consensus

The political changes taking place in Belgium and the Netherlands during the 1970s and early 1980s were not wholly created by the deterioration in economic performance. Rather, political instability resulted to a large extent from changing social values, such as the decline in religious devotion, and from the emergence of "new" political issues such as environmental protection. Changing political values were everywhere a destructive as well as a creative force. The May 1968 riots in France, the anti-Vietnam War movement in the United States, and the Green movement in Germany were all symptoms of what Ronald Inglehart terms "The Silent Revolution."[34]

Inglehart argues that the experience of prolonged prosperity removed strictly material concerns from the political agenda of young people. The generation that came of age during the economic miracle of the 1950s and 1960s was less concerned with class issues and financial security, and more concerned with quality of life. The post-materialist generation challenged political elites to address a wide variety of "new" issues such as environmental protection, family planning, and the like. Inglehart is careful to note that increasing economic security supported a gradual change in values throughout history, but is emphatic that the dramatic increase in material prosperity sparked a near-revolutionary change during the late 1960s and early 1970s. Moreover, as long as the postwar boom continued, electorates showed less concern with traditional materialist issues and greater enthusiasm for the emerging post-materialist agenda.

For most Western democracies, however, the change in social values during the 1960s and 1970s was alarming but not traumatic. The growing distance between elite and youth values did not deprive the political system either of its reason for being or of its "rules of the game." Because countries such as France, Germany, Great Britain, and the United States had largely pluralist political traditions, elites were more prepared to adapt to competition within a changing social environment.

In Belgium and the Netherlands, value change threatened the organization of society. The conflict in Belgium and the Netherlands was between the consociationalism that was and the pluralism that could be. Neither of these terms is a familiar subject of political dispute in most liberal democracies. In the United States, pluralism is the safeguard to liberty described in Madison's Federalist 10.[35] Madison argued that factions, which he understood to be "a number of citizens...who are united and actuated by some common impulse of passion, or of interest," would undermine the general good by bending the political process to the pursuit of their particular interest. Therefore, Madison believed that only a large union of diverse interests and ruled by elected representatives could overcome the disruptive influence of faction. Given a large enough political society, the particular interest of factions could not dominate the political process. Elected representatives would search for majorities across interest groups, and in doing so they would serve the general good.

For much of their history, the Belgians and the Dutch have looked at pluralism more skeptically. The tradition of elite-directed politics is stronger in both countries. The prevailing system of elites emerged during the transition to universal suffrage, and assumed a tight ideological framework for interest intermediation. Political scientists and sociologists argue that consociational systems were necessary to bridge the sharp cleavages existing within the two societies.[36] By the same token, the existence of competing ideological pillars is prerequisite to the functioning of consociational democracy. Some have even suggested that the ideological cleavages in Belgian and Dutch society are old enough and deep enough that conflict between them is more stabilizing than not. Like eccentric families, the two societies are happiest when quarrelling.

## Introduction

The consociational formulas in Belgium and the Netherlands are similar to each other: vertically integrated societies organized along ideological lines with overarching institutions able to facilitate negotiation and compromise by elites. The ideological components of this sociopolitical structure are familiar to any student of nineteenth-century European history. A Christian-Democratic group draws on the authority of the Catholic Church and, in the case of the Netherlands, the Protestant Reformation as well. A Liberal group accepts free-market traditions as an essential complement to its defining anticlericalism. And a Socialist movement struggles on behalf of the working classes while holding a rather skeptical opinion of Marxist-Leninist revolution and its anarcho-syndicalist variant.[37] Even within ideological clusters there are sharp divisions, as between Orthodox Reformed Protestants in the Netherlands and the less dogmatic Reformed or Catholic groups. In Belgium, there is a similar (sub-) division between the Jacobin-syndicalism of the Renardist branch of the General Federation of Belgian Trade Unions and the corporatist-reformism of the national federation's leadership.

In the "general model" for consociational democracy, each of the ideological groups is endowed with its own educational institutions; its own news media including papers, magazines, television, and radio stations; its own social groups such as marching bands and youth organizations; its own banks and credit institutions; its own health-care facilities; and, crowning it all, its own trade unions, employers' associations, and political party. In other words, these ideological groups are largely self-sufficient and self-contained. Although the members of different groups might share the same geographic space, they necessarily lead different lives. This explains why the formation of these ideological groupings is referred to as "pillarization" or, in Dutch, *"verzuiling."*[38]

Once established, these ideological pillars rely on a complex and authoritarian mechanism for the resolution of political disputes. Elites are expected to negotiate in the interests of the entire social pillar and nonelites are expected to accept the decisions of the leadership. For this to work, the pillars must be ideologically coherent, where ideology is understood to reflect a consistent system of values that allows for a high degree of predictability in decision-making. Elites must be ideologically rigid if they are to negotiate with the assurance that their followers will go along. Upward motion through the social pillar involves a continuous process of conditioning so as to strengthen the intergroup bargaining authority of group leaders.

What threatens the stability of Belgian and Dutch political life is not ideological conflict per se, but rather a breakdown of the structure for managing such conflict. This is where Inglehart's "Silent Revolution" comes into play. When there is a broad shift in societal values, particularly one creating a wedge between generations, the grass roots change but the political elites do not. In this sense, consociational democracy has a built-in weakness. Elites can be more flexible in dealing with their counterparts from other ideological groups than in dealing with their own followings. When elites have to accommodate their followers rather than each other, the process of decision-making between groups breaks down.

The system of ideological pillars only approached the ideal type described in theory during the 1940s and 1950s and arguably during the 1960s. Soon thereafter, the decline in religious devotion, the rise in standards of living, the spread of industrial democracy, and the softening of relations across the clerical–anticlerical divide began to take its toll on the discipline essential to vertical social organization. Where Belgian and Dutch societies could once be described as "pillarized" into ideological groupings of remarkable coherence and self-sufficiency, gaps suddenly appeared between elite and youth values within the pillars. Traditional political elites, however, were slow to recognize the changes taking place, and even slower to respond.

The same ideological rigidity that endowed elite decision-making with predictability made it difficult for elites to adapt to changes in societal values. Followers became more assertive and less deferential, and politics became more elite challenging and less elite directed.[39] From the end of the 1950s, support for traditional political parties declined rapidly in Belgium and the Netherlands

# Introduction

and the party systems of both countries witnessed a rapid growth of new political groupings. In the early to middle 1970s, the process of political disintegration culminated in a brief period of governmental instability simultaneous to, but not resulting from, the collapse of the Bretton Woods system and the first oil price shock.

Economic turmoil during the period from 1973 to 1975 brought about a partial reconsolidation of both party systems and, with it, a return to very traditional patterns in economic policymaking. While much of the rest of the industrialized world resorted to Keynesian stimulus to soften the 1975 recession, centrist governments in Belgium and the Netherlands continued with broad disinflationary policies designed to counter the impact of the oil price rise on domestic prices and wages. The Belgian and Dutch electorates remained with their traditional parties through the disappointing recoveries of 1977–8 but abandoned them in the aftermath of the second oil price shock.

The further collapse of support for traditional political parties sparked a dilemma. If elites were no longer able to negotiate on behalf of their following, and if voters no longer felt obliged to support ruling elites, how was the process for consensus building to function? The answer was not immediately obvious in the late 1970s. Elites, lacking confidence in the support of their followers, perceived little room for compromise in political negotiation. Followers looking for pluralist representation at elite levels made elite perceptions a reality. Whenever compromise-minded elites chose to give ground in the interest of consensus, marginal voters defected and uncompromising activists took to the streets. Neither Belgian nor Dutch society could unite around a program for recovery, and both governments suffered from the classic symptoms of democratic dysfunction: burgeoning debts and deficits.

The situation began to turn around in the 1980s. Center-right governments were elected first in Belgium under Wilfried Martens and then in the Netherlands under Ruud Lubbers. The coalitions that were formed were not broadly based and yet they carried

# Introduction

a strong mandate to find a way out of the economic crisis. In turn, they adopted economic adjustment programs that were more majoritarian than consensual. The distribution of adjustment costs fell disproportionately on the many to the advantage of the few. But the strategies were effective both in terms of inducing economic change and in terms of garnering popular support. Deficits began to fall and the growth of government debt slowly stabilized at or below the growth rate for the economy. Support for traditional parties increased and the effective number of political groups stabilized or even declined. Although much of the electorate lost income as a result of state intervention in the economy, the center-right Martens and Lubbers coalitions were re-elected on platforms of continued austerity. By the end of the 1980s, Martens and Lubbers were still in office. Moreover, both succeeded in making a successful coalition change from center-right to center-left.

## Recovering from the Crisis

Even successful adjustment extracts a high political price. Superficially, this can be seen in the plight of the mainstream political parties of both countries. By the mid-1990s, the centrist Christian Democrats who were the architects of the adjustment strategy lost power in the Netherlands for the first time in more than 70 years. By the end of the decade, the same fate befell the Christian Democrats in Belgium—who had been in office continuously since the 1950s. And while the successor coalitions continued along much the same course of action, their popularity soon proved limited as well. Both the Netherlands and Belgium entered into a period of political turmoil at the start of the twenty-first century. Their ability to engineer a consensual adjustment strategy has been greatly impaired as a result. Fortunately, neither country has experienced a real economic crisis. As their economic performance begins to deteriorate, however, it may be just a matter of time before they do.

## Introduction

My argument in this book is that consensual adjustment is a wasting asset. The implication is that while the adjustments of the early 1980s were difficult to implement in Belgium and the Netherlands, they will be even harder to repeat. This argument is developed in five parts. Chapter 1 introduces a framework for small country adjustment inspired by Katzenstein's analysis. Chapter 2 explains why this framework was more successful in the Netherlands than in Belgium, at least initially. Chapter 3 examines the crisis of the 1970s. Chapter 4 examines the challenges faced in the 1980s and early 1990s. The Conclusion brings the argument into the new century and explains what this means for Belgium and the Netherlands and for our larger understanding of economic adjustment and political transformation in small states.

# 1
# The Politics of Economic Adjustment

The introduction sets out a classic story of shock and adjustment. Belgium and the Netherlands start out doing well, something bad happens—in this case both economically and politically—and then they adapt. But all West European countries adapt. Some countries have done better than others at different points in time. But none has failed, disintegrated, or disappeared. This is not the case with the countries of Central and Eastern Europe. The formerly communist countries have undergone dramatic transformations and some, like Yugoslavia or the Soviet Union, have literally ceased to exist. So while it is true that the challenges confronting advanced industrial societies are considerable, it is easy to understand that many believe liberal-democratic market economies are somehow resilient.

Such complacency is due to the way shock-adjustment stories are told. Before 1989, most analysts never really expected the communist world to disappear either. Moreover, the external challenges that the communist countries faced were not the problem. Rather, it was how those countries were put together. The world changed and communism changed too, but the adaptation was only partly successful, at least internally. The communist countries continued to fit with the global environment, more or less, and yet they no longer functioned well as communist countries. With successive challenges and successive adaptations, the internal contradictions

# The Politics of Economic Adjustment

of the communist system continued to mount. In the end, the communist countries imploded.

The failure of analysts to predict the fall of communism reveals a weakness in conventional narratives of economic adjustment. The difficult part in telling any shock-adjustment story is not pointing to the changes. Rather, it is figuring out what remains the same and whether the continuities are sustainable over time. This is what Peter Katzenstein does so well in his *Small States in World Markets*.[1] He looks across a range of different countries confronting different shocks at different points in time. Yet he finds that the pattern for adjustment is broadly the same. There are variations across countries. But they all share a common theme. More important, the pattern for success is self-reinforcing: it remains the same because it is successful, and it is successful because it remains the same.

My goal in this chapter is to build on the strength of Katzenstein's analysis. That task is easier said than done. Whoever made up the cliché about "dwarves standing on the shoulders of giants" was either being ironic or never actually tried to stand on someone's shoulders. It is difficult, inelegant, even dangerous. Worse, it is only possible to get a decent perspective once you stop thinking about what you are doing and instead start trying to make sense of the view.

In that spirit, this chapter elaborates a framework for interpreting the politics of economic adjustment in Belgium and the Netherlands. The framework is inspired by Katzenstein, but is not always true (or fair) to his vision. Indeed, it is easy to imagine that Katzenstein would find my interpretation of his argument overly restrictive. I would not disagree. In defense, I can say only that my use of Katzenstein's work is functional. It is easier to stand on someone's shoulders if you can get them to hold still.

The chapter develops in three sections. The first looks at the question of size in general terms. The second sketches the strategy for economic adjustment in Belgium and the Netherlands. The third explains how everything fits together politically. The third section also points out what can be allowed to change and what has to remain the same for the politics of economic adjustment to hold stable over time. In this way, the chapter sets up the historical narrative to follow.

## The Size of Nations

The key to understanding Katzenstein's argument about economic adjustment strategies is to recognize that *Small States in World Markets* is not about small states per se. It does not focus on very small countries like Iceland, Liechtenstein, or Luxembourg. Greece, Ireland, and Portugal do not appear in the index. Neither does Finland. Instead, as Katzenstein admits, the argument rests on an analysis of seven countries: Austria, Belgium, Denmark, the Netherlands, Norway, Sweden, and Switzerland.[2] What unites these countries is not that they are small. It is that they are corporatist: political and economic leaders negotiate strategies to respond to economic change, and they also bargain over formulas to share the costs of adjustment.

The seven countries that Katzenstein studies are corporatist. Yet they are also small. The average population among them is less than one-tenth the population of Germany and one-sixth the population of Britain, France, or Italy. But does it matter? An underlying theme in Katzenstein's book is that even the larger countries are small in an increasingly global economy. That is why it is interesting to study the economic adjustment strategies of small states in the first place. As large countries get smaller, they will have to look to the lessons of small states. At this point the relatively high gross domestic product (GDP) per capita of the smaller states becomes interesting. On average, the smaller countries are more than 10 percent wealthier per capita than their larger neighbors. The apparent political stability of the small states becomes interesting as well. The small states in Katzenstein's analysis have been effective in using "social coalitions, political institutions, and public policies [to] facilitate...shifts in factors of production that increase economic efficiency with due regard to the requirements of political stability." Put simply, they are a success.[3]

## The Politics of Economic Adjustment

The question is whether size and success are somehow related through the propensity to develop corporatist coalitions, institutions, and policies. If corporatism is necessary for success, and yet only small countries can be corporatist, then there is not much for large countries to learn. Alternatively, if large countries are becoming smaller, then perhaps large countries might learn to become more corporatist. In this case, the small states have a lot to offer in the development of effective structures and policies.

Both the question and the answer are confused by the contrast between conventional and economic notions of what it means to be "small." In conventional terms, a country is small if it has a limited population or output. In economic terms, a country is small if it is dependent upon access to world markets and yet unable to influence world market prices. The conventional meaning of the word small is relative. Denmark is small relative to the Netherlands and the Netherlands is small relative to Germany. The economic meaning of "small" is absolute. In the global economy, Denmark, the Netherlands, and Germany are all small. Finally, size changes in the conventional sense are rare and dramatic—like German unification or population growth in Turkey. Size changes in the economic sense are no less dramatic, but they are commonplace to the point of being cliché—like deepening of economic interdependence or "globalization."

Thanks to globalization, the larger countries of Europe are becoming small in economic terms. But corporatism only tends to emerge in countries that are small in the conventional sense. The reason, Katzenstein suggests, is historical.[4] The small states were able to develop corporatist institutions, practices, and policies for one of two possible reasons. Either they were small enough in the conventional sense to contain a relatively homogenous population, as in the case of the Scandinavian countries. Or they were able to graft corporatist practices on prior patterns of accommodation (like consociational democracy) between different groups, as in the case of Belgium, the Netherlands, Austria, and Switzerland. By trial and error, under conditions of excessive vulnerability and in the face of extreme adversity, the small states managed to make "a political virtue out of an economic necessity." They became corporatist in order to survive, and yet corporatism proved effective enough to move them from survival to success.

Unfortunately, this historically contingent analysis makes it difficult to foresee how such practices could transfer from one country to the next. To take one example, France is not as homogenous as the Scandinavian countries and it also does not have a well-structured politics of accommodation like the other small states. Lacking these preconditions, it seems hard to imagine that France could invent a new corporatist tradition. It also raises questions about whether French corporatism would actually work. Are small states successful because they are corporatist, or is small-state corporatism successful because of the particular advantages of being small? Within a historically contingent environment, it is possible to make empirically grounded arguments about small states and world markets, but it is not easy to sort out the direction of causality. Small states were successful in the past and they may well be so in the future. But there is no guarantee that they will be and there is also no guarantee that others would benefit from imitating the small country road to success.

Enter the economists. Alberto Alesina and Enrico Spolaore have developed a parsimonious theory that links the conventional and economic notions of size.[5] They argue that all communities face a trade-off between political diversity and economic efficiency. Large countries—in the conventional sense—are diverse but efficient. Small countries are homogenous but lack economies of scale. Nevertheless, small countries can escape their economic disadvantages by embracing world markets. By opening up their borders to trade, conventionally small states become small in the economic sense as well—meaning dependent upon world markets and yet unable to influence world market prices. But they can at least benefit from the economies of scale otherwise available only to larger countries. Indeed, to the extent that world markets are more efficient than even very large national economies, the small states come out ahead.

Of course, large countries can also benefit from embracing world markets. In a globalizing economy, they may have little choice other than to participate in the international division of labor. But the benefits of globalization do not change the burden of political and social diversity that is the disadvantage of being relatively large in the conventional sense. On the contrary, conflict over how the costs of adjusting to world markets will be distributed is likely to be more fractious and divisive in larger, more diverse, countries than in their smaller, more homogenous, counterparts. Alesina and Spolaore explain:

As the world economy becomes more integrated, the trade off between heterogeneity of preferences and economy of scale "tilts" in favor of small size, as in a world of free trade even small countries can prosper. Thus, as trade becomes more liberalized, small regions are able to seek independence at lower cost. A consequence is that the phenomenon of economic integration is intricately connected with political separatism.[6]

This argument sharpens the distinction between the different types of small states studied by Katzenstein—those that are more homogenous, and those that depend upon pre-existing formulas for accommodating diversity. The Scandinavian countries are small in all senses: population, trade dependence, and homogeneity. The consociational democracies are not. They are conventionally small and economically small, but they are politically and socially diverse. Hence, finding a way to adapt to the more integrated world economy should be more difficult for the consociational democracies than for their Scandinavian counterparts. Not only do they have to share out the costs of adjustment, but they also have to shore up the mechanisms that reconcile domestic diversity. Taken to its extreme, the implication of Alesina and Spolaore's argument is that Belgium and the Netherlands will succeed in one domain only at the risk of failing in the other.

## From Size to Strategy

As small countries, both Belgium and the Netherlands face a trade-off in confronting world markets. By implication, they also face a choice. And choice is the real focus for this analysis. For the rest of this chapter, I underscore the choices made in forging a strategy for economic adjustment. Those choices include both the framework for economic policymaking and the pursuit of specific instruments like regional integration or corporatist intermediation. Moreover, it is not enough for governments to choose a strategy; their choices must also be accepted by the electorate. Therefore, the chapter develops a set of general claims about how such electoral validation works as well.

The starting point for this analysis is the observation that Belgium and the Netherlands have embraced a cluster of policy preferences by choice and not necessity. That cluster includes free trade, fixed exchange rates, hard-currency policy, and accommodating (or stability-orientated) monetary and fiscal policy. And the choice is clearly influenced by the two countries' relative size and position in the world economy. But the governments of Belgium and the Netherlands could have made other choices or pursued other combinations as well. Neither Belgium nor the Netherlands was obliged to promote free trade any more than Albania. Switzerland has long pursued a hard-currency policy without adopting a fixed exchange rate. And, until recently, the Scandinavian countries have shown little reluctance to see their currencies devalue against their exchange rate targets. The choices made by Belgium and the Netherlands were not structurally determined. They were chosen, and for a reason. Belgium and the Netherlands adopted free-trade and hard-currency policies at the cost of maintaining an accommodating or stability-orientated monetary or fiscal policy because the Belgians and the Dutch believed that this cluster of policies offered the most effective means for economic control.

The Belgian and Dutch free-trade tradition is easily explained. Economists have long taught that free trade maximizes national

## The Politics of Economic Adjustment

welfare, particularly for countries that cannot influence their external terms of trade. Although both Belgium and the Netherlands rank among the world's top ten exporters by market share, they have little to gain from protectionist policies and much to lose.

The fixed exchange rate preference follows from the free-trade tradition. Fixed exchange rates create a favorable environment for international trade by stabilizing the prices of traded goods. Since Belgium and the Netherlands trade well more than half the value of their domestic production, the benefits of stable international trading prices are significant.

The practical or theoretical motives behind the hard currency preference are more complex. Part of the problem is that "hard" is a relative term, which means that having a "hard currency" holds different implications depending on the exchange rate regime. During the period of fixed exchange rates under the Bretton Woods system, a hard-currency policy meant that Belgium and the Netherlands were reluctant to see their currencies devalued against the dollar. When many of the world's currencies began to float more or less freely against each other during the early-to-middle 1970s, a hard-currency policy implied a general tendency for the Belgian and Dutch currencies to appreciate with the Deutschemark relative to other currencies. Finally, during the 1980s and 1990s, a hard-currency policy meant both that Belgium and the Netherlands were reluctant to see their currencies devalued within the European monetary system (EMS) and that there was a general tendency for the Belgian and Dutch currencies to appreciate against the other currencies in the EMS.

Possible explanations for the Belgian and Dutch hard-currency policies include a high dependency on imported inputs to production, a large import component in the average household consumption bundle, and a large amount of domestic debt denominated in foreign currency. When domestic manufacturers rely on imported intermediates or raw materials, a hard-currency policy holds down production costs. When domestic consumers typically buy a lot of imports, a hard-currency policy helps keep down inflation. And when the government has a large amount of debt denominated in foreign currency, a hard-currency policy lowers the domestic cost of servicing and repaying the debt. The relevance of each of these arguments obviously varies over time and with changes in production, consumption, and government borrowing. However, each of these arguments played a role in the Belgian and Dutch preference for hard currencies.

Belgian and Dutch reluctance to use the monetary or fiscal policy to maintain full employment follows from their preferences for fixed exchange rates and hard currencies. Attempts to expand domestic demand through increased government spending or expansionary monetary policy threaten the hard-currency and fixed exchange rate policies by drawing in imports and by increasing domestic inflation. In other words, the joint decision to pursue free trade, stable international trading prices, and a hard-currency policy effectively forecloses the use of monetary or fiscal policy to stabilize domestic demand. Monetary and fiscal policy accommodate the preferences for free trade, fixed exchange rates, and hard currencies. By implication, the two countries prefer to maximize welfare in the long run, as opposed to minimizing employment and output fluctuations over the short-to-medium term.

The preference for an accommodating macroeconomic policy reveals the extent to which choices in some areas restrict options in others. This is true in terms of stabilizing economic performance across the business cycle. It is also true for responding to periodic economic shocks. Belgium and the Netherlands have to respond to economic change within the parameters set by their preferences for free trade, stable exchange rates, hard currencies, and an accommodating monetary and fiscal policy.

This is the problem of economic adjustment. If the Belgians and the Dutch somehow find themselves producing things that the rest of the world does not want to buy, or producing at uncompetitive prices, they cannot use trade policy, floating exchange rates, competitive devaluations, or monetary and fiscal stimulus to respond. Instead, the two countries must find new markets, lower the relative cost of production, or change what they produce. The Belgians and the Dutch have addressed the problem of adjustment through two sets of instruments: regional integration and corporatism.[7] They have used regional integration proactively, to secure market access, to control relative production costs, and to insulate domestic producers from external shocks. And they have used corporatism reactively, to lower relative production costs, to shore up profitability and investments, and to shift productive resources from unprofitable activities to more profitable ones.

## Regional Integration

The Belgians and the Dutch use regional integration to facilitate adjustment. But the choice for regional integration encompasses much more than just economics. Therefore, it is necessary to take a broader perspective in order better to identify how the economic advantages of regional integration balance off against other factors. It is also necessary to create a distinction between regional integration and free trade. Analysts often refer to integration and free trade as though these are rough equivalents. Moreover, the two concepts are closely related. Yet having already explained that the Belgians and the Dutch believe in free trade, it is helpful to use regional integration to bracket something else. The difference is the number of actors or countries involved. A single country can open its borders to trade with the rest of the world. It takes at least two countries to start a process of regional integration. This distinction is important because it underscores the international political dimension of regional integration. When a country liberalizes its own trade, the politics is domestic. When one country engages with another to coordinate trade liberalization, the politics is still domestic, but it is international as well.

The introduction of international politics into the discussion provides another means to distinguish between large and small countries: large countries can often achieve their foreign policy objectives even when acting alone. Small countries cannot. Hence, in the 1920s, any discussion of small countries immediately evoked the image of neutrality. The small countries of Europe were neutral,

## The Politics of Economic Adjustment

both economically and politically. By the early 1930s, that situation began to change. Although still neutral in political terms, the small countries banded together in the interests of economic stability. The Oslo alliance represented a first, tentative effort at regional integration.[8]

The alliance foundered almost at its inception. While the small countries agreed that they should cooperate together, they could not agree upon their joint relationship with the outside world. To be effective, the alliance of small countries needed a champion, both economic and political. Germany was an obvious economic partner, but—as a Nazi state—an unsavory political choice. Britain was more concerned with the Commonwealth than the Continent. The United States, despite numerous entreaties, could not be shaken from its isolationism.

Lacking a champion, the alliance of smaller countries had little impact. Although it succeeded in stabilizing and increasing trade among the signatories, it could not influence global, or even large national, markets. When the alliance fell apart, it was forgotten by history. It was not forgotten by the smaller countries themselves. For Belgium and the Netherlands, World War II demonstrated that neutrality, even joint neutrality, was not a viable option. In the war's aftermath, Belgian and Dutch politicians recognized that they needed a new vehicle for the promotion of their interests. Fortunately for them, some of the larger countries of Europe recognized this as well. European integration, with its periodic oscillations between euphoria and disappointment, was the result.

The lessons learned by the Belgians and the Dutch were not perceived in the same way by other small countries. In this sense, the distinction between free-trade and regional integration is empirical as well as analytic. Belgium and the Netherlands have participated in European integration since the beginning. Austria, Switzerland, and the Scandinavian countries have not. Instead, these other small states chose to focus more explicitly on free trade—joining the European Free Trade Area (EFTA) instead of the European Community (EC). Therefore, the two points to consider are what regional integration had to offer above and beyond trade liberalization and what regional integration costs in return. Since almost all of the small European countries now participate in the European Union (EU), it is also necessary to consider how the benefits and costs have changed over time. In this context, the enlargement of the EU to include Austria, Sweden, and Finland—but not Norway or Switzerland—provides an important point of reference.

## Benefits

The benefits of regional integration are both static and dynamic, and they depend on the countries that are involved and the depth to which they are willing to integrate. Unpacking these benefits is not self-evident. The easiest place to start is with the notion of depth. Economists separate the process of regional integration into stages, with each stage bringing a new element of commonality to the two- or multi-country region. A "free-trade area" marks the absence of internal barriers to trade. A "customs union" adds a common external commercial policy. And a "common market" implies the liberalization of internal movements of productive factors, meaning labor and capital.

In general terms, the small country interest in joining a free-trade area is easy to anticipate. Regional integration offers small countries the choice between unilateral and collective trade liberalization. The advantages of joint action are clear. The small country not only lowers its barriers to trade, but it gets a partner country or countries to lower them as well. The static benefits derive from the one-off reduction of barriers to trade between the two (or more) countries. Large partners, or partners offering a large potential for increasing trade, in turn provide large static benefits.

The dynamic effects of regional integration derive from the greater level of competition among industries within the newly formed region and the greater level of investment within the member states. Relative size matters here as well. Both competition and investment levels stem from the characteristics of a larger market. Larger markets enjoy greater economies of scale and lower barriers to entry. Correspondingly, industries established within larger markets are both more productive and more profitable.[9]

The dynamic effects of regional integration are particularly important for countries with small domestic markets. In smaller markets, both competition and investment resources are scarce relative to larger economies. Small country industries face a competitive cost disadvantage and, when exporting to protected markets, unfavorable terms of trade. Once part of a preferential trading arrangement, small countries not only experience a favorable movement in their terms of trade, they also become more specialized, more competitive, and more attractive to foreign investors. While such effects are difficult to quantify, at least one estimate suggests that more than 50 percent of Belgian and Dutch growth during the 1960s resulted from membership in the EC. Of course, the lion's share of this improvement was due to the growth of export volumes. But not all of that growth can be attributed to static effects.[10]

These advantages of integration accrue rapidly to small countries for two reasons. First, small countries generally start off with lower aggregate external tariffs. At the signing of the Treaty of Rome in 1958, average tariff rates for the Benelux were less than 60 percent of those for France or Italy.[11] Similarly, during the negotiation of the European Economic Area (EEA) in the late 1980s and early 1990s, average external tariffs for the EFTA countries were 75 percent of those for the EC.[12] Therefore, the static effects of integration are achieved rapidly, and with a minimum of domestic adjustment. This is evident both in the superior performance of Belgium and the Netherlands during the 1960s[13] and in the rapid convergence of the EFTA countries on German economic performance after the conclusion of bilateral free-trade relations between EFTA and the EC.[14]

Small countries also benefit from the dynamic effects of regional integration more rapidly than do their larger counterparts. With few exceptions, small countries provoke little market segmentation in a free-trade area or customs union. Rather, small country standards and regulations tend to converge on those of their largest trading partner—much as do their monetary, fiscal, and exchange rate policies. This partially explains why the EFTA countries were content to remain outside the Community before the initiation of the 1992 program. Although not part of the Community's customs union, the EFTA countries were in many ways more integrated than several of the actual member states. As the research director of the EFTA secretariat observed in 1990: "When the original EFTA members lost their pivot country, the United Kingdom, EFTA's center was effectively transferred to inside the EC.... The EFTA countries are now present in the EC as invisible members."[15]

The static and dynamic effects of preferential trading relationships are a function of the degree of integration. A free-trade area, for example, benefits from the fall in internal tariff barriers but suffers under the imposition of rules of origin. Because the partner countries maintain separate national commercial policies, they have to force firms to maintain detailed records on where the products they sell were originally produced. Failure to do so would make it possible for firms operating in the country with the lowest tariffs vis-à-vis the outside world to get a competitive advantage over firms operating elsewhere in the free-trade area. Nevertheless, rules of origin are complex, costly, and inefficient. Any effort spent complying with the rules represents a net cost to firms and so damages their competitiveness relative to producers who do not have to comply with such red tape.

A customs union, with its common external commercial policy, offers an improvement. Rules of origin are no longer necessary, except to the degree to which trade among the member states is exempt from the common external policy of the union. A customs union, however, does not maximize the gains from integration. Harmonization of commercial policies does little to provide for the free movement of factors (namely capital). Nor does the harmonization of commercial policies address the problem of non-tariff barriers to trade. Even with a customs union, differences in national regulations and product standards continue to segment national markets, limiting competition, and inhibiting the free flow of goods. At the extreme case, market segmentation from non-tariff barriers can prevent most of the dynamic effects of regional integration.[16]

The logic of this argument can be followed all the way up through the creation of a common market. At each stage, the process of deepening integration by eliminating obstacles to trade and investment only underscores the significance of those obstacles that remain.

## Costs

Regional integration offers economic benefits, but it exacts political costs. These costs originate because different societies have different interests or values. In turn those different interests and values manifest in different market rules. Regional integration threatens to do away with those rules. In the process, regional integration threatens to injure the values or interests that those market rules protect. Taken to its extreme, regional integration can threaten the very identity of a society. And the extremes are often very close to the surface. When Sweden negotiated its entry into the EU in the early 1990s, a major political row erupted over snuff tobacco. Snuff is illegal in the EU, but very popular in Sweden. The Swedes regarded the prohibition of snuff as a threat to their national identity. Therefore, the Swedish government insisted that it be given a national exemption from the ban.

The snuff example reveals the extent to which regional integration is limited by the differences in interests and values across societies. Integration is easier when the differences in values and interests are small, and integration is more difficult when the differences are large. Consider the American-led controversy over Japanese retailing in the late 1980s and early 1990s. The Japanese like to shop in small mom-and-pop stores. However, the US government claimed that the small size of Japanese retail outlets represents a barrier to American exports. In the interests of free trade, the United States demanded that Japan permit the development of

## The Politics of Economic Adjustment

larger stores. Japan responded that doing so would mean departing from Japanese values and traditions, by undermining the entire class of small-store owners and by destroying the personal relationship between consumers and retailers. Despite the economic advantage to Japanese consumers of greater access to US products, the Japanese government proved quite unwilling to accept the political consequences of permitting larger stores. Thus even a very low degree of economic integration was thwarted by the large differences in interests and values between the United States and Japan.

As integration deepens, the differences in interests and values across society become more important. In turn, the rising political cost associated with getting rid of those differences (or even just ignoring them) represents an obstacle to deeper integration. Consider the requirements for building a common market from a customs union. A common market goes beyond a customs union by allowing for the free movement of factors as well as for the elimination of nontariff barriers to trade. Thus, rather than relying predominantly on a collective liberalization, the completion of a common market implies the legislation of common market rules. A common market for labor depends upon the existence of common standards for education and training, comparable systems for worker representation in collective bargaining, and so on. The liberalization of capital markets requires some degree of fiscal harmonization, and also offers the prospect that domestic industries will come under foreign control. Finally, the elimination of technical barriers to trade raises questions about why national regulatory structures differ and what is the best means for harmonizing them.

The EC dealt with each of these issues during the drive to complete its internal market during the late 1980s and early 1990s. Although the single market is now largely complete, it is instructive to note that the effort was only possible once the European Commission embraced the principle of mutual recognition—a doctrine stipulating that products fit to be sold in one country are suitable throughout the common market—rather than attempting to harmonize product standards across countries.[17] Ignoring the differences between countries turned out to be much easier than regulating them away.

The conclusion to draw is that some overlap of interests and values across countries is a necessary precondition for regional integration. Where the overlap is great, it is possible for the countries to integrate more deeply, as in the case of Belgium and the Netherlands within the Benelux. Where the overlap is more limited, only shallow forms of integration are possible, as in EFTA or North American Free Trade Agreement (NAFTA). Finally, where there is little or no overlap, integration is hardly possible, as between the United States and Japan, or perhaps a better example, between North Korea and the world. It is not enough that integration be economically advantageous, it must also be politically and socially acceptable.

## Cooperation

The political costs imposed by regional integration condition any country's decision to participate, whether the country is large or small. Countries in a given region need not proceed to further integration by the discrete stages anticipated in economic theory. At each stage, governments choose to lower tariffs, harmonize commercial policies, and liberalize the movements of labor and capital. They also choose how they will undertake such actions. While those choices are facilitated by growth in trade and advances in technology, they remain, nevertheless, more political than inevitable.[18]

As a political process, regional integration does not necessarily imply full market liberalization—at least not in the short-to-medium term. In spite of often-inflated rhetoric, regional integration relies more on the practice of cooperation than on the ideology of market liberalism. This distinction is implicit in the famous "Monnet-Schuman" method for uniting the countries of Europe and in the functioning of the European Communities themselves.

# The Politics of Economic Adjustment

For example, the first great postwar experiment with supranational integration, the European Coal and Steel Community (ECSC), applied the principles of industrial organization as well as those of free trade. The Treaty of Paris not only made clear provision for the common market in coal and steel but also suggested that the ECSC function as a cartel, regulating production, pricing, and market shares for a significant portion of West European industry. The language of Article 2 of the Paris Treaty is instructive:

> The Community must progressively bring about conditions which will of themselves ensure the most rational distribution of production at the highest possible level of productivity, while safeguarding continuity of employment and taking care not to provoke fundamental and persistent disturbances in the economies of the Member States.[19]

The compromise between economic and political objectives was fundamental, not simply to the functioning of the ECSC but also to its success.[20]

Over time, the cartel function of the ECSC became more important than the common market for coal and steel.[21] Given the dramatic rise of steel production in the developing world followed by the liberation of Central and Eastern Europe, the member states of the ECSC were more concerned with managing the problems of domestic adjustment as with ensuring "the most rational distribution of production at the highest level of productivity." This concern was well placed. Even under managed conditions, one of the oldest coal producers on the Continent, Belgium, had to take the politically unpopular step of closing its last operational mine. That this closure sparked only minor protest testifies to the success of the process of gradual adjustment organized through the ECSC.[22]

Cooperation is also a principal component of the Rome Treaty, the Single European Act, and the Maastricht Treaty on European Union. Often this cooperation is focused on the objective of market liberalization, as during the Kennedy and Tokyo Rounds of General Agreement on Tariffs and Trade (GATT) negotiations.[23] But cooperation may also have the objective of increasing the competitiveness of the member states in world markets, or of enhancing the bargaining power of "Europe" on the world stage. Given the multilateral nature of such cooperation, each of these three objectives requires "a delicate balance of the national interests of the contracting parties."[24]

The willingness to cooperate represents a further political precondition for integration. It is not enough that countries share a common set of interests and values—or even that they translate these into a set of common objectives. They must agree on the means to achieve those objectives. Here again it is interesting to look at the 1992 program of the EC. Although France, Germany, and the United Kingdom (UK) were agreed on the need for a European common market, the UK initially rejected the use of majority voting to pass legislation through the Council of Ministers.[25] Had Margaret Thatcher refused to accept a reform of the Council's procedures, it is unlikely that the 1992 program would have come about. In this sense, her willingness to cooperate with the other member states was even more important to the success of the project than the consensus on the need for market liberalization among France, Germany, and the UK. A similar point could be made about the role of Spain and Poland during the negotiation of the European Constitutional Treaty.[26]

## Influence

A country's enthusiasm for integration increases when the gains are high, when the partners to integration share a common set of interests and values, and when the spirit of cooperation is strong. A country's enthusiasm falls off when the gains from integration are low, when partners to integration have different interests or values, and when the spirit of cooperation is weak. Using these general terms, it is also possible to suggest a trade-off between the different elements. High gains from integration can offset differences in values or interests, and so forth.

Such trade-offs were explicit in the EFTA countries' willingness to participate in the EEA, as well as in the decision of many EFTA countries to apply to join the EU. In fact, such trade-offs have been evident in each of the enlargements of the EC/EU, and on both sides of the negotiating table. Historic moments, like the negotiation of the Paris or Rome treaties, require a favorable conjuncture of all three elements—substantial benefits, common interests and values, and a willingness to cooperate. Moments of crisis, like the French rejection of the European Defence Community (1954), the "empty chair" (1965), or the breakdown of negotiations over the European budget (2005), suggest the absence of one or all of the three.[27]

Still there is another advantage that can influence a country's attitude toward regional integration, and that is influence. Moreover, the influence here is not limited to changing the actions or attitudes of partner countries. It extends to the elaboration of rules and procedures that constitute the environment for regional trade and commerce.[28] Once the EC embarked on its efforts to complete the internal market, the EFTA countries became concerned that the coordination of regulatory structures within the Community would place them at a competitive disadvantage. Rather than become the passive recipients of EU legislation, they sought some means to ensure that their own interests were represented in the legislative process. The decision to negotiate the EEA—and ultimately to apply for full membership in the EU—was the result.[29]

This notion of influence provides another balancing factor to add into the mix of motivations for participation in regional integration. In purely economic terms, the benefits of moving from the EEA to full EU membership were marginal, while the costs were high. Even at the time, existing members of the Community expected the EFTA countries to become net contributors to the transfer mechanisms between richer and poorer EU member states. Moreover, the EFTA countries had to increase their average external tariff rates and accept participation in the "community's system of contingent protection."[30] For the EFTA countries, full membership in the Community was both costly and illiberal. Nevertheless, any economic disadvantages associated with full membership in the EU were outweighed by the importance of gaining a stronger voice in European decision-making.

Even so, there are limits to the willingness of the small countries to cooperate within the community. Small countries choose to integrate with their larger neighbors in order to manage their external dependence and not to give up their identity as nations. For small countries, "commitment to multilateralism [is] not the opposite of neutrality: it [represents] a search for the same objectives but within a completely different international system."[31] The importance of this distinction was sharply revealed in the Dutch rejection of the Fouchet Plan (1962), in the Danish veto of the Maastricht Treaty (1992), in the Irish veto of the Nice Treaty (2001), and in the Dutch veto of the European Constitutional Treaty (2005). Faced with the choice, small countries have demonstrated a remarkable willingness to brave diplomatic or even economic isolation as a means to prevent the loss of national identity.

Here it is useful to return to the example of the Oslo alliance. The incentive for regional integration was clear. Given the economic and political turbulence of the late 1920s and early 1930s, the small European countries needed a vehicle for the promotion of stable diplomatic and trading relations. The lack of common interests or values between large countries and small was also evident: the smaller countries were fearful of German influence and were unable to raise the interest of either the British or the Americans. Finally there was the willingness to cooperate: although the small countries faced similar dilemmas of external vulnerability, they could not come to agreement on relations between the Oslo alliance and the outside world.

The Oslo alliance was doomed almost at its inception. After the war, the alliance was overtaken by the more general process of European integration. As before, for the small countries, as well as their larger neighbors, European integration represents a solution to the problems of economic dependence and political vulnerability.

## Choice

The Belgians and the Dutch use regional integration to help facilitate economic adjustment as a matter of choice and not necessity. Given their economic policy preferences, regional integration offers the best set of instruments available for ensuring market access and for maintaining relative cost competitiveness. Regional integration also offers the possibility for the Belgians and the Dutch to play an active role in shaping their economic environment. Nevertheless, such advantages do not come for free. And the price may have little or nothing to do with the requirements for economic adjustment. By implication, the Belgians and the Dutch may choose to abandon regional integration—or to scale down their participation in regional institutions—despite any economic advantages that may be on offer.

## Corporatism

The Belgians and the Dutch use regional integration proactively to shape their economic environment—for example, by getting their trading partners to lower barriers to commerce, by securing access to foreign credit, or by negotiating common market rules. They use corporatism reactively to implement specific policies, such as wage moderation, labor retraining and reallocation, or welfare-state reform. Regional integration helps the Belgians and the Dutch avoid the need for adjustment. Corporatism helps them to ensure that adjustments are made quickly and with a minimum of social conflict.

Making adjustments without conflict is challenging, particularly given the type of adjustments that need to be made. If the Belgians or the Dutch find themselves producing products at uncompetitive prices or that the rest of the world does not want, they need to find new markets, lower relative prices, or change patterns of production. Corporatism cannot help with finding new markets. But it can facilitate lowering relative prices or changing patterns of production. The challenge arises from what such actions entail.

Consider the difficulty of lowering relative prices. The trick is to convince domestic workers to accept a decline in real wages or real wage growth relative to their major international competitors. In its most moderate form, this entails asking workers to restrict wage increases beyond the rate of sectoral productivity growth and domestic inflation to a level that is lower than workers enjoy abroad. Domestic workers continue to benefit from productivity growth, and they are compensated for any erosion of incomes due to price increases, and yet they benefit less than their foreign counterparts. In a more aggressive form, workers may forgo productivity-based wage increases and yet continue to be compensated for the effects of inflation. Nominal wages increase, but the real value of these wages remains constant. In the extreme form, workers not only forgo any productivity gains but also surrender any compensation for rising prices. Nominal wages remain constant, but real (price-deflated) wages decline. The wage increases garnered by workers in competitor markets and the size of the relative cost adjustment required to restore price competitiveness for domestic industry determine how aggressively the policy should be set. The only question is how to get workers (and employers) to accept it.

A statutory price–incomes policy offers one mechanism to lower real wages. The government passes legislation (or, more often, uses administrative authority under existing enabling legislation) to set price and wage increases rather than allowing them to be determined in the marketplace. The danger with such a policy is that workers will go on strike or manufacturers will circumvent the price controls. Enforcement of statutory prices and wages relies on the policing powers of the state. If defection is widespread or well organized, the state has to choose between a vigorous enforcement of the policy or an embarrassing reversal. Usually, governments try these measures in sequence—by strengthening enforcement of the policy in the first instance and by caving into worker or industry demands once it becomes clear that enforcement has failed.

Workers typically greet any reversal of policy with demands for a huge increase in wages in order to compensate for the loss of real income they had to endure while the policy was in place. Manufacturers respond in kind. The end result is to leave the economy worse off. Two examples of this cycle of events could be found in the United States and the UK during the 1970s.[32]

A statutory price–incomes policy is not, however, the only recourse available to a government wishing to influence the levels of prices and wages in the domestic marketplace. Another option is for the state to participate in the collective bargaining between industry and labor. The range of state participation can be limited to an extension of the collective wage agreement to cover all relevant actors within the economy, much as with a statutory price–incomes policy but where the representatives of organized labor and industry are responsible for calculating the final numbers. State participation can also take the form of active involvement in the wage negotiations themselves. The government can set the parameters for what constitutes an acceptable rate of real wage growth, and it can co-opt, cajole, or coerce the social partners (meaning representatives of management and labor) to make sure that real wage growth remains in check.

This kind of active government involvement in wage bargaining is a type of corporatism, where corporatism is understood as:

> A specific socio-political process in which organizations representing monopolistic functional interest engage in political exchange with state agencies over public policy outputs which involves those organizations in a role that combines interest representation and policy implementation through delegated self-enforcement.[33]

Of course, this is not the only possible definition of corporatism. But it is the most useful definition to bring into a discussion of economic adjustment, because it underscores that government involvement in bargaining between the social partners is a tool used for the generation and enforcement of public policy. The policy being illustrated is a moderation of real wage growth. But it could as well focus on other problems related to adjustment, such as how to deal with the consequences of a permanent loss of competitiveness in a particular sector or industry, how to accommodate a sudden influx of women into the workforce, how to finance and encourage workers to undergo professional training, and what to do when particular labor market institutions cease to be affordable or generate perverse results.

Corporatism could fit a range of possible policies, but price–incomes policy is an area where it fits the best. This may not be obvious at first glance. As defined above, corporatism builds on three elements, two of them explicitly. The first is the existence of "monopolistic functional interest groupings" capable of self-enforcing the negotiated policy. For wage bargaining and price–incomes policy, this means centralized labor and employer organizations. The second is active state involvement. This implies not simply a functional competence to participate, but some sort of policy objective as well. The third element in the definition of corporatism is implicit. For corporatism to function, there must be some willingness to cooperate on all sides. Each of the three parties to negotiation must have an incentive to come to the table, and none of the three can afford to leave empty-handed.[34]

Viewed together, these three elements pose a number of difficulties. It is not immediately obvious why organized industry would choose to negotiate with organized labor, particularly at the highest level of centralization. Nor is it clear that the government can easily guide wage and price negotiations toward a predictable outcome. Finally, there is a question of where the will to cooperate originates and how it is maintained. Each of the three criteria holds problems internal to itself, and the combination of the three offers little suggestion of the dynamic working behind corporatist policymaking.

## Organized Business and Labor

The centralization of business and labor interests into national groups capable of self-enforcement suggests different problems of collective action.[35] Looking at industry, it is difficult to imagine why there would be centralization at all. There are strong reasons for collective action in business, but most of these are excluded by antitrust legislation.[36] Those reasons for industrial cooperation that remain are largely insufficient to guarantee a level of group discipline high enough to prevent defection from collective agreements. The higher the gains from defection, the less cohesive a national industrial federation is likely to be.

Turning to labor, there is a clear interest in national organization and peak collective bargaining. A larger union wields greater monopoly power over the workforce that it can bring to bear against employers. The collective action problem is manifested in the choice of the centralized labor federation to support either the interests of "insiders" or "outsiders."[37] Typically, a small trade union will care only for its own members, the insiders. In taking a stand during negotiations, a small trade union will tend to maximize real wages, even at the expense of unemployment. A very large trade union cares both for members and nonmembers, at least in effect if not by intention. This is so because the larger the union, the more any unemployment resulting from a real wage increase will be felt by union members.[38]

If the centralized labor organization acts like a small group, peak negotiations will be unlikely to result in a useful policy outcome. Rather than negotiating in the interests of the laboring classes, the union will act only on behalf of its membership. This observation is supported by econometric analysis correlating the degree of labor centralization with various indicators for economic performance. The results of that study led the authors to conclude that a danger exists when unions are "strong enough to cause major disruptions but not sufficiently encompassing to bear any significant fraction of the costs for society of their actions in their own interests."[39]

If the centralized labor organization behaves like a large group, negotiating in the interests of both members and nonmembers, it will suffer from a relative loss of cohesion. When the perceived gains from defection are high, constituent trade unions are likely to abandon centralized negotiations in favor of more self-interested direct action. This likelihood increases if the constituent unions believe that their federation leaders are acting as the co-opted agents of government when they participate in corporatist bargaining.[40]

The collective action problems associated with organized business and labor suggest the difficulties inherent to enforcing corporatist agreements. Even in the event that both groups negotiate in the interest of society, any large perceived gains from defection on behalf of either business or labor could undermine the principle of self-enforcement. This observation highlights the problems faced by government in promoting a corporatist framework for policymaking. It also underscores the importance of a willingness to cooperate. Where such willingness does not translate into tangible gains for the constituent elements of either employer or labor federations, the corporatist policies are unlikely to be a success.[41]

## The Role of Government

What can the government do to ensure a satisfactory policy outcome? Corporatism is, after all, a means to outline and implement public policy. The advantage of corporatism over a statutory price–incomes policy is that corporatism provides a less intrusive means of enforcement. Rather than responding to the rebellion of economic actors after the policy is announced, corporatism ensures their cooperation beforehand.[42] Given the problems centralized business and labor have with collective action, the government's role in providing a suitable forum for negotiation is critical.

The role of government encompasses several practical considerations. Some of these, like the provision of mutually acceptable statistical information, relate to technical competence. Others, like the selection of negotiating partners and policy targets, are more political. The government often has to choose partners with whom, and issues on which, there can be general agreement. This selection is crucial to the willingness to cooperate, and will necessarily depend on the prevailing economic situation and the desired policy outcome.

Even under the most favorable circumstances, however, the government has a further role to play in facilitating negotiations. In many cases, it has to provide side payments to industry and labor in order to enhance their abilities for self-enforcement. The combination of side payments and delegated self-enforcement distinguishes corporatism from the simple ratification of collective bargaining agreements. To understand how this works, it is useful to consider a "typical" example of corporatist exchange.

Imagine a society with three trade union federations and two employers' organizations. Economic conditions are poor, government balances are in deficit, and a coalition is formed with a mandate to impose austerity while at the same time stimulating growth and employment. This combination of targets implies a fairly drastic reduction in relative real wages in order to trigger an export- and investment-led growth. On the wage side, there are two possibilities. Either the government can impose wage restraint, through a statutory wage policy or declaratory wage ceilings—as when the Bundesbank announced explicit targets for acceptable wage claims—or it can offer concessions for union self-restraint. The government also needs to control prices in order to guarantee that any real wage reductions do not overshoot their targets. At the same time, the government needs to make sure that firms use any increase in profitability from lower real wages to improve their export competitiveness and to finance future investment. Given that domestic price increases are controlled by the policy, this is more difficult than it may seem at first glance. The government can provide financial incentives for firms to increase their capital formation or foreign market shares, but such subsidies threaten to aggravate the government's fiscal situation and offer no guarantee of success. Alternatively, the government can negotiate with industry as well as with labor.

The small number of trade unions and employer organizations in this hypothetical example increases the prospects for negotiation. The precise nature of the solution, however, remains unclear. In spite of price concessions by industry, labor stands to lose in real wage terms if the government is to succeed in its objective to increase private capital formation. Business, while holding a "privileged position" because of its power to determine investment levels, must harmonize its pricing decisions and sacrifice the choice between real and financial investments.[43] The government plays a conciliatory role. A possible agreement offers an increase in social outlays to counterbalance wage restraint, and a drop in payroll taxes to offset the impact of price restraint on profitability. Labor promises to adhere to the wage settlement, and industry commits to increase productive investment. In effect, the government is mitigating the degree of fiscal austerity in exchange for the wage, price, and investment concessions, which will allow austerity measures to achieve the desired outcome.

The solution is corporatist insofar as government, industry, and labor negotiate the content of the policy and so long as labor and industry recognize incentives for self-enforcement. Failure on behalf of labor to adhere to wage restraint could lead to a cutback in government social outlays, a rise in consumer prices, and the prospect of increasing unemployment, both in the present period because of high real wages and in the future because of low investment. Failure by industry to adhere to price and investment agreements suggests the possibility of labor unrest, a rise in real wages, and higher payroll taxes to support social insurance programs. In overall terms, arguments like these are persuasive. In individual terms, from the perspective of a constituent trade union or an individual firm, their persuasiveness depends on the particular situation to be faced.

## Cooperation

The literature on corporatism suggests many reasons why labor or industry might defect from centralized agreements. In tight labor markets, when aggregate unemployment levels are low, discipline within a large confederation of trade unions is difficult to maintain. Although the confederation itself might continue to negotiate on behalf of insiders and outsiders, the constituent trade unions, particularly those in profitable sectors, will see the promise of significant gains for their membership through defection from centralized negotiations. Such defection does not require a dramatic resurgence of some "romantic anarcho-syndicalist" ideology of conflict.[44] All that is necessary is a simple recognition that prospects for real wage increases are better in tight labor markets.[45]

Tight labor markets also provide incentives for industrial defection. On an aggregate level, industry benefits from real wage restraint in the face of the strengthened monopoly power of trade unions. At the firm level, however, real wage restraint diminishes the wage gap between skilled and unskilled workers. For firms in high-profit, high-productivity sectors, real wage restraint limits their ability to attract and hold a quality workforce. In an extreme case, the gains to be had from getting more skilled labor can more than offset the resulting increase in real wages. Defection from central wage agreements in order to attract skilled workers took place in the Netherlands in 1963 and in Sweden 20 years later.[46]

The government also loses authority in tight labor markets. Corporatism requires some form of policy mandate, which in turn requires some political recognition of the importance of corporatist arrangements. An explicit policy to hold down real wages is unlikely to find widespread popular support within a tight labor market. Support for austerity will be particularly lacking if the distribution of value added is skewed toward industry and away from labor.

In loose labor market conditions, when unemployment levels are high, the prospects for cooperation between labor, industry, and government are better. Trade union confederations use corporatism to enhance their bargaining power by elevating negotiations to the highest level of labor organization. Industry turns to corporatism to restrain social unrest. Although the relative bargaining power of industry is high in loose labor market conditions, such power is useless in the absence of negotiations. Corporatist arrangements may not result in the lowest possible real wage, but they do ensure that labor relies on arbitration rather than direct action. Finally, under loose labor market conditions, the government is likely to have a clear mandate for action. Economic issues will be at the fore of political debate, with unemployment, prices, and wages chief among them.

## A Corporatist Dynamic

The preceding analysis suggests that corporatism works better when economic conditions are poor, and corporatism works worse when economic conditions are good. When the national economy runs into difficulties, the government has a clear popular mandate to do something. The standard tools of fiscal, monetary, and exchange rate policy are likely to be insufficient for the task. Moreover, the government will not want to battle with organized industry and labor. Statutory policies risk problems of enforcement. The government, therefore, develops corporatist institutions to facilitate the implementation of an economic recovery policy. Labor participates out of concern for unemployment, and industry out of concern for social unrest.

As economic conditions improve, the motivation for establishing the corporatist framework loses urgency. The government's mandate for economic recovery yields ground to other, more pressing issues. Labor begins to chafe at wage restraint, and industry begins to focus on increasing productivity rather than holding down real wages. It is in the nature of bureaucracy, however, that institutions remain until overthrown. Revolt against the corporatist framework takes place during periods of prolonged economic prosperity, when industrial and labor discipline is lowest and when government policymakers are engaged with other issues and agendas. If the economy once again faces a downturn, it does so without the benefit of corporatist institutions for policymaking. Economic conditions deteriorate until the incentive exists to rebuild those institutions and start the corporatist cycle again.

The argument that corporatism works better in times of economic difficulty runs against much of the literature on corporatism.[47] Although generally eschewing the business-cycle approach to corporatism, Philippe Schmitter suggests that "modern corporatism is a 'fair-weather product,' whose emergence was greatly facilitated by the most protracted boom in real wages, productivity and total output in Western European history."[48] And Wyn Grant describes corporatism as "a phenomenon of small countries in prosperous times."[49]

Underlying the conclusions put forward by Schmitter, Grant, and others is the belief that corporatism can only function as a positive-sum game—when each of the parties to the negotiation can benefit.[50] This argument does not contradict that assumption. Rather, the argument assumes that, given the collective action problems associated with centralized business and labor, a positive-sum game is more likely in hard economic times than in good. This argument is consistent with the belief that corporatism is used by countries to offset their international economic dependence.[51] It is also consistent with the notion that hard economic times promote institution-building and good economic times give rise to institutional inertia.[52]

The argument that corporatism works better in times of economic difficulty is internally consistent and empirically plausible. It explains why corporatist institutions were established in many countries at the end of World War II, endured through the 1950s, fell apart in the late 1960s and early 1970s, and re-emerged in the early 1980s. It also provides one answer to the question of how Belgium and the Netherlands were able to respond to the need for economic adjustment.

## Choice

Corporatism is a bargaining framework that governments in Belgium and the Netherlands have chosen to use when implementing specific policies related to economic adjustment. They had other choices available. They could have turned away from their basic policy preferences and tried to respond with trade protectionism, competitive currency devaluations, or fiscal and monetary stimulus. But instead they chose to change relative prices by manipulating the growth of real wages. Industry and labor in both countries chose to go along with the policy and, indeed, to share much of the burden of implementation. Such choices are not self-evident. They are calculated. And the calculations are contextually specific. Just as with regional integration, it is possible to imagine that labor and industry would choose not to participate in corporatist bargaining. It is also possible to imagine that the government would prefer to work through a different policy framework or even to use different policy instruments. Corporatism and price–incomes policy have worked in the past. But that is no guarantee they will be used in the future.

## The Politics of Adjustment

Every aspect of the strategy for economic adjustment can be boiled down to some element of choice—for basic policy parameters, for regional integration, for price–incomes policy, and for corporatism. Such choices are interdependent. Given the preference for free trade, fixed exchange rates, a hard-currency, and accommodating monetary and fiscal policies, regional integration makes more sense than going it alone. Within a regional context, a corporatist price–incomes policy is a useful tool for lowering relative wage costs. Added together, these different elements constitute a strategy for adjustment that not only works, but works well.

Nevertheless, even after accounting for policy preferences, government action, and the participation of the social partners, the

# The Politics of Economic Adjustment

politics of this strategy for economic adjustment remains unclear. Who makes these choices, who evaluates them, and how are the evaluations translated into further action? The answers so far are vague. The Belgians and the Dutch have policy preferences. Belgium and the Netherlands engage in regional integration. Industry and labor participate in corporatist bargaining. The government plays ringmaster and the electorate votes.

Any discussion of the politics of choice is further complicated by two different tendencies in the literature on corporatism and on regional integration. The first tendency is to regard the choice for these instruments as politically self-destructive. Corporatist bargaining chips away at the state's authority by promoting the importance of trade unions and employers' associations, while regional integration threatens to supplant the state with a larger and more capable political organization. The second tendency is to view the choice for regional corporatism or regional integration as inescapable—a historical one-off. Corporatism delivers the institutions of the state into the hands of functional interests and regional integration strips the state of its sovereignty. At the juxtaposition of these two tendencies in the literature, the state is not only less desirable, it is also less significant and progressively so. In this sense, the economic adjustment strategy effectively takes over the state. Democratic governance gives way to the combined institutions for corporatist bargaining and regional integration.

Cast in this extreme form, these two tendencies seem unreasonably pessimistic or optimistic, depending upon what view of national democracy the reader may hold. Like it or not, the national state is alive and well in Europe today. Therefore, it is necessary to rescue democratic politics from academic analysis and to use the language of state theory to help isolate where political choice takes place, by whom, and under what authority. It is also important to understand how such choices can be validated in one context and rejected in another. That in mind, the purpose of this section is to add more precision to the politics of economic adjustment by focusing attention on the relationship between followers and elites, while at the same time emphasizing the importance of maintaining and bolstering the legitimacy of the national state.

## Choice and Validation

Both corporatism and regional integration rely heavily on the participation of national governments. Governments negotiate price–wage agreements with industry and labor, and governments are the contracting parties in regional integration. But these governments are not free agents. Presumably, they represent the interests of the voters. Governments must also be able to deliver the public goods that the voters demand. Therefore, it is not enough to say that governments choose. It is important to understand how government choices represent the interests of their electorates, and also how they serve those interests.

## Corporatism

Political analysis of corporatist bargaining is haunted by the experience of World War II. Fascism in Germany and Italy coerced the harmonization of labor and employer interests, often by overt use of force. Once united under state control, the representatives of labor and industry became the tools of the ruling party. Rather than representing the interests of their constituencies, trade unions and employers' organizations became conduits for state intervention in society. State corporatism was particularly traumatic for the occupied countries, which saw in their own functional representatives the instruments of foreign domination. After the end of the war, the term "corporatism" fell out of use. Even political actors engaged in definitively corporatist behavior refused to acknowledge any similarity between their actions and corporatism per se.[53]

## The Politics of Economic Adjustment

Use of the term corporatism revived in the 1970s.[54] Nevertheless, political scientists remained concerned about its legitimacy in the context of a liberal democratic society. Concern among political scientists centers on whether functional interest groups, like trade unions or employers' associations, can play a truly representative role in policy formulation or whether they block out the representation of particular interests. Recall that the role of functional interest groups in corporatist bargaining "combines interest representation and policy implementation through delegated self-enforcement." Philippe Schmitter's definition of corporatism is even more to the point:

Corporatism can be defined as a system of interest representation in which the constituent units are organised into a limited number of singular, compulsory, non-competitive, hierarchically ordered and functionally differentiated categories, recognised and or licensed (if not created) by the state and granted a deliberate representative monopoly within their respective categories in exchange for observing certain controls on their selection of leaders and articulation of demands and supports.[55]

Schmitter argues that corporatism exists as a paradigm for interest representation in competition with pluralism. As an alternative for democratic pluralism, however, corporatism suffers from two important shortcomings. First, it raises the question as to whether functional interest groupings are truly representative. Modern society is far removed from the guild societies of the late Middle Ages. A citizen in a liberal democracy has many more interests than can be expressed by an employers' organization or a trade union. Thus while corporatism may be legitimately representative in a very limited number of contexts, it is doubtful that this legitimacy will extend to cover the entire political system. Even the groups responsible for implementing national price–incomes policies cannot be said to encompass all aspects of political life.[56]

The second problem with corporatism as a representative system is that it relies on functional interest groups to enforce policy outcomes. In the simple example of corporatist bargaining given above, the trade unions were responsible for the maintenance of wage restraint while the employers' associations were required to police the pricing and investment practices of their membership. This allocation of responsibility to functional interest groups poses a twofold dilemma: first, it makes a privileged class of the leadership of a functional interest group, by imbuing it with the authority of the state, and, second, it creates a conflict of interest between the representative and enforcement roles of functional interest groups. In essence, corporatism creates "intermediate sovereignties" between the citizen and the state; sovereign intermediates which, it is argued, divide loyalties, fragment society, and ultimately undermine the legitimacy of the liberal democratic system.[57]

Drawing on these shortcomings, Schmitter and others argue that corporatism is most successful when it is least intrusive, that is to say, when the representative and enforcement responsibilities of functional interest groups are minimal.[58] Once the representatives of functional interest begin actively to participate in policy formulation and, more importantly, implementation, they begin also to consume the legitimacy of the state. Given enough time, corporatist institutions necessarily self-destruct.

Behind this view that corporatism is self-destructive lies a certain theoretical understanding of state–society relations in a liberal democracy.[59] The two principal issues are whether employer associations and trade unions have a necessary "representative" function, and whether state reliance on functional interest groups for policy implementation fragments state authority. These issues clearly depend upon assumptions about the nature of state autonomy, sovereignty, and legitimacy.

For example, Schmitter argues that functional interest groups play a "representative" role in corporatism because they influence both the formulation and the implementation of government policy at the expense of legislative autonomy. Alan Cawson concurs, and goes on to point out that "if the essential feature of liberal democracy is the relationship between individual electors and sovereign parliament, then that of corporatism is the representation of functional interests, whether or not this is institutionalized in parliamentary form."[60] Both authors, moreover, believe that corporatism diminishes the state's legitimacy by depriving it of sovereign authority. The assumption made by both authors is that state sovereignty and governmental autonomy are one and the same.[61] Whenever public policy is made or enforced by nonstate actors, the state loses sovereignty. The legitimacy of public policy, then, becomes a question of the citizen's "representation [within] and control [over]" the process of governance, with democratic legitimacy being dependent on the balance between "participation and accessibility" on the one hand, "accountability and responsiveness" on the other.[62]

Under these assumptions, the limitations of corporatist institutions are easy to recognize. The more corporatism intervenes in the functioning of society, the more limited is the "representation and control" of the citizen within the state. The creation of an elite class of functional interest leadership shuts off "participation and accessibility," while the failure of functional interest to respond to the diverse concerns of the individual limits "accountability and responsiveness." Thus reliance or corporatism consumes the legitimacy of the state until the citizenry reacts by replacing corporatist institutions with democratic ones.

The argument that corporatist institutions are self-limiting and self-destructive is a powerful one. Nevertheless, it is contingent upon the assumption that state sovereignty is equivalent to governmental autonomy. If state sovereignty is not the same as governmental autonomy, corporatism cannot challenge state legitimacy. For example, while state sovereignty is absolute, governmental autonomy can be limited either by circumstance or design. Circumstantial limitations can be ascribed to anything that the government simply cannot control. Here an example might be economic dependence: no matter what the government of a national state may do, it cannot escape its dependence on global or even large national markets. Therefore, the state is often forced to cooperate with other states in order to accomplish its objectives, such as monetary policy coordination or joint interventions in the interests of exchange rate stability.

Intentional limitations of autonomy can encompass all aspects of governance that are delegated to nonsovereign actors. If parliament alone is sovereign, such delegation would include all aspects of administrative law, as well as the *"in loco parentis"* powers of the educational system, etc. Here it is not a question of what the government can or cannot do, but rather a question of whether some other actor in society can implement public policy more effectively, such as holding parents responsible for the actions of their children. In this context, it is important to consider that sovereign power can revoke any delegation of authority, even up to the point of taking juvenile delinquents from their parents' homes.

The primary objective of the government is to provide essential public goods, such as peace, order, justice, and solidarity. Faced with circumstances beyond its control, a government can form alliances without violating state sovereignty. Similarly, the government does not sacrifice state sovereignty when it delegates responsibility for the provision of public goods at home. The sovereign power of state is simply the ultimate right to make decisions about how public goods can best be provided. Under responsible government, however, the sovereign is not compelled to make every decision.[63]

There is good reason to believe that state sovereignty is characteristically different from governmental autonomy. Theories of the state stretching back to the Middle Ages make the assumption implicitly.[64] Max Weber, who argued that "a compulsory political association" is only a state "if and insofar as its administrative staff successfully upholds a claim to the *monopoly* of the *legitimate* use of physical force in the enforcement of its order," went on to point out that "today, the use of force is regarded as legitimate only so far as it is either *permitted* by the state or *prescribed* by it...."[65]

The observation that the government can delegate its autonomy significantly changes the nature of corporatist bargaining. If the state can assign its decision-making authority to a negotiating council composed of trade unions, employers' associations, and government administrators, then none of the negotiating partners need serve a representative function. The fact that leaders of trade unions and employers' associations do represent their constituencies is largely irrelevant to the legitimacy of the political process. Democratic representation takes place during the act of delegation, and not during the process of negotiation.

The standard for legitimacy remains the same, yet the decision under scrutiny is not the policy outcome but rather the choice of procedure for policymaking. Two questions are relevant. First, was the parliament representative of the public interest in deciding to delegate responsibility for policymaking to a corporatist institution? Second, was the policy outcome effective with respect to parliamentary, and by extension popular, objectives regarding the policy outcomes? The representative characteristic of parliament is dependent upon the nature of the political mandate, as well as on the range of policy options available. The effectiveness of policy depends on the ability of the corporatist institution to design and implement a policy program that achieves parliamentary objectives.

Once again, the successful use of corporatist bargaining relies on the prospects for collective action within and between industry and labor groups. In difficult economic times, corporatism benefits from a broad common desire for economic recovery, a limited number of policy alternatives, and the likelihood that negotiations will bring gains to all parties. In prosperous times, the mandate is less clear, the options more varied, and the interests of the negotiating parties less harmonious.

The responsibility of trade unions and employers' associations to implement public policy is an explicit part of the parliamentary choice for corporatist bargaining. Does parliamentary delegation of the enforcement powers of the state create a privileged class of functional interest elites? Certainly it empowers the leaders of trade unions and employers' associations to act in the public good, but it does not grant them any "privilege" to operate independently of parliamentary authority. Therefore, "as long as democratically elected legislatures can determine the limits of such rights and withdraw them if they have undesirable effects, the character of the state is essentially unchanged."[66] The relevant question is not whether delegated enforcement "privileges" functional interest elites, but whether these elites are capable of achieving the desired policy outcome. And, it is an affirmative answer to this question, which Walter Lippmann recognized as the great promise of organized labor, and which John Maynard Keynes believed to be the future of liberal democracy:

Labour is far from having achieved anything like its legitimate influence in the conduct of industry, and the best hope for future adjustment lies in the immense discipline that power will enforce upon the worker. (Lippmann)[67]

I believe that in many cases the ideal size for the unit of control and organization lies somewhere between the individual and modern State. I suggest, therefore that progress lies in the growth and recognition of semi-autonomous bodies within the State... bodies which in the ordinary course of affairs are mainly autonomous within their prescribed limitations, but are subject in the last resort to the sovereignty of democracy expressed through Parliament. (Keynes)[68]

Evaluation of the accuracy of Lippmann's or Keynes' analysis depends on whether labor and employers' associations are capable of enforcing public policy. It also depends on the recognition that corporatism is a tool for public policy and not an alternative to democracy.

Sadly, the fascist dictatorships of the interwar period relied heavily on the support afforded by corporatist bargaining. It was the governments themselves, however, which were undemocratic and therefore illegitimate. Here the arguments made by Schmitter and others are correct: corporatist bargaining is only as legitimate as the state which sponsors it. Victory by the Allied Powers ensured that West European governments would be subject to rigorous and continuous scrutiny with respect to their democratic legitimacy. While this scrutiny often includes consideration of the appropriateness of corporatist bargaining, reliance on such bargaining does not constitute prima facie evidence of illegitimacy.[69] Corporatism is a tool. Like any tool, it can be used and it can be abused.

## Regional Integration

If the term "corporatism" suffered from its association with fascism, the concept of the national state staggered under the weight of two world wars. Hence, while the economic advantages to European integration are important, the origins of the movement itself stem from the powerful desire to avoid another European war. The early "Europeanists," regardless of their educational formation, were not economists so much as politicians. Their political ambition was to shackle the destructive forces of nationalism in order to preempt any conceivable military confrontation between the states of Western Europe.[70]

In the late 1940s, the primary debate was over the means for European integration, and not the objective. Some supported a federal constitution like that enjoyed by the United States, while others argued for a progressive fusion of sovereign parliaments. None of these radical departures from the European system of national states could find the popular or governmental support necessary for success. In a sense, these proposals relied too much on a leap of faith: the citizens and officials of sovereign states were expected to transfer allegiance to a large, heterogeneous, and imprecisely defined notion of Europe. Winston Churchill manifests this tension most visibly. Although a vocal proponent of Europe in the late 1940s, Churchill neither brought his Conservative government into the ECSC nor would he align with the proposed European Defence Community.[71]

The experience of the early 1950s confirmed that the creation of Europe had to proceed by increments. States would relinquish to a supranational authority only those tasks that could not be accomplished at the national level: The ECSC was a success while the European Defence Community was a failure. But the defeat of the European Defence Community in the French Parliament was not the end of Europe even if it did indicate that there would be no radical abandonment of the national state.[72] Efforts at European integration shifted back to economic issues. Even those for whom the ultimate goal of the European Union remained unchanged accepted that its achievements would pass through intermediate economic objectives.[73]

The strategy of the European federalists was twofold. First, they sought to create supranational institutions, which would gradually assume the competencies held by the national states. Second, they hoped to imbue these institutions with sufficient legitimacy to permit a transfer of popular allegiance from the national states to the European federation. Yet both aspects of this strategy are paradoxical: national states, acting in the national interest, are expected to relinquish their definitive sovereignty and welcome an erosion of popular legitimacy. In the words of Ernst Haas, an early and persuasive advocate of this hypothesis:

[It is] a theory of international integration by indirection, by trial and error, by miscalculation on the part of actors desiring integration, by manipulation of elite forces on the part of small groups of pragmatic administrators and politicians in the setting of a vague but permissive public opinion.[74]

General de Gaulle brought this paradox into sharp relief with the proposal of the Fouchet Plan in the early 1960s. Rather than seeing the national states manipulated by an elite group of European federalists, de Gaulle indicated that it was the states themselves that possessed the greatest manipulative powers.[75] While the Fouchet Plan was ultimately defeated, so too was the "neo-functionalist" paradigm for regional integration. Even before de Gaulle's Fouchet Plan, Italian federalist Altiero Spinelli made known his concerns that the institutions of Europe were being reduced to "arenas in which every state seeks only national successes."[76] After Fouchet,

Hendrik Brugmans asserted that the re-emergence of nationalism in Europe had made the bureaucracy of the Community something of a scandal.[77] The supranational institutions of the Community lost much of their authority, and decision-making became subject to the so-called "Luxembourg compromise," which granted each member state the right to veto Community decisions that might affect its "vital" national interests.

In the years that have passed since the defeat of the Fouchet Plan, the Community has grown in both its intergovernmental and its supranational characteristics. The rigid dictates of de Gaulle's hard-won Luxembourg comprise have given way to more majoritarian procedures, even as the European Council of heads of state and governments has assumed an increasingly central role in the integration process.[78] A similar point applies to the development of public opinion. The populations of the member states have become more European while at the same time retaining important national differences, and functional interest groups have, on the whole, failed to organize in any durable way across national boundaries.[79]

For political scientists, this result represents an even greater paradox than the one implied by the neo-functionalist paradigm. National states have become more powerful as European integration has progressed. National sovereignty exercised within European institutions has become more "effective," and national governments more legitimate.[80] For the smaller countries of Europe, this paradox reaches its extreme. As one small country representative explained:

Where before sovereignty was understood in terms of national independence, now it should be understood in terms of membership within the European Community: Full members are fully sovereign, associated members only partially, and non-members are not sovereign at all.[81]

In order to resolve this paradox, we need to look again at the meaning of sovereignty. National sovereignty is the ultimate right to make decisions, which includes the ability to determine where decisions will be made. The definition with respect to international affairs should be the same as the definition with respect to domestic politics, where delegations of state authority are a necessary part of governance. A state can decide to participate in a regional organization just as it can decide to allow corporatist institutions to make and implement public policy.

The member states were sovereign when they chose to join the Community and they remain sovereign as long as they are free to leave the Community. Membership is legitimate insofar as it is voluntary and to the extent that it increases the effectiveness of state efforts to serve the national interest. For example, given the degree of a smaller country's dependence on the Community, the government of that country is most effective if it participates in Community decision-making, less so if it is only associated with the Community, and least effective if it attempts to ignore the Community altogether. The decision of Austria, Finland, and Sweden to become full members in the Community—despite the small economic advantages to be achieved beyond participation in the EEA—reflects this fact.

The real promise of European integration is not to replace the national state, but rather to increase the effectiveness of national economic policy in attaining domestic economic objectives. The member states of the EU, small and large, have chosen a path of integration that is grounded in economic cooperation. Should this result in the creation of a truly European community of values in competition with national societal differences, it is possible that "Europe" will replace the European system of national states.[82] That remains to be seen. For the time being, as long as the member states are free to leave the Union, no matter what the cost, they remain sovereign.

Participation in the process of European integration depends on the benefits of membership for the member states. As long as there are economic advantages to integration, as long as the partners to integration are acceptable, and as long as there remains a strong spirit of cooperation, the sovereign states of Europe will continue to participate enthusiastically. When these elements are not present, enthusiasm will suffer. At the extreme, the EU member states may even reconsider their participation in all or part of the venture.

## Legitimacy

The test for legitimacy in a liberal democratic society involves a simultaneous assessment of representation and effectiveness. Government which is not representative, no matter how effective, is likely to be insensitive to changes in the popular interest. Government which is not effective, no matter how representative, is likely to fail in the provision of essential public goods. Given these two extremes, it is easy to conclude that the governments of Western Europe, both within the Community and without, fall somewhere in between. They are representative and effective to a greater or lesser extent.

The same twofold test determines the legitimacy of both corporatist and European institutions: to what extent do corporatist or European institutions represent the desires of the national electorates, and to what extent are these institutions capable of responding effectively to those desires? Having relaxed the assumption that state sovereignty and governmental autonomy are one and the same, neither corporatist bargaining nor European integration necessarily challenges the national state. And neither corporatist institutions nor European integration can be taken for granted. Depending upon popular perceptions, any choice to rely on either of these two mainstays for small country adjustment may find itself severely lacking in popular support—and, indeed, the subject of populist opposition. Corporatism and regional integration do not threaten the state, but populist politics in a nation-state context may imperil the future of corporatism and regional integration.

Small-state adjustment strategies must not only work, they must also be perceived to work. The real challenge to the national state stems from its political and economic vulnerability. To the extent to which corporatist bargaining and European integration increase the effectiveness of national economic policy, they also increase the legitimacy of the state. There is no real paradox between the continuing viability of the national state and the government reliance on either corporatism or the EU. Rather, the continuing viability of the European state is testimony to the success of their postwar policies, including both corporatism and European integration. Europe has not discarded the nation-state. European nation-states have learned to adapt to their inevitable interdependence. The smaller states demonstrate adaptability in its extreme form. For them, the challenges were much greater, and so were the necessary adaptations.

## The Structure of Politics

Yet neither corporatism nor integration can shore up economic vulnerabilities for all time and in every respect. Therefore, it is important to look at how states adapt to economic change without consuming their own legitimacy or undermining their national identity, using corporatism and integration as instruments rather than as panacea. My contention is that the people respond to the need for economic adjustment by throwing their support behind effective government, even if its effectiveness comes at the price of representative government. The difficulty here arises when elites cannot agree on how to determine the general interest, whether by consensus or by majority. At such time, the meaning of representative government becomes confused because there is no clear division between particular interest and the general interest. Consequently, the people will tend to support whichever formula—majority or consensus—promises to be the most effective at identifying the general interest and providing the necessary economic adjustment.

The structure of relations between elites and between elites and followers plays a vital role in the identification of the common interest. American-style pluralism is not very good at consensus. Instead, elites compete with each other to form majorities out of a diverse but unfragmented electorate. Belgian and Dutch consociationalism is better at forging consensus than at carving out a narrow majority. Nevertheless, the structure of such relationships is more behavioral than institutional. Although institutions can encourage one type of decision-making over another, the structure of relations between elites or between elites and followers can change over time—sometimes very quickly. Hence the character of decision-making can change very quickly as well. For example, the Netherlands was a consociational democracy throughout the late 1940s and 1950s; however, Dutch politics was less consensual under some governments than under others. Belgian politics was deeply polarized during the 1940s and 1950s, and only began to arrive at consensual policies in the 1960s.

Such variations in the degree of consensus within consociational democracy should not be surprising. Relations between elites or between elites and followers can survive only so long as they adapt to meet the changing wants and aspirations of society. Small changes in societal interests or state institutions require slight adaptations—as when the alternation of power between conservatives and social democrats results in a modification of the tax regime, or when the privatization of government enterprises requires the development of active capital markets.[83] More significant changes require much greater adaptations. In response to the growth of finance capital in the late nineteenth century, for example, Walter Lippmann argued that a fundamental change in the structure of the American polity would make the difference between *Drift and Mastery*. Lippmann did not argue that Americans should reject pluralism for some other form of political organization, but he did insist that America had to find some formula to make pluralism work more effectively.[84]

Nevertheless, relations between elites or between elites and followers do not always adapt, or adapt successfully. To borrow from Peter Hall, "[there] is no teleology here. Hence, it is quite possible for actions and institutions to have consequences that may be detrimental to the long term survival of the system."[85] When elites fail to adapt to changes in society, the democratic system begins to suffer from "something that is altogether comparable to old age or organic debilitation."[86] In the words of John Kenneth Galbraith, the state falls prey to a "culture of contentment," which is completely at odds with the changing aspirations of society.[87] Taken to its extreme, the inability of elites to adapt to societal change can reinforce the institutional paralysis of the state. The more the state fails in its organizational function, the less society coheres, and the more difficult becomes the reconciliation of competing interests.[88]

The reverse can also take place: the society can refuse to accept changes initiated by the government. Here it is important to consider that the entrepreneurial state experiences the same limitations as the entrepreneurial individual. Where there is no support for an idea, there is no market. And where there is no market, the idea cannot succeed. It is not enough that the state have a monopoly of the legitimate use of force in society. As Ludwig von Mises explains:

The theorists and practitioners of power politics should [remember] Hume's famous arguments that all rule rests on power over minds; the government is always only a minority and can govern the majority only because the latter either is convinced of the legitimacy of the rulers or considers their rule desirable in its own interests.[89]

It goes without saying that some political institutions work better than others. However, the point to note is that when the government's action reflects societal interests, and society accepts and ratifies that government action, the result is political power. Weber, while arguing that the monopoly of the legitimate use of force defines the state, notes that "the use of physical force is neither the sole, nor even the most usual, method of administration." Instead, the use of physical force "is always the last resort when others have failed."[90] The government of a weak state relies on force to enforce compliance from the society. The government of a strong state can anticipate compliance, even before acting. The weak state, in

## The Politics of Economic Adjustment

enforcing its wishes on an unwilling society, consumes its own legitimacy. The strong state, in uniting societal efforts, strengthens its legitimacy.

Of course, no program for adjustment, and no governmental action, can go on forever. Societal interests change as old problems get solved and new problems arise. To the extent that the government is endowed with only limited resources, new interests begin to compete with existing policies. Should the government fail to recognize the nature of this competition, it will cease to benefit from popular compliance with its policies and will begin to feel pressure for action in some new area. Again the underlying structure of politics must adapt.

## Dependence

The problem of economic dependence exists on both sides of state–society relations: it limits government resources and it affects societal attitudes.[91] For an open and externally dependent country, discretionary fiscal and monetary policies often fail to respond adequately to societal claims. Moreover, in extreme cases, the danger of speculation can prevent governments from borrowing resources abroad, while competition with private investment for domestic capital inhibits them from borrowing excessively at home.

From the standpoint of society, the external determination of prices and wages constrains action regarding the distribution of income. Although world market forces always create winners as well as losers, such assignments are arbitrary and volatile. Each change of relative prices also changes relative wealth and position. In periods of global economic turmoil, the very fabric of society is strained. Economic dependence calls into question the cohesiveness of the nation and the desirability of the state.

Yet if international interdependence limits the ability of the state to act on its own, it also increases the incentives for government to act in concert with major nonstate institutions and actors in the society. That is the promise of corporatist bargaining. Put another way, corporatism can increase the effectiveness of government in serving the general interest. Although corporatism relies on the leaders of trade unions and employers' associations for enforcing public policy, it also offers a superior, and sometimes unique, way to reconcile societal claims and government resources. To paraphrase Peter Gourevitch, the state is stronger, but it is not necessarily more autonomous from society, precisely because the "state and groups borrow from each other the authority to do what they cannot do alone."[92]

However, corporatism is only an instrument and not a political system in its own right. Although elites may attempt to elevate corporatist bargaining to the level of national ideology, they are unlikely to succeed in doing so. As mentioned earlier, the diversity of societal interests cannot easily be contained in a limited number of functional interest groups. Moreover, the spirit of cooperation which is essential to corporatist bargaining will not be present at all times. Should popular interests arise in competition with corporatism, interest groups or the government may abandon it in favor of some other activity. Corporatism is not the key to change, but only one of many possible instruments.[93]

A similar point can be made with regard to regional integration. The advantages of integration are numerous. So too are its limitations. For both government and society, integration promises to facilitate the fulfillment of economic objectives, but also requires explicit compromises. Supranational institutions do not always give adequate attention to particular national considerations. Representatives of the member states must continually assert their claims in competition with one another as well as with the institutional imperatives of the supranational organization itself. Both the intergovernmentalist and functionalist views of European integration have their own distinct logic—a reality accepted in the integrationist literature since the early 1990s.[94]

Nevertheless, to the extent that the objectives achieved through regional integration outweigh the costs, government participation in regional or supranational institutions represents a successful adaptation. When the costs begin to threaten the society, or when intergovernmental cooperation appears no longer to work in society's interests, integration will be rejected.

## Effectiveness, Stability, and Change

Both corporatist bargaining and regional integration are tools for the promotion of the general interest: for the smaller states of Europe, as for their larger counterparts, corporatism and integration are responses to the problem of economic dependence. As responses, they are limited by the nature and the extent of the problem at hand. When corporatism and regional integration facilitate government efforts to fulfill societal objectives, they represent successful adaptations of the political formula. Moreover, through their success, they spark a virtuous circle of cooperation, effectiveness, and legitimization. In other words, not only is government action more effective, the state is strengthened as well.

This analysis makes the link between the economic and political success of the adjustment strategies pursued by the Martens and Lubbers cabinets in the 1980s. The center-right coalitions of both countries relied on corporatism and European integration to increase the effectiveness of their economic policies. And, through these efforts, they increased the popular legitimacy of the government as well. Although not everyone in Belgium and the Netherlands necessarily liked the center-right strategies for economic adjustment, "the people" were willing to support those strategies because they appeared to offer an effective response to the economic crisis.

The same analysis can also explain the transition from the center-right to the center-left at the end of the 1980s. As economic performance improved, popular preferences for strong and effective government diminished. Instead, the Belgians and the Dutch began to call for more "representative" and "responsive" government. In order better to meet these claims, Martens and

Lubbers found it necessary to shift to the center-left, increase their parliamentary majorities, and begin to focus on building a more broadly consensual policy strategy. In turn, this shift back to consensus carried a high price in terms of decisive economic policymaking.

As political societies change within a given nation, that state's relationship with—its attitude toward, participation in, and reliance on—corporatist bargaining and regional integration necessarily changes as well. For this reason, there is, or at least should be, no mystery regarding the shift from consensual to more majoritarian adjustment strategies in Belgium and the Netherlands. The breakdown of consociationalism in the late 1960s and 1970s necessarily implied that there would be a change in both countries' use of corporatism and European integration. When Dutch and Belgian society was consociational in the 1950s and early 1960s, corporatism was compatible with consensus and regional integration could be limited to the removal of barriers to trade. However, in the more pluralist Dutch and Belgian societies of the early 1980s, the structure of corporatist bargaining was much less consensual and the gains from liberalization were all but realized. The economic adjustment strategies devised by Martens and Lubbers were inevitably more majoritarian in character. They were nonetheless effective, and economic recovery and political stability were the result.

Yet in understanding this outcome, it is necessary to focus not on what has changed, but what has remained the same—and to ask whether these continuities are still sufficient to support the style of economic policymaking that Peter Katzenstein identifies with small states and world markets. The answer depends upon a retelling of the story of economic adjustment in Belgium and the Netherlands from its origins at the end of World War II. The two countries emerge from the war (and the Great Depression that preceded it) with similar political institutions and yet in very different positions, both economically and politically. They follow different developmental trajectories. And they converge—briefly—on a common crisis and response. After that moment of convergence, however, the two countries part company both in relation to one another and in relation to their own past. What remains of the similarities between them is recognizable as a legacy of consociational democracy. Whether such similarities are sufficient to support a further use of Katzenstein's small country adjustment model is nevertheless in doubt.

# 2

# Consensual Adjustment in Consociational Democracy

Every history has to start somewhere and this one starts at the end of World War II. As starting points go, the end of World War II is not arbitrary—or at least not entirely. Belgium and the Netherlands were always small in the conventional meaning of the word and they were already, by most accounts, both consociational. The two countries also displayed many of the preferences that shape their strategic choices for economic adjustment: free trade, stable exchange rates, hard currency, and accommodating monetary and fiscal policy. Nevertheless, the Dutch and Belgian governments only began to combine regional integration and corporatism bargaining in the late 1940s. And they were able to do so—to a large extent—because of the shared experience of global conflict. Hence the end of World War II is not as good a place as any to start this analysis. In fact, it is better than most.

The material in this chapter, and the chapters that follow, is historical. But the objectives are functional and not narrative. Specifically, the chapter is designed to fulfill three ambitions: to show how Belgium and the Netherlands adhere to the policy preferences for free trade, fixed exchange rates, hard currencies, and accommodating macroeconomic policies; to introduce the specific institutions used for corporatist bargaining and regional integration; and to illustrate how these institutions could be used to facilitate economic adjustment and why, sometimes, they could not.

## Consensual Adjustment in Consociational Democracy

A fourth ambition is implicit. This chapter includes a lot of details about names and policies that may seem extraneous to the larger argument. In some senses it is. Nevertheless, these details are helpful to underscore the fact that this is an argument about real people making real choices, that there were always a large number of actors involved, and that they had numerous options and instruments at their disposal—some more attractive and more effective than others. Moreover, as in the real world, every choice implies a trade-off and every trade-off looks different from different perspectives. Although we might agree with benefit of hindsight that some actions are better than others, no choice is right in any objective sense, and no instrument is effective in all contexts. By the same token, policy goals that seem imperative and absolute in one moment may come to appear irrelevant, inconvenient, and counterproductive in the next. Hence even the most successful politicians, the most selfless business leaders, and the most solidarity-oriented trade unionists are likely to find themselves being punished for their actions in the end.

The chapter has two sections—both of which are very long. The first sketches the experience of the Netherlands as a paradigmatic case of small-state adjustment within a consociational democracy. The second explores the very different experience of Belgium.

## The Netherlands

Adjustment is too weak a term to describe the requirements of the Dutch economy at the end of World War II. The country was in ruins. Occupying (and also allied) forces had destroyed much of the national endowment of machinery and rolling stock. Official estimates valued total war damage at 25 billion guilders, or more than five times national income for 1945 and three times national income for 1946. Labor productivity had declined 30 percent in relation to the interwar period, and a large proportion of the population was out of work and, indeed, starving.[1]

Reconstruction and stabilization programs absorbed much of the government's attention. However, the devastation of national capital stocks forced policymakers to concentrate on balance of payments stabilization and inflation control, rather than on income redistribution or demand management. Keynes had a strong influence on the practice of government fiscal policy, and yet finance ministers found it difficult to make effective use of countercyclical spending or tax concessions. Production for domestic consumption was too limited, and investment too dependent upon imported capital goods, to permit a government-led reflation. Inevitably, stabilizing the balance of payments took priority over stimulating aggregate demand in the determination of government revenues and outlays.[2] The constraints on monetary policy were stringent as well. Finance Minister Pieter Lieftinck had to restore the internal and external value of the guilder in the face of a huge surplus in the supply of money and a shortage of goods or services to spend it on. Consequently, the government had little recourse to expansionary monetary policy.[3]

In this context, the government quickly availed itself of both regional integration and corporatism in its attempt to manage the domestic economy. Wartime negotiations between the government in exile and representatives from Belgium and Luxembourg culminated in the formation of the Benelux customs union. Although the customs union would not enter into force until 1948, it was clear from the outset that Dutch access to more prosperous Belgian consumer markets would have a strong positive influence on the reconstruction of the Dutch economy. Also during the war, collaboration between Dutch workers and employers to resist German occupation developed into a Foundation of Labour dedicated to the promotion of the working classes and to the maintenance of social harmony.[4] The government lost little time in engaging the Foundation of Labour in national collective bargaining in order to control the growth of wages under the oversight and guidance of the Board of Government Mediators.[5]

However, the government's joint application of regional integration and corporatist intermediation foundered on a lack of consensus with regard to the objectives of Dutch economic policy. Policymakers could agree on the broad requirements for reconstruction, but not on the specific ambitions of policy measures. With respect to regional integration, the success of the Benelux revealed a strong underlying concern for political sovereignty. European federalists were relatively few in number in the Netherlands and had little influence on government policy.[6] Integration enthusiasts, to the extent they existed in policymaking circles, had practical rather than idealistic objectives. And these objectives centered on market access for Dutch exports. The Netherlands refused to deepen the Benelux through monetary integration or even the close coordination of monetary policies. The Dutch also rejected proposals to extend the three-country customs union to France, Italy, or Germany. Economic integration was not to serve as a vehicle for surrendering Dutch commercial policy to one or several of Europe's larger powers. Privileged access to part of Europe's marketplace, the Dutch reasoned, made little sense if paired with greater protectionism vis-à-vis the rest of the world.[7]

Progress in the development of corporatist institutions suffered from a broad popular rejection of government-dominated price–wage controls. Involvement of the Foundation of Labour in collective bargaining proved insufficient cover for what was really direct intervention in goods and factor markets. Trade unions chafed under the oversight powers of the Board of Government Mediators and began to struggle for greater influence in wage and price determination. The result was 210 strikes and 326,450 lost workdays on average per annum to 1949.[8] By the end of the 1940s, the political leadership of the Netherlands had to find a more stable and less authoritarian solution to the problem of maintaining international competitiveness.

Thus while the combination of regional integration and corporatist intermediation should facilitate adjustment, the Dutch government encountered significant difficulties during the early postwar period. Moreover, the need for adjustment was immense. Before the war, the Netherlands was primarily a commercial power, with a strong specialization in services like insurance and shipping. When the war ended, the Dutch recognized that further development of the manufacturing sector was necessary for the promotion of national economic welfare. Thus Dutch policymakers not only had to recover from the damage wrought by war, they also had to effect a fundamental transformation of the economy.[9] As it turned out, progress in the Dutch development of an export-manufacturing base—as opposed to stabilization or reconstruction—would have to wait until the early 1950s.

The purpose of this section is to explain the relationship between Dutch consociationalism and economic adjustment during the early postwar period. The argument has four parts. The first shows how agreement among elites on a consociational political formula was necessary for the adoption of an adjustment strategy. The second explains how the combination of corporatist price–incomes policy and regional integration promoted the transformation of the Dutch economy toward manufacturing for export. The third describes the breakdown of economic consensus in the late 1950s and early 1960s. Finally, the fourth part examines the changes which took place in the structure and functioning of the Dutch political economy after the completion of the adjustment process.

## The Political Preconditions for Economic Adjustment

The Dutch model for consociational democracy is perhaps the best-known example of a political formula combining a fragmented political culture and coalescent elites. In Dutch consociationalism, ideologically distinct subnational pillars (or political cultures),[10] composed of deferential followers and compromising elites, jointly negotiate public policy in the national interest. So long as followers are deferential and elites make sufficient compromises, consociational democracy adequately explains political stability in a society with deep internal cleavages like the Netherlands.

## Consensual Adjustment in Consociational Democracy

Nevertheless, consociationalism is not a permanent feature of Dutch political life. Changing social values can soften the cleavages within the national culture, compelling elites to adopt more competitive behavior. Of course elites can resist competing with each other, but then they risk alienating the electorate by offering them little from which to choose in the name of consensus. In other words, as society becomes less fragmented and more homogenous, elites must choose between a pluralist political formula and anomie.

Value change is not the only threat to consociationalism as a stable political formula. The possibility that ideological conflict might escalate out of control is destabilizing as well. As Seymour Martin Lipset pointed out, political movements which rely on the close ideological integration of their followers are likely to breed intolerance and, ultimately, civil strife. Where ideology is concerned, it is a fine line between the "give-and-take game of pressure politics" and "a mighty struggle between divine or historic truth on one side and fundamental error on the other."[11] If, in a fragmented political culture, elites try to adopt a competitive and more pluralist political formula, they run the risk of creating a centrifugal situation, ideological conflict that can tear the society apart.

Thus, restraining the forces that knit subnational political cultures together is as important for elites as adapting to the softening of political cleavages.[12] Consociational democracy represents a delicate balance between forces that break down subnational political cultures and the forces which forge subnational cultures into competing ideological groups.[13] Too great a momentum in either direction undermines the stability of the political system.

Only by recognizing the dynamic nature of consociational democracy can we understand the politics of the Netherlands at the end of World War II. The specter of German National Socialism lessened the fervor of many Dutch elites for the consociational system. Political leaders, particularly Socialists from the western provinces, feared that the ideological segmentation of Dutch society would lead to either civil strife or an authoritarian regime. From their exile in London, these elites worked to establish a Dutch Peoples Party capable of bridging the gap between the various secular and nonsecular ideological groups. Such a bridge would overcome ideological divisions and bring the disparate elements of Dutch society under one political roof—not in the form of utopic depoliticization, but in a competitive pluralist political formula like that found in the Anglo-Saxon world.[14]

Their efforts at changing the Dutch political formula from consociationalism to pluralism were ill timed. The long process of liberation benefited Catholic leaders in the southern provinces who desired to retain the consociational framework. Catholics rallied to the renamed Catholic Peoples Party (KVP) in December 1945, and in doing so upset plans for a cross-ideological union. The Socialists changed names (to *Partij van de Arbeid*, PvdA) in order to pick up the banner of reform, but the orthodox *Anti-Revolutionaire Partij* (ARP) and moderate *Christelijke Historische Unie* (CHU) Calvinists retained their old consociational structures. Consequently, the Dutch Peoples Party failed to overturn the consociational system. Willem Schermerhorn headed the first postwar government as a leader of the movement for political renewal, and yet his premiership did not receive popular legitimation at the polls. In numerical terms, the 1946 elections returned a close approximation of the Second Chamber of 1939.[15]

However, such numbers are misleading. The 1946 Chamber was different from its predecessor in that the two main parties—the Catholic KVP and the Socialist PvdA—no longer agreed on whether consociationalism or pluralism was the correct political formula. Moreover, statements by the Catholic leadership only served to deepen the division. Soon before Schermerhorn's reform movement failed at the polls, Catholic leader C. P. M. Romme suggested that liberal democracy be replaced with a more corporatist state. His suggestion was immediately rejected by Socialist ranks and quietly dismissed within his own party. Democratic institutions may have left the Netherlands unprepared for war, but state corporatism was an unacceptable bulwark for peace. After the 1946 elections, the PvdA refused to join a cabinet under Romme's leadership.[16]

## Consensual Adjustment in Consociational Democracy

Conflict between Catholics and Socialists over the merits of consociationalism effectively closed the door on consensus building. This was unfortunate because healing the Netherlands from its long and bitter occupation should have allowed for a national coalition government dedicated to economic reconstruction and adjustment. Functional interest groups, with the exception of the Communist trade union *Eenheidsvakcentrale* (EVC), saw little interest in confrontation. The largest trade union federation, the Socialist *Nederlands Verbond van Vakverenigingen* (NVV), suffered under the stigma of wartime collaboration and was therefore eager to show patriotism through self-restraint. The confessional trade unions, the Catholic *Katholieke Arbeidersbeweging* (KAB) and the Protestant *Christelijk Nationaal Vakverbond* (CNV), were willing to forgo confrontation with employers in the interests of social stability.[17] And, the largest federation of employers' organizations, the *Centraal Sociaal Werkgeversverbond* (CSWV), was willing to cooperate with trade unions as an alternative to class conflict.[18] After the 1945 dockworkers' strike in Rotterdam, employers were unanimous that social unrest was the greatest threat to economic recovery.

In spite of the prospects for broad cooperation, however, Catholic L. J. M. Beel had to bring together a narrow Red-Rome (PvdA-KVP) coalition in order to hold the Socialists to governing responsibility and to prevent a radicalization of the left along class lines. The situation was not ideal for the Catholics, but they accepted it as necessary for the political stability of the country.

Participation in the Beel cabinet saw the Socialist PvdA begin to soften its stand on political renewal and to revert from a competitive pluralist party back to a party of consociationalism. Indeed, sharing governing responsibility with the Catholics left almost no other choice. Socialist ministers, particularly Willem Drees, found it difficult to meet the demands of a broadly based constituency in wide-ranging negotiations. Ministers, Drees believed, had to retain the liberty to make compromises in cabinet discussions, and therefore could not take direction from diverse interests within the party.[19] However, while it is possible to take followers for granted in a party unified by a single ideology, it is more difficult in a diverse party.

With the inclusion of nonsocialist groups in the PvdA, Drees could not ignore the demands of party sub-factions without risking their defection. Nevertheless that is what he chose to do. As a result, Liberal activists within the PvdA began to fear for the loss of their political identity, and more left-wing elements agitated for a return to class struggle.[20] Satisfying both wings of the party was impossible. In the end, the PvdA remained true to its socialist origins and, in 1947, the Liberal group left the party to found a more ideologically coherent organization—the Liberal *Volkspartij voor Vrijheid en Democratie* (VVD).[21]

The departure of the Liberals gave more ideological coherence to the PvdA, making it possible for Socialist leaders to negotiate more effectively with their Catholic, Protestant, and even their Liberal counterparts. However the Socialists still aspired to create a more pluralist formula for the Netherlands, more because they feared an outbreak of ideological conflict than because they found consensus building somehow distasteful. When early elections were called in 1948, the PvdA remained committed to participation in the government as well as to political reform. Return to opposition, the party leadership feared, would only benefit the extreme left and would give responsibility for economic policy to the center-right.[22] Continued participation in the government, they felt, was the only effective counter to the danger of ideological extremism.[23]

The difficulty for the Socialist leadership was in joining a cabinet that commanded a sufficient number of parliamentary votes to pass legislation for constitutional reform. The PvdA had lost seats in the 1948 election,[24] and a narrow Red-Rome coalition could not guarantee the necessary two-thirds majority.[25] The party leaders were loathe to share governing responsibility with anyone other than the Catholics, and were particularly reluctant to see the Liberal VVD in the cabinet. Each party added to the cabinet placed greater negotiating demands on the governing parties,

## Consensual Adjustment in Consociational Democracy

thereby strengthening the consociational characteristics of party organizations. Leaders had simultaneously to find a basis for compromise and to ensure top-down discipline within their subnational pillars. Such requirements ran directly against the objectives of political reform. There was, however, little alternative.

The Catholic KVP again played the crucial role in forming the government. A first attempt by Beel foundered on Socialist objections to the participation of the Liberals. The second attempt, made jointly by J. R. H van Schaik (KVP) and Willem Drees (PvdA), was more successful.[26] Drees, a Socialist, became minister-president in spite of the PvdA's numerical inferiority in parliament, and the Liberals were allowed to control the foreign ministry. This surprising arrangement was perhaps the only means to bring together a cabinet with a sufficiently broad constituency in parliament: the Catholics, Socialists, Liberals, and moderate Calvinists together controlled 78 of the 100 seats, 11 more than required for constitutional reform.

Formation of the Drees–van Schaik cabinet marked the return of the Socialists to the consociational fold. The PvdA had no choice but to accept the give-and-take of multiparty politics organized around subnational cultures. Consequently, Drees had to maintain a certain distance between governing elites and party activists. Attempts within the PvdA to transfer the seat of the party from Amsterdam to The Hague met staunch resistance from Socialist ministers and, in particular, from the minister-president.[27] Those members of the PvdA serving in the cabinet had to retain their room for compromise with the Catholics, Liberals, and Calvinists, and therefore could not afford close interference from party activists. PvdA cabinet members also had to rely on the top-down discipline of the Socialist pillar to enforce bargains struck within the government.

Granting Drees the minister-presidency exacted a high price from the Catholics. Nevertheless, Drees' leadership of the government was a necessary sacrifice if the Catholics were to hold the PvdA to governing responsibility outside of a narrow Red-Rome configuration. Romme was reportedly furious with van Schaik for offering the minister-presidency to the PvdA. Yet he soon acknowledged that this concession was essential to effective cooperation and political stability.[28]

Once the Socialists abandoned their claim to political reform, the Drees–van Schaik cabinet succeeded in building a broad consensus around full employment as the principal objective of economic policy. The government's 1949 "First Report on the Industrialization of the Netherlands" provided a blueprint for action.[29] The role of government was "to create an industrial environment which [could] minimise the risks facing industry and stimulate the dynamism of private enterprise."[30] The report showed little enthusiasm for massive state intervention in the marketplace or for state control over productive resources. Rather, the report reflected the prevailing Dutch sentiment that economic planning should be suggestive and not binding.[31] Entrepreneurship and market forces were to be the driving forces for industrialization.

The 1949 report on industrialization provided the outlines for government policy. The 1950 Industrial Organization Act provided the institutional framework.[32] The Drees–van Schaik cabinet built on the 1945 initiative of the Foundation of Labour to involve labor and employers' groups in the formation of economic policy. Involvement was to take place at the national and industrial levels. The 1950 Act provided for a Social and Economic Council to be comprised in equal proportions by representatives of the trade unions, the employers' associations, and the state.[33] As an independent organization, the Council's role was to give timely advice to the government on all facets of economic policymaking.

Agreement on the 1949 First Report and on the 1950 Industrial Organization Act was possible for two reasons: one economic and one ideological. The economic problems to be faced had a direct impact on confessional and nonconfessional constituencies alike. Unemployment made few ideological distinctions. Moreover, because families developed around single-income households, unemployment was a principal determinant of regional and societal income disparities. In 1948, the dispersion of income across socioeconomic groups compared more closely to Mexico than to any industrialized country with the exception of the British-occupied zone of Germany. By 1950, inequality in the distribution of Dutch income had diminished little if at all.[34] The confessional strongholds to the South and North were particularly hard hit. Unemployment among males was above average, and exacerbated in importance by the large size of Dutch families. Per capita income in southern provinces of North Brabant and Limburg, for example, was more than 10 percent below the national average. Income in the rural provinces to the North and East was lower still.[35]

The second reason for cooperation between the secular and nonsecular groups was ideological. The danger that communism would emerge from social conflict threatened all points of the political spectrum. Communists scored well in the first postwar election, garnering almost 11 percent of the vote—primarily from Socialist constituencies. The advent of the Cold War cooled popular enthusiasm for Communism, but concern among elites about a broadening of class struggle remained. In 1949, the leadership of the Catholic and Socialist parties signed a joint appeal for cooperation in the struggle to preserve democracy.[36] The 1950 Industrial Organization Act provided the institutions for such cooperation to take place. At the same time, the Act addressed the ideological ambitions of the Socialist and confessional parties. The delegation of policymaking authority to nongovernmental actors appealed to socialist aspirations for economic democracy as well as to the notion of private responsibility in Jacques Maritain's influential theory of personal socialism.[37] The delegation of authority also reflected the 1931 papal encyclical, which promoted the doctrine of corporate responsibility for the general good.[38] Agreement on the 1950 Industrial Organization Act marked the end of any serious attempt at political reform. Indeed, the institutional mechanism set out in the Act reinforced lines of authority in consociational groups from the top down. Before World War II, constituent trade unions and employers' associations had significant independence in relations with their national federation. The balance of power began to shift toward the national federations with the creation of the Foundation of Labour in 1945. The constituent industries or trade unions retained control over their respective finances, but the national federations gained considerable power in collective bargaining.[39] The 1950 Industrial Organization Act further strengthened consociational elites by distinguishing between recognized and unrecognized interest groups at the national level. Unrecognized federations or insubordinate constituent unions could expect neither sympathy nor assistance. Minister-President Drees made this point brutally clear in his 1950 reaction to wildcat strikes over price increases: "the government," Drees proclaimed, "will not deviate from its position that the settlement of labor conditions will be handled with the recognised labor federations which are prepared to follow the rules of the game."[40]

Upon assuming the minister-presidency of the four-party coalition, Drees and the PvdA agreed to adhere to the rules of consociationalism—coalescent elites governing a fragmented society. However, the underlying tension between the adoption of corporatist institutions and the creation of a corporatist state remained. Efforts to extend corporatist institutions beyond the level necessary for policymaking at the national level were met with little enthusiasm. Although the 1950 Industrial Organizational Act permitted the creation of specific industrial boards, these never found sufficient support to be established. Critics—primarily among the Liberals—successfully argued that cooperative industrial boards would undermine the entrepreneurial basis of the economy and result in too great an intrusion of the state in society. The "logical" result of such industrial boards would be inefficient at best and undemocratic at worst. With few exceptions, institutionalized cooperation at the industrial level did not take place.[41]

Consociational democracy took root but consensus politics had its limitations, particularly with respect to the promotion of social welfare. In spite of the center-left coloration of the Drees–van Schaik cabinet, ideological differences between Socialists and Catholics prevented the rapid expansion of the welfare state.

# Consensual Adjustment in Consociational Democracy

Conflict simmered between socialist aspirations for increased state welfare provisions and Catholic desires to manage social concerns within a confessional framework. Spending on welfare programs increased, but continued to be channeled through the ideological pillars rather than through the state. Inaction at the state level favored the consociational status quo by strengthening the social importance of subnational political cultures. Citizens forced to appeal for welfare assistance would turn to organizations offering ideological reinforcement as well as economic support.[42]

In summary, the political configuration of the Netherlands at the end of World War II was favorable to the promotion of full employment through industrialization. The objective, however, lacked the means for its achievement. Once the PvdA relaxed its efforts at political reform, the possibilities for consensus politics improved. Moreover, the consociational framework supported a particular institutional solution to the problem of industrialization. Consociational politics supported corporatist policymaking, just as corporatist institutions reinforced the overarching consociationalism.[43]

## Consensual Adjustment

The Dutch strategy for full employment through industrialization was a curious mixture of dirigiste and free-market instruments, Keynesian and classical influences. The compromises inherent to Dutch economic thought were incorporated into the "magic" triangle of objectives adopted by the government: full employment, price stability, and balance of payments equilibrium. However, as two economists later pointed out, "strictly speaking only the first [is a goal] in the proper sense of the word, the latter two are more to be considered as constraints."[44] Indeed, the distinction between objectives and constraints provides the unifying theme for interpreting the blend of instruments developed by the Dutch for the management of their economy.

Industrialization, per se, represented only part of the solution to unemployment. The Dutch recognized early on that domestic output would have to find foreign demand. Securing access to foreign markets, therefore, was a particular concern for the government. The Netherlands had long advocated free trade and Dutch governments had regarded free trade as a cornerstone of commercial policy since the 1840s. The outbreak of competitive mercantilism of the 1920s and 1930s, however, forced the country to experiment with protectionism.[45] As a way of preserving national income, the experience proved disappointing and reinforced Dutch convictions regarding the virtues of free trade.

Yet how could the Netherlands open foreign markets for its exports? The need grew urgent during early postwar years for three basic reasons. First, turmoil in the Dutch East Indies threatened to deprive the Netherlands of an important source of national income.[46] Second, the poor state of Dutch productive capital made the economy's reconstruction even more dependent upon imported machinery, particularly from the "dollar zone." Third, the servicing of foreign debts incurred during wartime burdened already scarce reserves of foreign exchange.[47] Thus, the Netherlands had to export to recover, and it had to secure market access to export.

The pursuit of regional integration was, for the Dutch, a logical corollary of the need to secure market access. The early experience of the Benelux customs union showed larger-than-expected gains from trade creation and smaller-than-expected losses in otherwise sheltered sectors of the three economies. In terms of Dutch national income, formation of the Benelux was a tremendous success.[48] Yet it is important to consider that the politics of consensus reduced regional integration to a means rather than an objective in and of itself. Neither the Drees–van Schaik cabinet nor any of its predecessors was prepared to abandon the national state in favor of some supranational grouping.

The contrast between Dutch objectives in economic integration and the Dutch approach to security cooperation underscores the importance of national interest in regional integration. The Liberal foreign minister in the Drees–van Schaik cabinet—D. U. Stikker—proposed the creation of a Europe-wide customs union at the same

## Consensual Adjustment in Consociational Democracy

time that he strove to limit the North Atlantic Treaty Organization (NATO) alliance to the United States plus the six signatories of the 1948 Brussels Pact (Benelux, France, Italy, and the UK). His reasoning was consistent: economic integration to maximize market access; security cooperation to maximize political influence. That he failed on both counts merely reveals the constraints on smaller countries in international negotiations.[49]

The Dutch emphasis on integration to secure market access solidified in the aftermath of the 1949 First Report on the Industrialization of the Netherlands and the 1950 Industrial Organization Act. One of Stikker's successors, J. W. Beyen, put forward an ambitious proposal to transform the Coal and Steel Community into a full customs union during the ill-fated negotiation of the European Political Community (EPC) which ran parallel to the proposed European Defence Community (EDC). The Drees cabinet was virtually unanimous that acceptance of the Beyen plan by the other five countries be a precondition for Dutch participation in the EPC. Again the Dutch failed, but their single-minded determination succeeded in placing the question of market access at the center of the European project.[50]

Efforts to secure market access through integration were a necessary component of the strategy for industrialization. So too was the Dutch attitude toward domestic inflation. After the war, Finance Minister Lieftinck enacted a radical reform of the guilder in order to soak up excess liquidity generated during the occupation. Lieftinck's monetary stabilization policies continued through the late 1940s, and succeeded in restoring the Dutch currency's ability to fulfill each of the three tasks of money: as a reliable store of value, means of exchange, and unit of account. When Lieftinck nationalized the Dutch central bank, however, he adamantly refused to allow that organization to place monetary stability above the other objectives of economic policy.[51]

Hence, the Dutch perspective on domestic inflation was (and still is) less doctrinaire than the German—whether embodied in the Bank deutscher Länder or its successor, the Bundesbank.[52] The Dutch central bank pursues price stability with due regard to other elements of the Dutch economic consensus and not as a higher objective. The Bank's mandate is "to regulate the value of the Netherlands monetary unit in such a manner as will be the most conducive to the nation's prosperity and welfare, and in doing so to keep the value as stable as possible."[53] The minister of finance retains the ability "to coordinate the monetary and fiscal policies of the government and the policy of the central bank."[54]

The limited mandate of the central bank in combination with the prospect of ministerial instruction has not eliminated conflict between central bank presidents and finance ministers. Nevertheless, the bank's first president, Marius Holtrop, only rarely came into disagreement with social democrats Pieter Lieftinck and Hendrick Hofstra.[55] Indeed, the right of ministerial instruction has never been used. The reason for this is fundamental to understanding Dutch monetary policy. As one assistant to the Governing Board of the Dutch central bank, Emile den Dunnen, explained:

An effective monetary policy is possible only if there is fundamental agreement between the central bank and the Government on the basic principles of this policy; the more objective these principles are, the better can policy be sheltered from political influence.[56]

Bank's President Holtrop encapsulated the objective principles of monetary policy in his analysis of the "liquidity ratio"—a uniquely Dutch understanding of the monetary economy which focuses on the ratio of liquid assets held in the economy to national income.[57] When the economy holds excess liquidity, the balance of payments moves into deficit and the bank will intervene to slow down the creation of liquidity to the minimum level necessary to maintain the growth of national income. Alternatively, when the economy experiences a liquidity shortfall, the balance of payments moves into surplus and the bank will allow a gradual increase in liquidity beyond the rate of growth of national income.

In practice, emphasis on the liquidity ratio under the Bretton Woods system led the bank to give greater emphasis to exchange-rate stability than to domestic price stability. When the balance of payments came into surplus, putting upward pressure on the exchange rate, the bank was willing to accept some increase in domestic inflation as a corrective measure.[58] When the balance of payments came into deficit, the bank tried to slow down domestic inflation rather than allowing a depreciation of the exchange rate. The Dutch central bank demonstrated an extraordinary reluctance to devalue the guilder after 1949. The opinion of the bank was (and remains) that devaluation serves speculative and not productive interests.[59]

For the Dutch to create a favorable industrial environment required more, of course, than foreign market access or exchange-rate stability. Access to foreign markets only mattered to the extent that the Dutch could export at competitive prices. Competitive exports in turn necessitated that the Dutch government obtain some control over the movement of domestic prices and wages. Given the preoccupation of the central bank with the external value of the guilder, the government required some instrument other than monetary policy for the manipulation of prices and wages.

The 1950 Industrial Organization Act inaugurated a new process for price–wage determination. The Social and Economic Council drew on advice of the Foundation of Labour and the resources of the Central Planning Bureau in order to prepare proposals for wage and price increases to take place over the coming year.[60] Such proposals could establish the limits of permissible increases, they could call for mandatory increases, or they could recommend freezes. The council submitted these proposals to the Board of Government Mediators for approval and, if approved, to the Foundation of Labour for collective bargaining and for implementation.

Dutch price–wage policy was an early and overwhelming success. The government called for real wage cuts in 1951 in response to the sharp economic downturn and the crisis in the balance of payments. The national federations participating in the Foundation of Labour obliged: the trade union federations agreed to accept nominal wage increases of 5 percent in spite of a 10 percent increase in the cost of living, and the federation of employers' associations promised not to pass these wage increases through to prices, and not to increase prices in compensation for the rising of "non-essential materials."[61]

The pattern of events was typical of the new system for economic policymaking: the Social and Economic Council recommended a 5 percent reduction in consumption and a 25 percent reduction in capital investment as part of its February report, the government altered its tax and spending policies accordingly, the national bank raised its discount rate, and the Foundation of Labour gave its consent to wage and price reductions. It was only the price–wage reductions, however, which the then Finance Minister Pieter Lieftinck singled out as "very important."[62]

Lieftinck's comment brings the discussion of Dutch early postwar management of economic constraints full circle: the government focused attention on the balance of payments while making aggressive efforts to gain market access. Monetary authorities defended the external value of the guilder while relying on price and wage controls to ensure export competitiveness. In the broad language of the 1949 First Report in the industrialization of the Netherlands, this combination of measures worked to mitigate the risks faced by Dutch manufacturers. Although aspects of Dutch economic policy were interventionist—price–wage policies in particular—industrialization relied more directly on entrepreneurship than state support.

The objective of Dutch economic policy was, and remained, the promotion of full employment. Market access, balance of payments stability, and competitive labor costs were immediate to the promotion of full employment. Though Dutch policymakers, particularly on the left, recognized the need to redistribute income, redistribution remained a secondary and longer-term goal. The distribution of income would begin seriously to compete with unemployment for political attention only when full employment became a reality.

The full-employment objective of the adjustment policy should not obscure the liberal foundations of Dutch economic policy, because these are the assumptions which Catholics, Protestants,

## Consensual Adjustment in Consociational Democracy

Socialists, and Liberals used in negotiating their consensual adjustment strategy. Put another way, no matter what the political coloration of the government, the Dutch remained committed to entrepreneurship and free markets. Indeed, this commitment predominated in the context of regional integration, where the government rejected both domestic calls for trade protection and French and Italian pretensions to build a fortress Europe. The Dutch did not choose to pursue full employment through Keynesian instruments like deficit spending or expansionary monetary policy. Rather, they focused attention on the supply side of the economy, lowering costs, and encouraging investment in order to create more jobs.

### Centripetal to Centrifugal

Until 1954, Dutch price–wage policy benefited from the larger consensus on full employment through industrialization. The number of strikes fell to an average of only 66 per year for 1950–3, with a correspondingly low annual total of 72,563 lost man-days of work.[63] Hourly labor costs stabilized at 60 percent of those in Belgium and 75 percent of those in Germany.[64] The government did not devalue the guilder after 1949, nor did it revert to protectionism as a means to shore up the balance of payments.[65] Moreover, as mentioned previously, the government strove for the creation of a European customs union to serve as a vehicle for providing access to European markets.

While agreement on the objective of full employment remained, however, support for price–incomes policy began to falter in 1953. The wage and price restraint of 1951–2 had its desired effect; growth accelerated while the balance of payments moved into surplus. Consequently, employers' associations called for a relaxation of strict discipline and trade unions began to strive for a more equitable distribution of income. The Social and Economic Council supported these claims in 1954, advising the government that wages should increase in line with the growth of national output, rather than the rise in the cost of living. The Council's objective was to focus government attention on the wage share in national income. The result was a series of "prosperity" nominal wage increases, by 9 percent in January 1954 and by 6 percent the following October.[66]

However, the government's ability to use wage–price negotiations to stabilize the balance of payments weakened, as it began to focus on the wage share of national income. Problems arose because different parts of the workforce contributed differently to economic growth. Given historically tight labor market conditions, both employers and a growing number of trade unionists called for a greater differentiation in wage increases based on relative productivity by sector. Only the socialist NVV retained its conviction that "solidarity" should be the guiding principle for wage formation.

The attitude of the NVV, however, proved critical to the continued functioning of price–wage policy. When the government faced a deterioration of the balance of payments in 1957 as a result of excess domestic consumption, it called for another decrease in real wages. The trade union federations, led by the NVV, complied. For the second time in less than a decade, the government succeeded in stabilizing the balance of payments on the basis of voluntary cuts in the wage rate.[67]

With respect to the continuing viability of price–incomes policy, the real wage cuts of 1957 were a Pyrrhic victory. Employers' associations and trade-union federations suffered from membership disaffection and responded with increased calls for wage differentiation. The NVV was a principal loser, suffering an almost 7 percent decline in membership from 1957 to 1959. Disenchantment with the government's incomes policy culminated when the Socialist PvdA left the government, elections were held, and the Dutch returned their first center-right government in postwar history.[68]

The political shift of the governing coalition from center-left to center-right marked the end of consensual adjustment. Although the government retained support for corporatist intermediation and regional integration, the government's objectives for both

## Consensual Adjustment in Consociational Democracy

instruments necessarily changed. For example, the signature of the Rome Treaty in 1957 allowed the government to relax its activist posture with respect to gaining market access through European integration. During the early 1960s, the Dutch negotiating strategy within Europe was to defend the progress made in trade liberalization among the member states of the Community, while supporting the British application for membership. This twin-track approach resulted in an about-face with respect to the Dutch position on supranational institutions. Where the Dutch had objected to the creation of a High Authority for the Coal and Steel Pool, Foreign Minister Luns emerged as a strong defender of the Commission of the Economic Community during the negotiation of the Fouchet Plan. While Luns's position strengthened the institutional position of the Netherlands as a smaller country in the European Community, it also heralded more than a decade of stagnation in the process of integration.[69]

The fulfillment of employment objectives allowed a similar relaxation of price–wage controls. For example, in 1959, the Dutch government again changed the emphasis of its incomes policy in favor of wage differentiation. This time, however, the advice of the Social and Economic Council centered more on sectoral productivity growth rates than on the wage share on national income. The result was far from optimal. The Central Statistical Bureau did not possess sufficiently accurate productivity measures to make the new emphasis in wage–price policy workable.[70] Meanwhile, the economy was booming. From 1959 to 1960, seasonally adjusted productivity increased by 14 percent and industrial production by 15 percent. Unemployment fell dramatically as the demand for labor increased. In 1959, there were 71,000 unemployed and an average of 32,500 vacancies. By 1960, there were only 46,000 unemployed and 56,000 vacancies. Wage growth accelerated as workers tried to make up for lost income and as employers resorted to "black" wages to attract and retain scarce labor resources.[71]

Problems first emerged in the service-sector industries, particularly transport. Although service-sector productivity increased much more slowly than manufacturing productivity, both sectors were in competition for the same pool of workers. General wage increases without corresponding price increases for services threatened the financial viability of service providers. Service-sector employers responded to government calls for price restraint by trying to hold down the growth of wage costs. Transport strikes broke out almost immediately, followed by a rash of strikes in the building sector—strikes which were larger than any since 1945. The government and the Board of Government Mediators tried but failed to control the pace of events. There were 121 strikes and over 467,000 lost workdays during the course of 1960. As a result, wages increased by more than 8 percent while consumer prices increased by slightly over 2 percent.[72]

In October 1960, the government asked for advice from the Social and Economic Council on a third reform of the price–wage system. The advice finally came two years later but the era of effective wage–price control was already near its end. Control within the national federations of workers and employers had diminished considerably in the face of ever-tightening labor market conditions. Employers were compelled to resort increasingly to "black" wages, even as the revaluation of the guilder and the shortening of the workweek put a strain on profitability.[73]

The break came at the beginning of 1963, as the government was inaugurating its new price–wage policy. One of the large metal industries defied the government to announce a higher-than-permitted wage scale for the upcoming year. Disciplinary action by the government and expulsion from the employers' association only heightened tensions. The wage explosion of 1964 followed, bringing with it the end of effective government control over the growth of prices and wages through corporatist intermediation. Where the hard economic times of the late 1950s had created a favorable environment for corporatism, the prosperity of the early 1960s proved its undoing.

As mentioned earlier, the period from 1962 to 1964 also witnessed stagnation in the drive for European integration. Dutch opposition to de Gaulle's Fouchet Plan peaked in 1962 just before the French president rejected the first British application to join the Communities. Dutch–French relations soured within the community, and helped set the stage for the 1965 "empty chair" crisis and all that was to follow.

In summary, economic policymaking and the consensual adjustment strategy had been focused on the promotion of full employment by controlling wage costs and encouraging job-creating investment. The singular nature of this objective gave a unity of purpose to the various instruments of economic policy, as well as a harmony of function. This functional harmony in turn reflected and reinforced the broader political consensus generated through the disciplined participation of ideological pillars (and particularly elite leadership) in the process of consociational democracy.

However, once the government succeeded in promoting full employment, the Dutch again revealed tendencies that were evident during the late 1940s—tendencies that included the rejection of state intervention in price and wage setting, and guarded enthusiasm for European integration. Such a reversal was only natural given that the objectives of economic adjustment had been realized. Nevertheless, the collapse of the institutional framework for consensual adjustment brought with it a series of changes with respect to economic policymaking, as well as changes in the structure and functioning of the Dutch political economy.

## The Transformation of the Dutch Political Economy

By the late 1950s, the consensual adjustment strategy lost its unifying theme—full employment. Corporatist price–incomes policy no longer benefited from the disciplined participation of employers' associations or trade unions, and regional integration no longer found an easy international environment for collective trade liberalization or broadening market access. Productive investment and the reasonable distribution of income emerged as competing objectives at the center of Dutch economic policymaking, and the functional harmony of economic policy instruments dissolved in the competition for wealth.

The management of economic constraints, balance of payments equilibrium and domestic price stability, demonstrated the first signs of strain during the transformation of the Dutch political economy in the 1960s. Given the central bank's emphasis on the liquidity ratio, the government responded to shortfalls in the balance of payments by slowing down the creation of domestic liquidity. In the 1950s this was accomplished through concerted price–wage restraint, and supported by "gentlemen's agreements" with the representatives of the commercial banking system regarding the level of required reserves to be held at the central bank. During the 1960s, concerted price–wage restraint was no longer available. Real consumption wages increased by almost 7 percent each year, far exceeding the growth of output or of labor productivity. These wage increases reflected the competition between income redistribution and productive investment, with the result being an increase in the adjusted wage share of total output from 68.7 percent in 1964 to 71.3 percent in 1969.[74] Although the price–wage policy had succeeded in sharing burdens during the early postwar periods, it did not survive the emergence of prosperity.[75] The final blows fell during the period from 1969 to 1971. The government twice attempted to impose wage and price controls and twice withdrew under pressure from the trade unions and employers' associations.[76]

The struggle between capital and labor over the distribution of value added deprived the government of its primary instrument for controlling the growth of domestic liquidity, corporatist price–wage controls. The gentlemen's agreements with domestic banks proved insufficient for the task of slowing down liquidity creation. Interest rate manipulation to change the cost of credit had little impact on a domestic banking system with access to large stocks of foreign assets, and so the central bank began to rely increasingly on direct credit restrictions to control the development of domestic liquidity—telling the banks how much they could lend and to whom.[77]

Yet reliance on direct credit restrictions was not without problems. Although such restrictions did succeed in controlling the rate of domestic liquidity creation, they were too rigid in their application. Quantitative restrictions telling banks how much credit they could create did not easily allow for a qualitative assessment of who should receive credit, nor did they provide for rapid reaction to changes in international liquidity.

By 1965, the central bank admitted that, although the Netherlands had become an "autonomous source" of inflation, it (the bank) was powerless to tighten credit for fear of precipitating a liquidity crisis. Indeed, such a crisis almost arose in response to the Bundesbank-induced German recession of 1966, and the Dutch central bank released its hold on the credit policies of the commercial banks. However, relaxation of direct credit controls provoked a round of difficult discussions between the central bank and the representatives of the commercial banking sector about the future use of domestic credit restrictions. These discussions failed to produce a change in policy and the bank reintroduced direct controls in 1969 as the German revaluation pushed the Dutch economy toward overheating.[78]

The new credit restrictions proved too little too late. Foreign speculation that the guilder would follow the Deutschemark's revaluation sparked a massive inflow of short-term capital, which greatly increased domestic liquidity. Under the prevailing rules of the Bretton Woods system, the bank was powerless to stop the capital flow increasing the quantity of Dutch currency in circulation and so it resorted to floating the guilder in May 1971 and closing domestic capital markets the following September.

Competition between labor and industry over the distribution of income also placed new strains on domestic fiscal policy. During the 1960s, the government attempted to serve as intermediary between representatives of capital and labor by erecting a more formal welfare state to correct for the failings of private provision of social insurance. For example, 1965 saw the passage of a "national assistance act" providing subsistence income for the poor, a "national health insurance act" providing for mandatory medical coverage, and an "unemployment provisions act" extending the time period for income support in the event of job loss; and 1967 brought in a worker's disability program (WAO, the wet op de arbeidsongeschiktheidsverzekering).[79]

Although many of the employment-related social insurance programs drew financial support from employer and worker contributions, the general welfare schemes relied on government coffers. Therefore, increasing the state's role in welfare provision shifted the balance of government spending from discretionary to nondiscretionary categories and limited the room for fiscal maneuver. Government balances moved into deficit in 1963 and net borrowing fluctuated at around 1 percent of GDP throughout the 1960s. In percentage terms, the two fastest-growing budgetary categories of government outlays were for interest payments and transfers to firms or individuals. Off-budget expenditure on social insurance increased by more than 43 percent over the same 1963 to 1970 period, matching total government outlays for final consumption.[80]

Thus without cutting back on the development of the welfare state, budgetary officials could do little to slow down the rate of economic activity. The 1966 recession in Germany arrived on the heels of a slight contraction in Dutch government spending. As the national bank released its credit restrictions, spending authorities began to loosen the reins on fiscal policy.[81] The result was a call by Catholic leader W. K. N. Schmelzer for the stabilization of government accounts in the 1967 budgetary memorandum. Schmelzer's efforts succeeded primarily in bringing down J. M. L. T. Cals' Confessional-Socialist coalition and provoking the worst electoral performance for the Catholics up to that point in postwar history.[82] Fiscal stimulus continued largely unabated throughout the period of "overheating" and credit restrictions in 1969, and into the final collapse of price–wage restraint in 1970 to 1971. Moreover, the failings of price–wage restraint, credit restrictions, and fiscal policy reinforced each other. The poor functioning of any one instrument placed greater strains on the other two, with the result that none of the three could be used to stabilize the economy.[83]

## Consensual Adjustment in Consociational Democracy

The economic changes that followed the collapse of the consensual adjustment strategy were complicated to deal with in and of themselves. At the same time, however, changes in the political side of the political economy made matters even more difficult. For example, Schmelzer's attack on budgetary policies of the Cals' coalition was symptomatic of tensions emerging within the Catholic and Socialist pillars. The "de-confessionalization" of the electorate, marked by a dramatic drop in attendance at religious services and emerging conflicts between the Dutch Catholic Church and the Vatican, ushered in a renewed questioning of the consociational system and calls for political "renewal." Dutch political scientist Bart Tromp summarized the critiques of consociationalism in two observations: first, the parties did not seem accountable enough to the voters because the lines of discipline ran from the top down, and second, the continuous process of compromise collapsed the differences between party positions, leaving the voters with little to choose from between one party and another.[84]

The 1960s drive for political renewal assumed different manifestations on right, left, and center of the political spectrum. Among the confessional parties of the center-right, the Catholics sought to build a Christian-Democratic union in order to stave off the rapid decline in their electoral fortunes. The share of the vote garnered by the KVP dropped from 31.9 percent in 1963 to 26.5 percent only four years later. Vote shares for the Calvinist CHU and ARP, however, remained roughly constant and so the two smaller parties were reluctant to make a tight union with the Catholics.[85] A breakaway Radical Peoples Party (PPR) emerged from the ranks of the KVP and the ARP in 1967 to capture almost 2 percent of the vote in the 1971 elections. Still, however, the confessional parties could not be shaken from their "strategic paralysis," and the Catholics continued to lose voters at a rate of 5 percentage points of the electorate with each polling.[86]

Political renewal on the left combined a curious mixture of traditional socialism and emergent post-materialism: a self-proclaimed "New Left" arose among the youth membership of the PvdA to challenge the ideological consistency of the "old guard." This New Left called for a more participatory party organization and for closer links between the PvdA and the Pacifist Socialist Party. New Left activists had insufficient support to capture the leadership of the PvdA, but they did succeed in winning a number of important concessions from the party's strategists. In 1969, the PvdA announced that it would no longer enter into ruling coalitions with the Catholics and began to campaign for a left-right polarization of the electorate. Many of the older members of the party broke off to form a more centrist organization called "Democratic Socialists '70," while others, like Pieter Lieftinck and Willem Drees senior, simply retired from political life.[87]

Political renewal from the center, however, posed the greatest and most purposeful threat to the consociational system. Soon after Schmelzer's attack on the Cals' government, a new party called Democrats '66 (D66) emerged with the expressed ambition to "explode" the traditional party system. The rapid success of this new center party, which garnered 4.5 percent of the vote in 1967, catalyzed the transformations taking place on the right and left and reinforced the growing polarization of the electorate. Attempts to build a bridge between D66 and the PvdA ran contrary to New Left ambitions and therefore failed in the creation of a broad-based progressive center. From its isolation in the center, therefore, D66 became a way station for voters seeking a change from traditional confessional or socialist party affiliations. Thus D66 increased the liquidity of the Dutch political marketplace, even as it intensified the competition between right and left.[88]

By the late 1960s and early 1970s, increased political competition combined with macroeconomic policy failure to undermine the last remnants of the social partnership between management and labor, as well as the corporatist inclination of the labor movement itself. Where the combination of economic hardship and consociationalism had supported corporatist intermediation, the combination prosperity and pluralism undermined it. Even the institutions established by the 1950 Industrial Organization Act became deadlocked, and the Social and Economic Council ceased to function adequately. As Steven Wolinetz explains:

> Rather than operating as a forum for discussion and discovery of an underlying consensus the Social and Economic Council functioned more like a British-style Parliament in which opposing sides stated positions known in advance.[89]

Attempts within the Socialist trade union movement (NVV), to agree on a 1972 "social pact" accepting wage restraint to stave off inflation, provoked threats of wide-scale defection. The trade union leadership could no longer guarantee the level of discipline necessary to control the growth of wages and prices.[90]

In summary, the consensual adjustment strategy of the 1950s relied on a number of political factors. Consociational democracy provided a framework for national consensus building, and the prospect of full employment offered a focal point for cooperation. Broad-based coalitions under the leadership of socialist Willem Drees forged a plan for economic adjustment around domestic corporatism and regional integration. In due course, the plan worked, and the Netherlands moved into the latter half of the twentieth century with a freshly industrializing economy having access to a large European marketplace.

The realization of full employment, however, brought this period of consensual adjustment to an end—and, with it, the privileged position of Dutch macroeconomic policymakers. Regional integration no longer afforded immediate returns in the form of increasing market access and gradually devolved toward a more technocratic concern for exchange-rate stability. Corporatist intermediation lost focus, and divided between the objectives of productive investment and a reasonable distribution of income. Simultaneously, the discipline afforded by consociational democracy dissipated, and the electorate renewed calls for political reform. The institutional framework for consensual adjustment was ill-prepared for the realization of its objective or for the end of ideology.[91] Once the cleavages in Dutch political culture began to soften, conflict emerged between Dutch elites over the correct formula for relations among themselves and with society. Dutch politics became more competitive, policymaking became less consensual, and the constraints operating on monetary and fiscal policy increased even as the prospects for a further round of consensual adjustment diminished.

## Belgium

Belgium ended World War II very differently from the Netherlands. Occupation had wrought destruction in the Belgian economy, but not havoc. Belgium had a strong foreign reserve position thanks to reverse lend-lease credits earned through hosting Allied liberation forces and gold stocks repatriated from France. Belgium also retained large capacities for coal and steel production, industries which at the same time provided the building blocks for speedy reconstruction and a steady source of export income. Therefore, reconstruction in Belgium was not as difficult as in the Netherlands. Charles Kindleberger, who reported on the Belgian economy for US Marshall Plan authorities, once compared the situation in that country to "killing the cat by stuffing it with cream"—using abundant exports and a strong currency position to finance job creation, welfare provision, and the import of scarce consumer goods.[92]

In spite of their relative prosperity, however, Belgian politicians—both Flemish and Walloon—were well aware that their economy required significant adjustment. Belgium was one of the earliest industrialized countries in Europe. Consequently, its industrial structure reflected the needs of the nineteenth century more than those of the latter half of the twentieth century. "On the eve of the Second World War," Alan Milward records, "coal (production) still employed more than 10 percent of the national industry labor force and still accounted for about 12 percent of the value of all industrial production."[93] These

## Consensual Adjustment in Consociational Democracy

figures changed little up through the early 1950s, in spite of widespread (and widely acknowledged) financial problems with Belgian coal mining.[94]

Belgium's political situation was different from the Netherlands as well. Whereas Dutch elites sought to overturn consociational democracy, elites in Belgium were preoccupied with the shifting balance of power between Flanders and Wallonia, and—since the country has almost no Protestant population—between the Catholic Church and the nonconfessional pillars. Making matters worse, the stigma of collaboration fell more on Flemings, Catholics, and Monarchists, than on Walloons, Liberals, or Socialists. As a consequence, linguistic, religious, and ideological distinctions hardened, and prospects for broad-based consensus fell by the wayside.[95]

The purpose of this section is to show how Belgium came to adopt a consensual adjustment strategy only during the 1960s. The lateness of Belgium's adjustment is surprising because it had many of the same institutions (or institutional possibilities) as the Netherlands during the mid-1940s. The Belgian government was the driving force behind the Benelux during its wartime exile in London. Belgian business and labor signed a Social Pact in 1944, promising to cooperate across class lines toward the establishment of a welfare state, and also participated in national labor councils. Nevertheless, neither regional integration nor corporatism was harnessed to the cause of economic adjustment. Indeed, until the late 1950s, the Belgian government relied on participation in the European Coal and Steel Community to slow down changes in the productive structures of the Belgian economy, even as the need for adjustment became manifestly apparent.

The reason for Belgium's late adjustment is to be found in elite behavior, and particularly in the centrifugal combination of competitive elites ruling over a fragmented political culture. In this sense, the Belgian example underscores the political requirements for successful adjustment—when elites cannot agree on how they will interact with each other or with society, they have little ability to control developments in the domestic economy. Moreover, the

Belgian case highlights the fact that both corporatism and integration function as policy instruments, which are not necessarily bound to the cause of economic adjustment. Regional integration became a pawn in the competition between elites, providing German-financed subsidies to Walloon and Brussels-based holding companies. Finally, and perhaps most important, the Belgian example further illustrates how the relationships among elites and between elites and followers limit the use of either corporatist bargaining or regional integration: institutional configurations designed to accommodate one political situation may not function adequately in another.

The argument has five parts. The first examines the political and economic environment from 1945 to 1950 in order to explain how competition between Belgian elites temporarily created a centrifugal political situation with government coalitions alternating both right and left, and between nonsecular and secular. The second section describes the period of polarization from 1950 to 1958, when fundamental ideological and regional conflicts resulted in the manipulation of the ECSC by the special interests of Walloon business and labor. The third section looks at the foundations of Belgian consensual adjustment during the period from 1958 to 1961, and the shifting balance of regional interests between Wallonia and Flanders. The fourth part makes the link between the strengthening of Belgian consociationalism and the consensual adjustment process during the early to mid-1960s. Finally, the fifth part describes the breakdown of consensual adjustment in Belgium during the late 1960s and early 1970s.

## Reconstruction in the "National" Interest

On the surface, early postwar Belgian economic policies mirrored those in the Netherlands. The government managed the growth of prices and wages through statutory measures, while the social partners met in national labor conferences to discuss the development of Belgian social welfare and to plan for institutionalized cooperation. At the same time, the trade unions and employers' associations initiated a process of centralization at the national level: the four major independent trade union federations, the socialists, communists, "Renardist"-syndicalists, and one of the public-sector unions, joined to form the General Federation of Belgian Trade Unions (FGTB-ABVV) in April 1945;[96] the confessional unions split along functional lines, with a political and a more traditional Confederation of Christian Trade Unions (CSC-ACV), while still retaining considerable national cohesion; and employers united in the Federation of Belgian Industry (FIB-VBN) in April 1946.[97]

The Belgian government responded to the 1944 Social Pact between business and labor with the creation of a national agency for social security, and the passage of a number of statutes toward the creation of a welfare state. Institution building culminated in 1948 with the creation of a three-tier structure of bilateral organizations uniting the representatives of management and labor: a national Central Industrial Committee (CCI-CRB) to advise the government about the general direction of economic policy, sectoral councils for collective bargaining, and industrial councils for labor collaboration in management decision-making.[98]

Conditions seemed ripe for close cooperation. Even within the communist syndicates, the watchwords for the reconstruction period were *eerst produceren*—"first produce" and worry about control over productive resources later.[99] When communist self-restraint began to wear thin in 1948, the FGTB-ABVV expelled the communist unions for continued resort to direct action, and the concept of worker-control virtually disappeared from the language of Belgian syndicalism.[100]

Nevertheless, Belgian price–incomes policy failed to evolve as an instrument of economic policy. A general explanation for this failing is that economic conditions never deteriorated sufficiently to induce all parties to accept corporatism at the same time and in the same manner. Thus, while management, labor, and government expressed interest in close collaboration, they were reluctant to accept the constraints that corporatism implied. Management feared the loss of autonomy, government ignored the advice of the social partners, and labor wanted greater control over the pace and development of social welfare.[101]

The failure to implement price–incomes policy also resulted from divisions within industry, labor, and government. For example, much of the manufacturing sector of the Belgian economy was controlled by a small number of large holding companies like the Soiété Générale de Belgique, the Banque de Bruxelles, Paribas, and Coppée. Therefore, while firm management participated in corporatist intermediation, the real decision-makers were within the holding companies and were unlikely to be represented. Representatives of government and labor could not be sure that agreements reached with industry would be accepted by the holding companies, which controlled investment decisions. More troubling still, the capacity of holding companies to accept losses in one sector in exchange for profits in another sector obscured the holdings' true interests in trilateral negotiation. From the standpoint of government and labor, the holding companies were unreliable and unpredictable negotiating partners.[102]

As "social partners," the working classes were similarly disunited and therefore unreliable. Socialist leaders disagreed about whether corporatist intermediation was a means to obtain control over the distribution of income or an end in and of itself. André Renard, who emerged from the 1940s as the leader of the left of the Socialist trade unions, argued that negotiations with industry and government should be used to strengthen labor's control over the distribution of income. Louis Major, who assumed the leadership of the center, maintained a more corporatist outlook. The ideological struggle between these two poles within the FGTB-ABVV compromised the national federation's ability to control its membership in the interests of effective bargaining.[103]

The deeply felt syndicalist traditions of the left-wing FGTB-ABVV also brought the Socialists into conflict with the confessional and liberal trade unions. During negotiation of the 1948 institutional reform legislation, for example, Socialists argued that industrial councils should be consulted on financial and investment

## Consensual Adjustment in Consociational Democracy

**Table 2.1.** The regional structure of Belgium (1947–9)

|  | Belgium | Brussels | Flanders | Wallonia |
|---|---|---|---|---|
| *Production* (percentage of total output) | | | | |
| Agriculture | 10.5 | 1.5 | 15.5 | 9.3 |
| Manufacturing | 54.4 | 46.6 | 51.6 | 62.3 |
| Services | 35.1 | 52.1 | 32.9 | 28.4 |
| *Political alignment* (percentage of national vote in 1949 elections) | | | | |
| Catholics | 43.6 | 31.0 | 54.4 | 31.2 |
| Liberals | 15.3 | 24.9 | 13.3 | 14.9 |
| Socialists | 29.8 | 29.4 | 24.3 | 38.4 |
| *Relative wealth and size* | | | | |
| GDP per capita index Belgium = 100 | 100 | 132 | 88 | 103 |
| Population share (percentage) | 100 | 15 | 50 | 35 |

*Source*: Chaput and de Falleur (1961a) and Delruelle et al. (1970).

decisions, while Catholics preferred to restrict the competence of the councils to social matters and working conditions.[104] Tensions mounted as a result of the struggle for membership between national federations. In 1945, the ratio of Socialist to Catholic trade union members was 1.88:1. By 1947 that ratio was down to 1.37:1 and continued to drop through the end of the 1940s. Consequently, collaboration between the national trade union confederations in the interests of the working classes was difficult at best.[105]

Finally, divisions existed within government itself. Table 2.1 provides data for the composition of regional output and electoral alignment. As can be seen, government representatives had to address the needs of three distinct regional economies, possessing different levels of income and holding different ideological beliefs. The Brussels region relied heavily on financial services, supported Liberals and other secular parties, and possessed more per capita wealth than the rest of the country. Flanders was poorer, more agricultural, and more Catholic. Wallonia was more socialist, more industrial, and only moderately wealthy.

These divisions within industry, labor, and the government resulted in elite behavior that was more competitive than consociational, though elements of both formulas were present.

### Consensual Adjustment in Consociational Democracy

Consequently, the government was ruled by two-party coalitions made up of all three possible combinations of Liberals, Socialists, and Catholics—usually directed against whichever party happened to be in the opposition. Belgium was not ruled in the "national" interest per se, but instead alternated between defending the mature industries of Wallonia, promoting the industrialization of Flanders, or catering to Brussels finance.

When the Socialists and Liberals joined forces against the Catholics during the period from 1945 to 1947, for example, the government expanded already elaborate programs to subsidize coal and steel. The basic terms of the agreement—which included special welfare provisions for mine workers, price supports and subsidies for unprofitable mines, and energy price concessions for the steel industry—had emerged during wartime negotiations between the social partners and government representatives. Given the relative importance of the coal industry to the national economy, it is possible to suggest that "consensus" on the further subsidization of coal extraction represented a "national" consensus. However, the regional distribution of benefits clearly favored Walloon producers and the Brussels-based holding companies, which controlled them. More efficient Flemish coal producers made net contributions to the system, both in terms of higher taxes on production and in terms of forgone profits.[106]

When Catholics and Socialists joined forces in 1947, the Brussels banking sector came under attack through the nationalization of the Belgian National Bank. During its first 100 years, the National Bank was owned jointly and exclusively by the financial sector. Nationalization of the Bank, therefore, indicated both a consolidation of state control over the economy, and an important shift between "the commercial nature of the Bank," and "the Bank's importance for the public good."[107] From the perspective of the financial sector, however, nationalization of the Bank represented a powerful constraint on their influence over the monetary economy. The principal changes made in the Bank's statutes provided for state—rather than shareholder—appointment of the Bank's regents and governors. Thus, even though the terms of the government's debt-for-equity swap to obtain controlling interest were favorable to existing shareholders, Liberal opposition to nationalization was intense.[108]

Another change of government in 1949 brought Catholics and Liberals together against the Socialists. This time, the target was to end the subsidization of Walloon coal mining. The government announced an ambitious program to phase out price supports and to liberalize the domestic market for coal. Here also it would be possible to argue that the "consensus" in favor of rationalizing the coal industry was clearly in the "national" interest. However, given the disproportionate impact that coal reform would have on the Walloon economy, the draconian measures put forward by the Catholics and Liberals could never find support south of the linguistic border. Indeed, the political viability of the 1949 coal rationalization plan was never put to the test. In 1950, the return of King Leopold III and the subsequent negotiation of the Schuman Plan rendered the government's proposals both politically and economically obsolete.[109]

Nevertheless, it is interesting to speculate whether adjustment would have occurred in the absence of interregional economic competition. The answer is probably yes. Like the Dutch, the Belgians were averse to state intervention in the marketplace. Even after World War II, Belgian finance ministers, like Gaston Eyskens, invariably strove to balance government accounts in spite of their commitments to the development of the welfare state and to the promotion of the working classes. Welfare-state provisions, and particularly coal subsidies, were not intended to increase domestic demand, and have even been described as an early experiment in supply-side economics.[110] Therefore it is conceivable that the country would have moved away from its excessive reliance on coal and steel production had those industries been evenly distributed across linguistic and regional groups.

In this context, it is worth noting that the nationalization of the Belgian Bank in 1948 was a rare and important departure from free-market traditions.[111] However, the revised statutes of the Belgian National Bank contain no mention of the need to balance price stability with the other objectives of government economic policy, because they contain no mention of price stability at all. Price stability was already ingrained in the underlying Belgian economic consensus and required no institutional support. As mentioned previously, the principal changes brought about through nationalization were the royal appointment of the Bank's governor as well as of a government commissioner with responsibility to monitor the actions of the Bank on behalf of the minister of finance. This commissioner was given the right, subject to ministerial review, to suspend any Bank activity, which might be against the law, beyond its charter, or contrary to the interests of the state.[112]

The relatively dependent position of the Belgian National Bank made little difference in the functioning of Belgian monetary policy or, indeed, economic policy more generally. While the ideological colorings of ruling coalitions did influence the focus of industrial policy, this did not result in an inflationary bias or a recurrent pattern of stop-go.[113] There was little chance for Keynesian business cycles to take hold in a country which was so slow to adopt Keynesian economics. Indeed, the classical inclinations of Belgian economic policymakers—on the left as well as on the right—led them to attach great importance to the stability of the frank both at home and abroad.[114]

When unemployment began to emerge at the end of the 1940s, the Belgian government faced the prospect of devaluing its currency within the Bretton Woods system. Given that the reconstruction of the rest of Europe was virtually complete, the mainstays of Belgian production faced increasing competition. Nevertheless, the government in 1949 chose to devalue by significantly less than its major trading partners. The reason was straightforward—the control of domestic inflation.[115] For the Socialist opposition, however, government actions were not stringent enough. Any devaluation, they argued, would accelerate inflation, lower exports, increase unemployment, raise the cost of imports, and lower tax receipts.[116]

The liberal foundation of Belgian macroeconomic policy—encompassing free trade, balanced budgets, price, and exchange-rate stability—was perhaps the only point of agreement between industry, labor, and the government. This same liberal foundation also found support from the regions of Brussels, Wallonia, and Flanders. Nevertheless, the Belgian liberal traditions did not seem to apply to coal and steel production. The costs of changing over from the mature industries of the nineteenth century to the growth industries of the latter twentieth century were too high to be supported by Wallonia alone. And the government could not find a consensual arrangement for sharing those costs across either the social partners or the regions. Belgium refused to accept the need for adjustment, and turned away from its liberal foundations in order to thwart the dictates of the global market.

## Polarization and Conflict

The return of Leopold III in 1950 brought the period of three-way regional competition to an end and deepened the cleavages between confessional and nonconfessional parties. The link between the King and the Catholic Church was a complicated one, and was inextricably bound to the tensions between Wallonia and Flanders arising from wartime collaboration. The King had defied his own ministers and capitulated to German forces during World War II. Consequently, while the government of Belgium established itself in London, the King remained in the country throughout the period of occupation. Soon after the Normandy invasions, the German forces removed the King from Belgium and thereby prevented him from participating in the liberation of the country. The parliament refused to accept the King's return to power in July 1945 and appointed his brother as regent the following September. A five-year stalemate followed, with the government unwilling to accept responsibility for the King's return but similarly unwilling to strip him of his title.

The Catholic-Liberal Eyskens' government finally succeeded in calling a referendum on the return of the monarch in March of 1950, and the vote split significantly across geographic regions and linguistic groups: Flanders for, Wallonia and Brussels against.[117]

This division mitigated the political importance of the absolute majority in favor of the King's return, and Eyskens dissolved the parliament to call for early elections. The same regional divisions apparent in the referendum resulted in a slight overall majority for the Christian Democratic PSC-CVP (50.9 percent of the seats) and the formation of the first homogenous Catholic government of the postwar period. Prime Minister Jean Duvieusart called for the King's return and thereby attempted to put an end to the so-called "Leopold Question."[118]

However, Duvieusart's unilateral restitution of King Leopold destroyed whatever elements of Belgian consociationalism that may have existed during the early postwar years: by forcing the majority wishes of one region (Flanders) and one party (CVP) upon the whole of the country, Duvieusart eliminated the possibility for cooperation between the secular political parties and the Catholics. Relations soured throughout the system of ideological pillars and particularly between Catholics and Socialists. Left-wing Walloon syndicalists under the control of André Renard launched a major offensive against the economic and political organization of the state and seized control over the city of Liège. Ultimately, the government had to call in the army to restore order. Even after Leopold abdicated in favor of his son Baudouin, cooperation between secular and nonsecular groups was impossible.[119]

The conflict between confessional and nonconfessional groups shifted away from the monarchy to focus on the relationship between the state and the Catholic school system. Church–state relations had long been a point of tension in Belgian politics, resulting in a polarization between secular and nonsecular political groups. In the nineteenth century, most of the battles were won by the (secular) liberal bourgeoisie. The political balance changed after World War II, and the Catholic governments began to provide state subsidies to raise teacher salaries and lower fees in Catholic schools. The anti-Catholic opposition protested these measures and overturned them after obtaining power in the elections of 1954. Political conflict escalated until a tenuous 12-year truce was called in 1958: the Catholic Eyskens' government retained the right to subsidize religious education but agreed to use state funds to establish nondenominational schools as well.[120]

Because of the Royal and educational disputes, conflict between confessional and nonconfessional parties effectively overwhelmed three-way regional economic competition in political importance for the period from 1950 to 1958. Geographic support for the Belgian government alternated between Flanders and Brussels/Wallonia. However, the government could not claim a preponderant majority in either event. As a consequence, economic policymaking was reduced to the fundamental agreement on free-market principles with a minimum of state intervention.

The regional standoff had little impact in terms of the general development of the economy. Due primarily to its balanced fiscal position and the modest devaluation of the frank, Belgium was better placed to overcome the inflationary stimulus of the Korean War than was the rest of Europe. While growth slowed relative to Germany and the Netherlands, price inflation remained among the lowest in Europe. During the period from 1953 to 1955, the cost of living rose by only 2 percent in Belgium, compared to 4 percent in Germany, 6 percent in the Netherlands, and 10 percent in Great Britain.[121]

The failure of social partnership in Belgium, however, was striking. Here it may be useful to make the contrast with what was then going on in the Netherlands. In the Netherlands of 1951, the rise in inflation and deterioration of the balance of payments led to close social cooperation ending in real wage cuts. In Belgium of 1950, rising inflation and deteriorating balance of payments led to a long summer of discontent, the capitulation of management in collective bargaining, and increases in real wages. Where the Netherlands emerged from extreme poverty to promote full employment through industrialization, Belgium enjoyed relative prosperity and yet could not manage its distribution. When the Belgian trade unions pressed for higher wage claims in April, the national federation of employers balked. This started a round of increasing social tensions that finally culminated in the April 11, 1954, elections, the fall of the Christian-Democratic government of Jean Van Houtte, and its replacement by a Socialist-Liberal coalition under the leadership of Achiel Van Acker.[122]

Soon after the April elections, the representatives of management and labor tried again to start nationwide cooperation. They signed a joint "productivity declaration" on May 5, 1954, which made three pledges: incomes would rise with the rate of productivity increases; workers would refrain from strikes as anything but a last resort in collective bargaining; and both parties, management and labor, would support the government in its efforts to sustain corporate profits and increase productive investment. The agreement originated out of concern for the relatively poor international competitive position of Belgian industry as well as for the high rate of domestic unemployment.[123] Its success was, however, limited. Social tensions increased in 1956 as the Renardist left wing of the FGTB-ABVV began to struggle for greater autonomy within the national federation. Economic activity slowed yet again, and strikes broke out in the "hot summer" of 1957.[124]

Polarization between confessional and nonconfessional parties was particularly damaging to Belgium's prospects for diminishing its excessive reliance on coal and steel production. Plans developed within the Catholic-Liberal Eyskens' government in 1949 threatened to exacerbate already tense interregional relations and therefore had to be shelved. The combined opposition of Walloon labor and Brussels holding companies proved insurmountable, and even Flemish Catholic governments found themselves having to subsidize Walloon coal mining.[125]

However the European Coal and Steel Community (ECSC) offered an unexpected means to square the circle. The Flemish Catholic government nominally continued with its plans for reconstruction of the coal industry, but drew additional financial and market support from the other countries of Europe, and particularly Germany. When conflict between Walloon economic interests and the government's declaratory restructuring policy re-emerged in 1953, the High Authority of the ECSC conceded additional financial support to prevent a further explosion of social unrest in Belgium. This and similar incidents effectively ensured that the rationalization of Belgian coal mining would not take place—at least until the government could gain some leverage over the union of Walloon- and Brussels-based economic interests, or until conditions in European and world coal markets made it financially impossible for Belgium to continue producing coal.[126]

The irony here is apparent. Participation in the ECSC was intended to help Belgium make the transition away from its nineteenth-century economy. However, the polarized Belgium of the 1950s lacked the capacity for consensus building necessary to promote such a difficult adjustment. As a result, the Belgian government used the support of the ECSC to delay rather than to accelerate adjustment. For theorists who argue that European integration assists governments in the implementation of unpopular but necessary policies through the "advantages of tying one's hands," Belgian manipulation of the ECSC must seem perverse. Nevertheless, domestic political stability required that the homogenous Catholic governments of the period from 1950 to 1954, and the Social-Liberal coalition of 1954–8, avoid a transformation of the economy which could have inflamed a devastating interregional conflict. In this context, European integration played a more important role than the "tying one's hands" argument anticipates—by offering much-needed, albeit temporary, respite from the dictates of global market forces.[127]

## Changing the Structure of Interests

Belgian room for maneuver dissipated during the late 1950s. Metal workers in Wallonia took to the streets in 1957 with demands for higher wages only shortly before the collapse of the market for European coal. Caught between labor unrest, wage increases, and slackening demand, the Belgian economy went into a tailspin. By the time elections took place in June 1958, Belgium was headed into a deep recession and the coal industry was tumbling into crisis.[128] This combination of factors put an end to Belgian manipulation of the ECSC and brought the period of avoiding adjustment to a close. As Alan Milward explains:

The adjustment of Belgian coal mining to the realities of an interdependent world was not brought about through the supranational machinery (of the ECSC) but more brutally through the old familiar mechanism of bankruptcy. Ironically, after delaying the use of the supranational structure to help in a rational restructuring of the industry, the Belgian government found itself facing the coal industry's collapse at the very moment when de Gaulle's seizure of power in France confined all Community action to the strict letter of the Treaties of Paris and Rome and so prevented further recourse to the Community's financial resources.[129]

However, the manifest failings of the Belgian economy—including the crisis in the coal industry—were not enough to promote a consensual approach to the national problem of economic adjustment. Because elites still did not agree on how they would cooperate with each other, they remained trapped in a centrifugal political competition. Evidence for this can be found in Belgium's brief flirtation with Keynesianism. The Catholic, and later Catholic-Liberal, Eyskens governments responded to poor economic performance by using deficit spending to provide greater subsidies for structural reform. These efforts were only partially successful at mitigating the 1959 recession, and the resulting public deficits were perceived as an increasing burden on national prosperity. Eyskens quickly withdrew the subsidies and launched a major push for budgetary consolidation.[130]

Deficit spending to promote economic activity ran counter to the liberal foundations of Belgian macroeconomic policy. Therefore, the fact that Eyskens even tried to resort to Keynesianism signaled his inability to nurture agreement between regions and social partners to share in the cost of adjustment. Deficit spending, in this context, was Eyskens' attempt to replace cooperation with government fiscal intervention. That Eyskens recanted almost immediately, moreover, reflected the strength of the underlying liberal, free-market consensus as well as the difficulty of applying demand management in an open trading economy.

Eyskens was more successful elsewhere. In 1958 he finally succeeded in healing divisions between secular and nonsecular parties with the signing of the "school pact." This agreement paved the way for the Liberals to enter into a coalition with the Catholics (also in 1958) and started to reintroduce cooperation between elites from different ideological constituencies. Nevertheless, two fundamental conflicts re-emerged as constraints on national consensus building. To begin with, the old struggle within the Labor movement between corporatists and syndicalists intensified as André Renard began to agitate increasingly for direct action against industry and the government, and in favor of greater worker control of the economy. Strikes broke out in the coal-mining regions of Wallonia as a response to threatened government pit closures in the winter of 1958–9 and drew support from other industrial trade unions across the whole region.[131]

A second problem to re-emerge was three-way regional economic competition. By 1959, relatively fast economic growth in Flanders brought the level of per capita GDP up to that in Wallonia. However, the Flemish ratio relative to Brussels fell to less than 60 percent. The Flemish economy industrialized during the 1950s, but remained heavily dependent upon agriculture, light production (textiles, etc), and services. Wallonia retained its attachment to heavy, mature industries, and so grew more slowly than either Flanders or Brussels. In short, the regional economies of Belgium were not converging, but rather following very different trajectories.[132]

Looking to the future, Wallonia and Flanders needed investment and Brussels needed investment opportunities. The newly formed Catholic–Liberal coalition began to prepare for a new round of structural reform in 1959 and 1960, involving a decreased role for the central government, defensive restructuring of the mature industries in Wallonia, and a foreign-investment-led modernization of Flanders. The combination of the Paris and Rome treaties provided an appropriate context: within the Coal and Steel Community, Belgium could draw on Community financial resources to supplement its own subsidiaries for the reconstruction of Walloon coal mining; and, as part of an emerging six-nation customs union, Belgium was ideally situated to attract foreign firms as well as to benefit from the opening up of neighboring markets. Indeed, the European Economic Community (EEC) offered the perfect resolution for Belgium's dilemma—foreign investors willing to provide much-needed capital and also willing to share risks with existing Belgian holding companies. Consequently, the 1959–60 economic expansion program offered generous incentives to foreign investors looking to find a central manufacturing location in Europe's newly created common market.

However, in spite of the manifest promise of European integration, close cooperation between the social parties remained essential to the success of any restructuring. Social and political unrest was a powerful deterrent to foreign direct investment no matter how convenient Belgium's location was in the Common Market. Therefore, the government created an Office for Economic Planning in October 1959, and began preparations for the creation of a National Council for Economic Expansion to incorporate the social partners more closely into economic policymaking.[133] Management and labor seemed prepared to cooperate. In May 1960, representatives from both sides of the social partnership signed the first "interprofessional" (nationwide) agreement in collective bargaining; trading real wage increases in line with productivity growth for the promise of social stability.[134]

The rapid acceleration of political developments in the Belgian Congo, however, prevented the government from taking decisive action until November 1960.[135] By that time, agitation for a change of leadership with the Christian Democrats and for a new coalition with the Socialists undermined the ruling Catholic–Liberal coalition. Dissension also emerged within the ranks of the left, as the continued growth of Renardist syndicalism threatened the cohesiveness of the Socialist FGTB-ABVV. Consequently, the proposed "single act for economic expansion, social progress and financial reform" (hereafter "single act") became a point of contention rather than solidarity. Strikes broke out on December 16 among public-sector workers and quickly spread throughout

## Consensual Adjustment in Consociational Democracy

Wallonia and parts of Flanders. The national trade union federations refused to call for a general strike, and yet the manifestations rapidly grew to become the largest social protest in postwar Belgian history, with almost 5.5 million workdays lost. In total, 700,000 workers participated in over 300 different demonstrations during a five-week period.[136]

The Eyskens' government refused to submit, and gradually broke the strikes through a combination of police action and administrative sanctions on public-sector employees. Renard responded with the mobilization of Walloon separatist forces and an official plea for regional autonomy within a Belgian federation. This action confirms the suspicion that elite competition in a fragmented political culture is centrifugal and therefore unstable. However, it was the competition between elites, rather than the Belgian state, which ultimately gave way.

Renard's declaration of Walloon autonomy highlighted the need for elite cooperation and pushed the mainstream of the Socialist Party closer to the Christian Democrats. Louis Major and the moderate leadership of the Socialist trade union federation abandoned syndicalist direct action and isolated Renard on the left. Subsequently, Eyskens succeeded in passing his "single act" through parliament. However, he was not able to ensure the success of his own adjustment program. Instead, a new Catholic–Socialist coalition came to power under the leadership of Theo Lefèvre and Paul-Henri Spaak.[137] Thus, while the center-right had been able to reintroduce elements of consociationalism, only the center-left was able to reshape the pattern for elite behavior.

The Lefèvre–Spaak coalition could build a more consociational relationship between elites because the winter strikes of 1960–1 finally put to rest (at least temporarily) the conflicts between regions and within the labor movement. The first of these conflicts crystallized in the struggle between Wallonia and Flanders, as well as between the advocates of the unitary Belgian state and the proponents of economic federalism.[138] In essence, the dispute centered on the relationship between geography, power, and regional interdependence. By 1961, Flanders was more prosperous than Wallonia as well as being the most populous region in the country.[139] The balance of power between the French- and Flemish-speaking regions had changed decisively. Flemish politicians could be sure to protect as well as to promote their interests in a unitary Belgium. For Walloon politicians, however, the prospects were less certain. As long as Flemish elites agreed to cooperate, the regional interests of Wallonia would be protected if not actively promoted. However, should the Flemish rely on their strength in wealth and population, Wallonia would be better served by a more decentralized economic policy. Hence the most combative elements of Walloon political life felt compelled to be the most federalist as well. In the end, Flemings and unitarists won the field.[140]

The conflict within the labor movement was between corporatists and syndicalists. Among the Socialists, the isolation of the Renardist syndicalists placed Louis Major firmly in control of the FGTB-ABVV. Major soon began promoting the doctrine of corporatism as opposed to direct action. At the same time, the discipline of the confessional trade unions during the winter strikes gave the ACW-MOC new authority in dealings with the government and with industry. Such authority was essential to the social partnership given that the confessional trade unions by this time had the largest membership. These changes within the labor movement altered the balance between the syndicalist and corporatist traditions in labor relations, thereby permitting a form of close cooperation between management, labor, and government, which hitherto had been impossible.[141]

In summary, the center-left Lefèvre-Spaak coalition could encourage consociational patterns of behavior at the same time that it implemented Eyskens' program for economic adjustment. The major obstacles to elite cooperation in Belgium had been removed and a coalition on the center-left was best able to bridge those obstacles that remained. The Rome-Red government offered a bargaining partner which was approachable for business and labor alike and, because it brought together the ruling parties of Wallonia and Flanders, it was also able to dampen concern that one region would promote its economic fortunes at the expense of another. The period of polarization came to an end, and Belgium at last entered into its golden age of political stability and economic prosperity.

## Consensual Adjustment in Belgium

The Belgian strategy for economic adjustment combined corporatist intermediation and regional integration to enormous benefit for the country. The 1960s were a bountiful period for the Belgian economy. Real output grew at an average rate of 4.9 percent from 1961 to 1970, and inflation held at an annual average rate of only 3.4 percent.[142]

However, the Belgian strategy for adjustment was in many ways less rigorous than the Dutch. Whereas in the Netherlands, labor exchanged social harmony and concerted wage restraint for the promise of full employment, in Belgium labor conceded "only" social harmony, and gained both full employment and a greater share of value added. Consensus in the Dutch case centered on the objective of full employment, and so labor initially accepted wage increases, which were below the growth of productivity. Consensus in Belgium formed around the objective of increasing real labor income. Even at its most rigorous, Belgian wage bargains accepted the level of productivity growth as a baseline for wage increases rather than as a ceiling.

In fact, corporatism often failed even to restrain wage increases to the level of productivity growth. The reason is simply that labor market conditions did not allow for that outcome. The rate of unemployment fell off sharply at the start of the 1960s, and the bargaining position of labor strengthened. The relative power of labor was perhaps most evident in the collective wage agreements reached in the spring of 1962. The influence of the Belgian National Bank on the leadership of the confessional trade unions was considerable, and trade union leaders were eager to demonstrate their ability to control their respective constituencies. Nevertheless, collective bargaining agreements awarded real wage raises to the labor force in the face of falling profits and rising inflation.

Nominal employee compensation increased by 7.2 percent in 1962 and 8.0 percent in 1963, while GDP price inflation accelerated from 1.7 percent to 3.0 percent, and growth slowed from 5.2 percent to 4.4 percent. The result was an increase in the adjusted wage share of GDP of almost 1 percent, from 69.5 percent to 70.3 percent—at that time, the highest such ratio in postwar Belgian history.[143] In this sense, productivity-linked wage restraint was no more successful in Belgium during the 1960s than in the Netherlands after 1958.

Because of aggressive wage setting on the part of the trade unions, moreover, Belgian corporatism was also less successful in controlling inflation than Dutch corporatism. Consequently, the government had to insist on the application of price controls even though (and because) wage growth remained relatively high.[144] When inflation emerged during the period 1963–4 the government imposed no fewer than 26 individual price restrictions, mostly on foodstuffs, and began to call for restrictions on the growth of commercial credit.[145]

Belgian corporatism did succeed, however, in emphasizing the importance of collective bargaining for the resolution of labor disputes. This was no small accomplishment. The average number of workdays lost each month due to social unrest fell to 23,000 during the period from 1962 to 1969—a figure which was lower than the monthly average for any year in the 1950s.[146] Those strikes which did take place were spontaneous and usually resulted in the capitulation of management. Less frequently, strikes were the responsibility of nontraditional labor groups, which then had to face the united opposition of employers and trade unions, as in the 1964 doctors' strike.[147]

Moreover, the social harmony garnered through corporatism was an essential counterpart to regional integration as a means to attract foreign investors. During the period from 1965 to 1968, Belgium benefited from an unprecedented net inflow of

## Consensual Adjustment in Consociational Democracy

investment capital—totaling $614 million in only four years.[148] In turn, this investment had a powerful effect on the real economy. Gross fixed capital formation increased to an average 21.9 percent of GDP during the 1960s from an average of 16.5 percent in the 1950s and foreign investment accounted for fully one-half of the total net investment in manufacturing between 1960 and 1972.[149]

Toward the middle of the 1960s, however, cooperation between the social partners began to show signs of strain. Wage claims made by the trade unions in 1964 met considerable resistance in collective bargaining. Although an estimated 26 percent of all employers were suffering from a labor shortage relative to existing capacity, they were loathe to accept wage increases in the face of tightening monetary conditions.[150] Labor markets suddenly tightened further with the passage of a law reducing the workweek from 48 to 45 hours on July 15, 1964.[151] As the labor market tightened, the economic and bargaining power of labor increased and so employers were forced to accept nominal wage increases of 9.7 percent in 1964 and 9.5 percent in 1965.[152]

Tight labor market conditions explain at least part of the relative strength of trade unions in Belgian corporatism during the early 1960s. Further explanation, however, requires a deeper understanding of the disciplining forces at work within the Belgian ideological pillars. The installation of the Lefèvre–Spaak coalition ushered in a new period of governmental stability through the introduction of a consociational patterns of behavior. Nevertheless, even as Belgian elites learned to cooperate with each other in their governance of a fragmented society, the ideological cleavages in Belgium began to dissolve. The truce between the confessional and nonconfessional pillars of Belgian society after the signing of the 1958 "school pact" freed the Liberal Party from its strict anticlericalism and allowed it to redesign its platform to attract Catholic as well as secular voters.

Once the Liberals began to line up to the right of the Christian Democrats, they completely transformed the structure of the Belgian political system, making it more stable but also more competitive. Belgian politics became more stable because the Catholic dominance of the political center prevented any future polarization between confessional and nonconfessional ideological groups.[153] However it became more competitive because the Liberal Party's decision to break with its traditional strict anticlericalism made it easier for voters to move from one traditional party to another. Put another way, political stability in terms of relations among elites came at the price of coherence within the ideological pillars.

The new mobility of the electorate was particularly evident with respect to the Catholic Party. Most of the voters attracted to the Liberal Party were Catholics: from 1958 to 1965, the Catholic share of the vote dropped from 46.5 percent to 34.5 percent, while the Liberal share increased from 11.11 percent to 21.6 percent. The result was not completely negative for the Catholics. The shift of the Liberals to the right assured that the Christian Democrats would serve until 1999 in every subsequent ruling coalition as the hegemonic center between the Liberal right and the Socialist left.[154] It also sparked a marginal movement to the left for the Christian Democrats and a strengthening of the links between the Christian Democratic Party and the confessional trade unions—particularly in Flanders.

Despite this new mobility, the Lefèvre–Spaak government was able to shore up the cleavages in Belgian society by strengthening the institutions within the ideological pillars. For example, when the government made far-reaching reforms in the provision of national health and disability insurance and a number of other welfare-related programs, these reforms did not result in an expansion of the welfare state. Disbursements continued to channel through the ideological pillars—through insurance "mutuals" and trade unions—and thereby increased the institutional importance of the pillars themselves.[155] In this way, developments in Belgium during the 1960s paralleled developments in the Netherlands in the late 1940s and early 1950s. The consensual adjustment strategy evolved in tandem with an institutional consolidation of the ideological pillars even as the cleavage structure of Belgian society came into question.[156]

## Consensual Adjustment in Consociational Democracy

In summary, the Belgian adjustment strategy relied on a change in elite behavior from competition to cooperation. Moreover, the success of the strategy derived from the act of cooperation more than anything else. Nevertheless, such success was qualified. The adoption of a consociational formula also resulted in a softening of the cleavages in Belgian political culture, creating the possibility for future elite competition in a more pluralist political environment. Welfare-state reforms succeeded in strengthening the institutional role of the ideological pillars and perhaps prolonging the usefulness of Belgian consociationalism. Even so, the results were only short-lived.

### The End of Adjustment

Cracks began to emerge in the Belgian economic adjustment strategy as early as 1965. Although it can hardly be said that Belgian adjustment had run full course, and that the economic needs of Wallonia, Flanders, and Brussels had been realized, four developments whittled away the cooperative adjustment strategy based on social harmony and imported capital and gradually made it unworkable. First, conflict between linguistic groups undermined the cohesion of the national political parties, as well as relations between them. Second, the acceleration of inflation ran counter to the liberal preferences at the center of Belgian economic policy. Third, discipline within the labor movement began to wear thin, and once again the leadership shifted away from corporatism and toward direct action for the resolution of labor disputes. Fourth and finally, the breakdown of the Bretton Woods system made international capital flows, domestic price stability, and exchange rate targeting increasingly incompatible.

Increasing tension between Flemings and Walloons exacted a high price in terms of the solidarity of the national trade union federations as well as in terms of the cohesiveness of the national political parties. The 1965 elections witnessed a resurgence of Flemish nationalism, as well as a proliferation of smaller regional parties in Wallonia and Brussels.[157] Most important, a group of disenchanted Walloon Catholics within the confessional trade unions broke off from the CSC-CVP. Relations between Catholic trade unionists and the Christian Democratic Party had always been stronger in Flanders than in Wallonia. Thus as tensions rose between the two linguistic groups, it was the Walloon Catholic trade unionists that manifested the first signs of disaffection. Moreover, their defection from the Walloon Christian Democrats heightened divisions between Christian Democrats in Wallonia and Flanders. In 1968, the CSC-CVP separated into regional political parties, the CSC for Wallonia and the CVP for Flanders.[158] While the Christian Democrats—broadly speaking—remained at the center of the Belgian political spectrum, leadership of the Christian-Democratic movement divided unevenly across two parties rather than concentrating in one.

The change in politics was accompanied by changes in the economy. Inflation accelerated in the immediate aftermath of the 1965 elections and the National Bank raised the discount rate, its primary monetary instrument, from 4.75 percent to 5.25 percent, imposed advanced notification requirements on all price increases, and negotiated a voluntary 12 percent limitation on the creation of commercial credit.[159] The system of concerted wage bargaining continued to function, however, as long as there was sufficient productivity growth to lessen the strain on corporate profits. The trade union federations formed a "common front" with respect to the further elaboration of the welfare state in October 1965, and the influence of the Catholic trade unions within the Flemish Christian Democratic Party (CVP) smoothed the transition from the center-left to the center-right in 1966.[160]

Nevertheless, the rise in domestic inflation contradicted the fundamental liberal, free-market consensus at the heart of Belgian economic policymaking and, in doing so, drew the attention of economic policymakers away from the cause of adjustment and toward the necessity for stabilization. Monetary conditions eased in the early months of 1968, but tightened again in the months preceding the French franc's August 1969 devaluation.

## Consensual Adjustment in Consociational Democracy

In February 1969, the National Bank raised its discount rate on foreign exchange certificates and followed this with general increases in the discount rate in March, April, May, and July. Going into August, the discount rate stood at 7 percent for "certified" credits and 9 percent for those uncertified. A political crisis broke out over the projected size of the government deficit and speculation was rampant that the Belgian frank would be devalued.[161]

The solution to the exchange rate crisis emerged through close cooperation between Prime Minister Gaston Eyskens, National Bank Governor Hubert Anciaux, Budget Minister André Cools, and Finance Minister Jean-Charles Snoy et d'Oppeurs. Instead of yielding to pressure for devaluation, this group of four agreed to begin pushing for a revaluation following the line of the Deutschemark. Although the revaluation never came to pass, Eyskens' public comparison of the Belgian and German economic positions was sufficient to calm the markets. Experts in the press remained skeptical, but the crisis had ended.[162] The National Bank raised the discount rate yet again in September, and credit conditions remained tight until October 1970.

As in the Netherlands, the death throes of the strategy for consensual adjustment came in the form of a series of wage "explosions." The mild recession in 1967 sparked a significant increase in the rate of unemployment and set the stage for the politically important Ford strikes of 1968. The government responded in December 1968 by legislating in favor of monopolistic labor representation at the sectoral level. Far from strengthening the power of the national labor federations, however, government legislation exacerbated concern among independently minded constituent unions.

Thus, while the government worked to achieve greater regional autonomy through constitutional revisions, important divisions began to emerge between the national trade union leaders and their constituencies. The establishment of a national Planning Bureau in July 1970, supplemented by regional organizations for economic policymaking, coincided with increasing disillusionment on the shop floor and massive social unrest.[163] The relationship between the two events is circumstantial and yet their coincidence is important: while national leaders worked to consummate a system for centralized cooperation between the social partners, the grass roots lost the desire to cooperate. More than 2 million workdays were lost during the 1970-1 period. Although the national leadership of business, labor, and government tried to restart the social cooperation of the 1960s, the golden decade had ended and, with it, what little control the government had over the size of wage claims and over the transmission of wage increases into higher prices.

Underlying the divisions within the labor movement was a gradual shift of attention away from reforming Belgian economic structures and toward concentration on creating a more progressive Belgian society. The first signs of this transformation had been evident in the 1965 "common front." The rate of transformation accelerated, however, once the leadership of the national labor federations changed over from the wartime generation— represented by August Cool (ACW) and Louis Major (FGTB)—to a generation more heavily influenced by postwar experiences—Jef Houthuys (ACW) and George Debunne (FGTB). This newer leadership was more willing to accept the progress made in economic adjustment and to devote more attention to—in their own words— progressive causes. For the social partnership, the effect was much the same as had been the achievement of full employment in the Netherlands. Corporatist intermediation ceased to benefit from a focused objective, and collapsed in a series of independent and often spontaneous disputes.[164]

In summary, Belgian adjustment relied on social harmony and imported capital to meet the investment needs of both Flanders and Wallonia. Corporatist intermediation ensured harmonious labor relations, and European integration increased the availability of foreign capital. On the surface, at least, the strategy seemed to offer a perfect combination. However, the consensus on increasing real labor incomes through wage increases linked to productivity growth was inherently unstable. Tight labor market conditions nurtured excessive wage claims, increasing underlying inflationary

## Consensual Adjustment in Consociational Democracy

pressures and decreasing the return to capital. The different types of investment across regions also gave rise to variable productivity growth rates; highly productive and newer industries in Flanders fared better than the mature industries in Wallonia, even where Walloon heavy industries were subsequently restructured. National wage setting had different implications for diverse parts of the country and thereby undermined the broad-based consensus. The period of Belgian adjustment came to a close when the strategy for adjustment no longer served regional interests or the social partnership, and when the government became preoccupied with conserving price and exchange-rate stability.

On the political level, however, the breakdown of consensual adjustment did not result in a return to the polarization of the 1950s. Rather, the transformation of the Belgian party system that started in the early 1960s with the shift of the Liberals to the right continued. Belgian politics became more competitive, and the breakdown of the consensus on increasing the real income of labor simply added to the competition. The growth of regional parties, and the regional division of national unions like the Christian Democrats, brought a new element of competition into play. Thus the 1970s promised to make it more difficult for Belgian policymakers to arrive at consensus positions.

# 3
# The Implications of Change

The 1970s and early 1980s were a time of economic and political turmoil for Belgium and the Netherlands. The collapse of the Bretton Woods system, the oil price shocks, the global recession of 1975, and the decline in international trade were powerfully unsettling influences on the two economies. Moreover, a change in social values complicated relations between elites by causing some to pursue more competitive behavior as others remained committed to consensus building. While elites debated how they should relate with each other and with society, they found little opportunity to forge agreements on what to do about the economy.

The purpose of this chapter is to explore the implications of economic and political change for economic adjustment in Belgium and the Netherlands. My argument is that both sources of change—the economic and the political—caused a shift in the style of politics from consociational to pluralist and in the style of policymaking from consensual to majoritarian. These changes were a matter of degrees and not absolutes. Belgium and the Netherlands did not suddenly become smaller versions of the United States—and, indeed, it is worth questioning whether even the United States lives up to the ideal types that terms like "pluralism" and "majoritarianism" imply. Even so, the shift in Belgium and the Netherlands was enough to place the representatives of traditional labor interests (high real incomes and full employment) in the minority.

## The Implications of Change

The chapter has two structural peculiarities. The first is that the analysis reiterates some of the material introduced at the start of the book. However, this time the focus is on the process of adjustment rather than on the underlying mechanisms for economic and political change. The second is that the historical narratives for Belgium and the Netherlands are woven together. Although this risks narrative confusion, it reflects an important coincidence in real-world events. Whatever their differences during the early postwar period, Belgium and the Netherlands had converged on a similar political and economic situation by the late 1960s and early 1970s. Both faced a depillarization of their national political cultures, which caused a rise in competitive behavior among elites, and both confronted the acceleration of domestic inflation without the benefit of effective price–wage control. By narrating their accounts together, it is easier to bring these similarities to the fore.

The chapter has five sections. The first examines the collapse of the Bretton Woods system and the decision to tie the frank and the guilder to the Deutschemark within the European snake mechanism. The second draws attention to the relationship between profitability and employment as well as to the impact of that relationship on the relative position of industry in wage bargaining. The third looks at how the rise of domestic inflation and unemployment provoked a contradiction between the welfare state and the liberal market economy. The fourth studies the demise of left-wing solidarity in a context of changing social values and increasing political competition. Finally, the fifth section brings the four lines of analysis together in an explanation of the crisis years during the late 1970s and early 1980s, when discussions about the appropriate relations between elites and society collided with attempts to devise a coherent strategy for economic adjustment.

### From Bretton Woods to the Deutschemark

Soon after the Bretton Woods system broke down in August 1971, Belgium and the Netherlands chose to peg their currencies to the Deutschemark within the European "snake" mechanism—an informal agreement to limit exchange rate fluctuations between participating currencies. For both countries it was a fateful decision. Once having tied their currencies to the Deutschemark, they soon found themselves converging on the strict monetary policies of Germany. Belgium and the Netherlands also saw their currencies appreciate against the dollar and, as countries began defecting from the snake, against many of their larger European trading partners as well. Simply put, the decision to peg to the Deutschemark provoked a number of fundamental changes in the economic policies of Belgium and the Netherlands—making them at the same time more austere and less competitive. The question to ask, then, is why they opted for fixed exchange rates.

Part of the explanation for pegging to the Deutschemark lies in the deep liberal, free-market traditions of the Belgians and the Dutch. Exchange-rate stability had long been a priority of Belgian and Dutch monetary policy by the early 1970s, even among the parties of the left. Here it may be useful to recall Socialist opposition to the 1949 devaluation of the frank and the determination of the Drees cabinets to bolster the external value of the guilder. In both instances, the Belgians and the Dutch expressed concern that a weak currency would accelerate domestic inflation through higher import prices and thereby undermine the purchasing power of labor income. Even then, the trade-off between a strong currency and export competitiveness was obvious. Consequently, both countries had developed price–wage policies within the broader framework of the Bretton Woods system—the Belgians, for political reasons, later than the Dutch. These policies controlled the development of domestic prices while a strong currency stance in the Bretton Woods system helped to limit the influence of import prices on the domestic economy.

The combination of a strong currency and price–wage controls worked only so long as wage constraint provided for export competitiveness. By the late 1960s and early 1970s, however, control over domestic inflation had lost much of its effectiveness

## The Implications of Change

in both countries, but particularly in the Netherlands. Import price increases remained low relative to export price inflation for the largest trading partners, but domestic prices accelerated by a magnitude commensurate with developments elsewhere. Nevertheless, stable costs and prices remained essential to profitable trade in both countries. Given the huge share of exports in domestic production, which was 53.9 percent in Belgium and 42.3 percent in the Netherlands in 1970, failure to maintain cost competitiveness posed a significant threat to economic prosperity.[1]

A second reason for pegging to the Deutschemark is to be found in the nature of Belgian and Dutch inflation. Like many countries in Western Europe, Belgium and the Netherlands exhibited many of the symptoms of imported inflation during the collapse of the Bretton Woods system.[2] Both countries ran current account surpluses on average throughout the 1960s and early 1970s, and the export of capital provided only partial compensation.[3] In the period from 1960 to 1967, Belgium and the Netherlands gained an average of $175 million and $142 million in foreign exchange each year. From 1968 to 1973, the annual accumulation of foreign exchange increased to $423 million and $589 million, respectively. The net foreign asset position of Belgian and Dutch monetary authorities more than doubled from 1960 to 1973.[4]

As the Bretton Woods system began to collapse, the foreign transmission of inflationary pressure became more important and also more difficult to control. Inflation almost doubled in the OECD by the end of the 1960s and the price of traded goods increased almost as fast as the general price levels in most advanced industrial economies. Inflation was not simply a national phenomenon, it was an international one as well. The large and growing volume of international trade and capital movements coordinated inflation rates across countries in a way that inhibited the preservation of "islands of stability." Traditional policies for controlling inflation at the national level throughout the OECD were either not working well enough or they were simply not working. Growing popular awareness of the impact of rising prices on real income raised the danger of built-in acceleration. Inflation began to feed on itself as more and more economic actors struggled to shield their earnings. Worse, popular resentment of rising prices undermined the credibility of government policy, lowering the effectiveness of measures for financial control. The Secretary-General of the OECD summarized the situation in December 1970:

> The essence of the problem today is that the cumulative economic, social and political consequences of inflation, which up to now some may have regarded as tolerable, could begin to build up rather quickly... This is why such a heavy responsibility lies on informed opinion to stress the dangers in the present situation, and the urgent need to give a higher priority to price stability.[5]

The situation in Belgium and the Netherlands was particularly disturbing. As very open economies, Belgium and the Netherlands were characteristically more vulnerable to the transmission of inflation from abroad. The import share of the GDP in 1970 was 51.3 percent in Belgium and 44.2 percent in the Netherlands.[6] Rising traded goods prices had immediate impact on more than half of all intermediate goods used in production as well as a similar proportion of capital goods and consumer durables.[7] Inflation in the traded goods sectors also had a knock-on effect through rising wage claims, thereby exaggerating the importance of collapsed price–incomes policies and the loss of domestic price–wage control. When manufacturers attempted to pass increasing cost burdens on to consumers through price rises, workers responded with higher wage claims. The result by the early 1970s was an incipient price–wage spiral, which, though not fully developed, promised further inflation in the years to come.

Going into the first oil price rise, neither Belgium nor the Netherlands could rely on cooperation between the social partners to inhibit the development of a price–wage spiral. Moreover, restrictions on the movement of international capital had only limited effectiveness in restraining the monetary transmission of inflation through accumulated foreign reserves.[8] In short, the challenge of emerging price inflation represented a significant constraint on domestic economic performance, even as the breakup of Bretton Woods exacerbated the weakening of domestic price control.

When US President Richard Nixon closed the gold window, policymakers in Belgium and the Netherlands perceived little alternative to pegging to the Deutschemark. Of course, they could have set monetary instruments to target the growth of domestic prices. But given their liberal traditions, their extreme openness to international trade and the loss of other instruments for controlling domestic inflation, both countries focused attention on exchange rates instead. The decision to peg to the Deutschemark followed soon thereafter.[9]

Pegging exchange rates to the Deutschemark changed the hierarchy of macroeconomic targets from a more balanced consideration of price stability in relationship to growth and employment to a more narrow consideration of exchange-rate stability on its own. Where both countries had accepted some leeway in domestic inflation in order to achieve other economic objectives before 1972, this became more difficult as any inflation differential with Germany threatened to undermine the exchange rate peg. Increasingly, the Belgians and the Dutch had to accept the single-minded determination of the Bundesbank. The Deutschemark exchange rate emerged as the primary target of short-term monetary policy, with only longer-term considerations working toward a balance between full employment, stable growth, and international payments equilibrium.[10]

Deutschemark exchange rate targets also increased government resistance to nominal wage growth for two reasons. The first of these is simply that nominal wage increases fed domestic inflation and the governments of both countries needed to match German price performance in order to maintain the stability of the Deutschemark exchange rate. The second reason for increased resistance to nominal wage increases was concern about export competitiveness. Competitiveness was more of a problem when the frank and guilder were pegged to the Deutschemark than when both currencies participated in the Bretton Woods system. Most industrialized countries had been pegged to the dollar under the Bretton Woods system. Therefore maintaining a stable exchange rate with the dollar translated almost directly into a stable effective exchange rate across the whole of Belgian and Dutch exports. After Bretton Woods system fell apart, most currencies began to float more or less freely against each other and the Deutschemark generally appreciated. Thus, a stable exchange rate between Belgium, the Netherlands, and Germany meant an appreciating exchange rate vis-à-vis the rest of Europe.

The short-lived European snake broadened the zone of monetary stability for Belgium and the Netherlands, but soon fell prey to differences in national economic strategies. Once France, the UK, and Denmark left the snake, Belgium and the Netherlands were virtually alone in their acceptance of the dictates of German monetary policy.[11] Consequently, when the frank and the guilder appreciated with the Deutschemark in relation to France and the UK, Belgian and Dutch exports became less competitive in French and British markets. This loss of competitiveness increased the importance of wage restraint to export industries and strengthened government resistance to wage growth.

In summary, the end of the Bretton Woods system reinforced the liberal free-market tendencies of the Belgians and the Dutch and began to put traditional labor interests in a minority position. By the mid-1970s, both the fight against domestic inflation and hard-currency policies emerged as a constraint on wage bargaining. The breakdown of political control over price–wage setting, moreover, meant that government was less able to rein in domestic inflation even as the need to do so increased. Each time the representatives of labor succeeded in negotiating (or garnering) large nominal wage rises, government resistance to future wage claims hardened. This hostile interaction set the stage for a major conflict between government and labor in both countries by the end of the decade.

## Value-Added and Corporate Profits

Inflation was not, however, the only challenge confronting the Belgian and Dutch economic policymakers. The governments of both countries also had to face a rise in the rate of unemployment. In the six years starting 1968, the figure for Dutch unemployment doubled over what it had been in the early to mid-1960s. The growth of Belgian unemployment was lower in proportional terms, but the starting point was higher. Average annual unemployment rates in the Netherlands and Belgium were, respectively, 0.7 percent and 2.1 percent during the eight years from 1960 to 1967. Unemployment during the next six years averaged 1.5 percent in the Netherlands and 2.3 percent in Belgium. These rates of unemployment were not high in comparison with developments elsewhere. Aggregate measures for the seven largest industrial countries and for the smaller European countries of the OECD were almost a full percentage point higher than the Belgian rates during both periods.[12]

The disconcerting aspect of Belgian and Dutch unemployment was that it occurred while growth rates and the ratio of gross fixed capital formation to total output remained high. In other words, the economies were producing more and investing more, and yet somehow were creating fewer jobs relative to the size of the active population. Part of this phenomenon was due to the increase in the size of the active population, through the growing number of women entering the workforce through the coming-of-age of a large group of postwar baby boomers, but not all. In the Netherlands, the active population grew more slowly in the six years starting 1968 than in the eight years proceeding. The growth of the Belgian labor force was greater after 1968, but only marginally.[13] Moreover, in relative terms, the active populations in Belgium and the Netherlands were unusually low. By 1973, the ratio of active to total population in Belgium and the Netherlands was at least 5 percentage points lower than for France, Germany, the UK, and the United States.[14]

Part of the rise in unemployment also stemmed from the increasing difficulty changing jobs or finding first-time employment.[15] Possibly this resulted from greater demands for skilled labor in an advanced industrial economy, or from poor access to information about employment possibilities, or even from an increasing willingness among workers to spend more time looking for better or better-paying jobs.[16] Nevertheless, as a phenomenon unto itself, the deterioration of labor market efficiency hardly accounted for all of the change in unemployment in either country, even in combination with the growth of the active population.[17] More correctly, the increase in labor market friction was not the source of unemployment but rather a symptom of larger changes taking place.[18]

By the late 1960s and early 1970s, an increasing part of Belgian and Dutch unemployment arose as a result of structural changes in the Belgian and Dutch economies. Two economists for the Dutch Central Planning Bureau, H. Den Hartog and H. S. Tjan, first popularized this interpretation using econometric analysis in 1974. They contended that the nature of production changed during the 1960s such that any given level of output required fewer labor inputs; this change, they argued, was responsible for much of the rise in unemployment.[19] In other words, the productivity of labor increased in the Netherlands while the prospects for employment fell.

Den Hartog and Tjan argued that production became more capital-intensive because real wage growth led the growth in labor productivity, rather than the other way around. Labor in the Netherlands became so expensive that industries began to apply more capital-intensive techniques. The wage explosions of the early 1960s caused the growth of real compensation to leap ahead of the growth of productivity. When first the giant firm Philips (1965) and then the Social and Economic Council (1969) agreed to index wage movements to the cost of living over multiyear contracts, the gap between wage and productivity growth hardened, leading to a perpetual worsening of the ratio of labor to capital costs.

## The Implications of Change

Following this line of reasoning, it is possible to suggest why the pre-1973 increase of unemployment was less dramatic in Belgium than in the Netherlands: the increase in real compensation per employee accelerated earlier in the Netherlands than in Belgium. The early collapse of Dutch price–incomes policy contributed greatly to the rise of unemployment in that country. The more modest achievements of Belgian social cooperation forestalled similar developments until the end of the 1960s. The gap between real productivity and real compensation growth doubled in Belgium from the period before 1968 to the period after, while that same gap narrowed in the Netherlands by almost 40 percent. Given the lag between the time when investment decisions are made and the time when they are realized, the rapid acceleration of Belgian real employee compensation during the early 1970s had effect by the middle of that decade.[20]

The emergence of structural unemployment should not have come as a great surprise to economists in either country. As early as 1963, the Dutch Social and Economic Council argued that a rise in labor costs ahead of the growth of productivity was essential to release the tension in the labor market.[21] Similarly the Eyskens "single act" of 1961 foresaw a growth in worker productivity as one means to mitigate the emerging capital surplus in Belgium. The controversial aspect of Den Hartog and Tjan's analysis was the identification of excessive capital deepening as the principal cause of unemployment. It is one thing to assert that unemployment retains a structural component, and quite another to argue that the structure of the economy does not allow for a decline in the rate of unemployment.

The emergence and growth of structural unemployment represented a significant challenge to policymakers.[22] No matter how much income or the propensity to consume out of income increased, employment was limited by the product of the amount of physical capital and the labor required to work it. In order to resolve this dilemma, policymakers not only had to increase the volume of physical capital, they also had to change the nature of investment from labor-saving to labor-intensive.[23] Changing the nature of investment, however, required a change in the relative cost of labor or, more explicitly, a decline in the real employee compensation relative to the cost of capital.[24]

When the economy was growing and labor productivity was increasing, policymakers needed to slow down the growth of real wages and nonwage labor costs to below the increase in labor productivity. There were, however, two important complications. First, industry was unlikely to scrap existing plant until the underlying capital was either physically obsolete or until the relative cost change between capital and labor was sufficient to warrant both the scrapping of existing machinery and its replacement by more labor-intensive machinery.[25] Second, real wages do not mean the same thing to workers as they do to employers. Even if real consumption wages—wages deflated by consumer prices—had remained constant, real production wages—wages deflated by producer prices—would have continued to increase. In the period from 1968 to 1973, consumer prices in Belgium increased on average 1.5 percent more than producer prices per annum. Similarly, during the period from 1971 to 1973, producer prices trailed consumer prices by 2.3 percent in the Netherlands.[26] In order to provide manufacturers with the appropriate investment incentives, workers had to experience an even greater slowdown in the growth of real consumption wages than employers would witness in terms of real production wages. Under the best of circumstances, the decline in the relative return to labor would have to be considerable to increase the rate of total employment.

The reaction to Den Hartog and Tjan's diagnosis of structural unemployment within the economics profession was immediate and heated. Neo-Keynesians accepted that employment depended in part on the influence of relative wage costs, but argued that employment was far more dependent upon the level of aggregate demand. If the government held down wage costs, they reasoned, the result would be a fall in aggregate consumption, provoking a further drop in demand for labor and a rise in unemployment. Much of the discussion centered on the specifications of the econometric models used to diagnose the origins of unemployment, but, as one commentator remarked, "the central question (remained): in which measure neo-Keynesian (and) in which measure neo-classical"[27]—to what extent could they rely on the manipulation of aggregate demand to combat unemployment, and to what extent did they have to accept the need for supply-side measures. In the end, virtually all sides of the debate were in agreement that a better understanding of the causes of unemployment required further empirical analysis.

The consensus on the need for more study offered little direction for policymakers. Although both the Dutch and Belgian governments accepted the existence of a relationship between high real wage costs and high unemployment, this acceptance did not result in an immediate and strong consensus on the need to bolster corporate profitability. Nor did the acceptance of the relationship between high wages and high unemployment translate into an obvious policy program.[28] However, one thing was clear. Throughout the 1970s, the wage share of GDP remained high in Belgium and the Netherlands. Whereas during the 1960s, the average adjusted wage share was 70 percent in both countries, that average had climbed to 75 percent in the 1970s.[29] Gradually, by the end of the 1970s, policymakers began to acknowledge the need to bolster corporate profits. Doing so, however, would require taking the unpopular step of lowering the compensation for workers.

## Inflation, Unemployment, and Budgetary Reform

The simultaneous emergence of inflation and unemployment presented Belgian and Dutch policymakers with the problem of stagflation in the early months of 1973. This paralleled developments elsewhere in the OECD, but with three important qualifications: Belgian and Dutch monetary authorities had to converge on the more rigorous German standard for domestic price inflation; cooperation between the social partners, which had long been an essential support for policymaking in both countries, had broken down; and the structural component of Belgian and Dutch

## The Implications of Change

**Table 3.1.** Various indicators of fiscal stance

|  | General government balance ||| Peak-cycle or structural balance ||| Mid-cycle, inflation-adjusted balance |||
|---|---|---|---|---|---|---|---|---|---|
|  | 1973 | 1974 | 1975 | 1973 | 1974 | 1975 | 1973 | 1974 | 1975 |
| Belgium | −3.5 | −2.6 | −4.7 | −4.8 | −4.4 | −3.9 | −2.2 | 1.1 | 1.4 |
| Netherlands | 0.6 | −0.4 | −3.0 | −0.1 | −1.1 | −0.9 | 0.7 | 0.1 | 0.4 |
| West Germany | 1.2 | −1.3 | −5.7 | −1.3 | −0.5 | −3.4 | −0.6 | −2.3 | −5.0 |

*Source*: Price and Muller (1984, Tables 1, 2, and 8).

unemployment had risen and was continuing to rise. Tensions mounted as first the Germans and then the Dutch revalued within the European snake mechanism.[30]

Then came the oil price shock and, with it, a fivefold increase in the international price of oil. A barrel of crude oil worth less than $4 in 1972 cost more than $20 in 1974.[31] The response from Belgian and Dutch monetary authorities was characteristically conservative. Whereas much of the OECD began to loosen monetary conditions and rely on fiscal stimulus to counteract the drain on domestic incomes,[32] Belgium and the Netherlands focused on price and exchange-rate stability. Policymakers expressed more concern for overheating and inflation than for the stabilization of aggregate demand. Indeed, in comparison with Germany, the Belgians and the Dutch were extremely rigorous in their struggle to rein in domestic inflation. Short-term interest-rate differentials with Germany rocketed from negative 5.6 percent in Belgium and negative 4.7 percent in the Netherlands in 1973 to positive 0.8 percent and positive 0.6 percent in 1974.[33]

The difference in fiscal policy was less acute, although still indicative of the relatively conservative attitudes of the Belgians and the Dutch. This is not wholly evident in the figures for general government balances, but does show up in more technical measures of fiscal stimulus presented in Table 3.1. Belgian and Dutch authorities reacted to the first oil shock by changing the structure of government outlays such that the excess of expenditure over revenues would be smaller for any given level of national economic activity. Thus although both Belgian and Dutch authorities did

## The Implications of Change

attempt to mitigate the influence of the oil price shock on domestic incomes—largely through increased transfers to households—the effects of fiscal policy were not countercyclical. The peak-cycle, or structural, balance illustrates the slightly procyclical effect of Belgian and Dutch fiscal policy by showing what the balance on government accounts would be if the economy were to achieve optimal levels of growth and employment. The narrowing of structural deficits in Belgium during 1974 and 1975, and in the Netherlands during 1975, corresponds to an effective (albeit modest) tightening of fiscal policy. Symmetrically, the broadening of the German structural deficit indicates a loosening of fiscal policy in that country.

Mid-cycle, inflation-adjusted balances tell much the same story, but include the effects of inflation on the value of outstanding government debt. Economists often regard this measure as the best indicator of government fiscal stance because it illustrates the total impact of the government on the wealth of the private sector, and therefore on the level of private-sector demand. In Belgium and the Netherlands, the government subtracted from private-sector wealth in spite of large government deficits, while in Germany the impact of government fiscal policy was the reverse.[34]

These technical measures of government fiscal stance illustrate the constraints under which Belgian and Dutch policymakers had to perform. In choosing to emphasize inflation and exchange targets over demand stabilization, the governments of both countries inadvertently moderated the countercyclical effects of fiscal policy. The continued acceleration of domestic inflation further magnified the impact of government moderation on aggregate demand, inducing a subtraction of private wealth equal (at mid cycle) to 1.4 and 0.4 percent of Belgian and Dutch GDP during the deepest recession in postwar history. When inflation began to decelerate during the recovery of 1976, the effects on net fiscal stimulus changed direction. As Belgian and Dutch policymakers turned their attention to the stabilization of government accounts, implying a mild fiscal restraint, 1976 inflation-adjusted government balances plummeted to a deficit of 1.2 percent of GDP in the

Netherlands and of 2.5 percent of GDP in Belgium. The lesson here was clear, at least with the benefit of hindsight. Fine-tuning economic performance was impossible under rapidly changing economic conditions. Yet apart from making minor policy alterations, neither Belgian nor Dutch policymakers were capable of outlining a coherent plan for adjusting to the changed world economy.[35]

The social partners hardly asserted more convincing economic leadership. Trade unions reacted to rising prices during the 1975 recession with even higher nominal wage claims. Employers lacked bargaining power in spite of loosening labor-market conditions or the growing awareness of the relationship between profitability and unemployment, and real employee compensation grew in Belgium by 5 percent in 1974 and 4 percent in 1975, and, in the Netherlands, by 6 percent in 1974 and 2.8 percent in 1975.[36] As the currencies of both countries continued to appreciate with the Deutschemark, real wage increases further subtracted from the competitiveness of Belgian and Dutch exports during a time of weak corporate profitability and falling international demand. Moreover, the inability of manufacturing industries to raise prices in the face of international competition shunted the bulk of inflationary pressure onto the sheltered sector of the economy. This fueled consumer demand for imports, which were relatively cheap, while it dampened enthusiasm for domestic production, which was relatively expensive. Rising unemployment and falling current account balances were the result.[37] To be sure, this experience was repeated throughout many of the European countries.[38] Nevertheless, it made for a striking contrast to the 1950s in the Netherlands and the 1960s in Belgium.

Without the cooperation of the social partners, government strategy oscillated between alleviating (the burdens of) rising unemployment, stabilizing and improving corporate profitability, holding down inflation and defending the Deutschemark parity, and, finally stabilizing the balance between government expenditures and receipts. On the one hand lay the social objectives of the welfare state (full employment and rising living standards), and on the other hand lay the requirements for an efficient market economy (corporate profitability and international and government balance).

The competition between the welfare state and the market economy was more pronounced in Belgium than in the Netherlands. The growth of Belgian government outlays gathered momentum from efforts to buy the reconciliation of linguistic and regional disputes, as well as from the ambitions of social progressives. In 1970, general government expenditure accounted for only 38 percent of GDP while by 1978 government outlays accounted for more than 50 percent of domestic product. The Catholic-Liberal Tindemans cabinet called for budgetary reform in the late Autumn of 1976, but succeeded only in uniting the trade unions against the government. Elections in the Spring of 1977 forced Tindemans to form a new coalition with the Socialists rather than the Liberals, and the growth of government outlays continued unabated.[39]

Government finances in the Netherlands showed greater flexibility, thanks to large revenues from natural gas exploitation. Thus, while government expenditure grew from 42 percent of GDP in 1970 to 53 percent of GDP in 1978, this growth did not wholly translate into higher tax burdens or public-sector borrowing requirements. The windfall was short-lived. Dutch authorities recognized that gas revenues were limited in duration: the Netherlands could not remain a net exporter of energy indefinitely. The center-left Den Uyl government initiated a plan to limit the increase in government outlays to only 1 percent of national income per annum. Such measures were not draconian. Taken to its logical extreme, a rule limiting the growth of government outlays to only 1 percent of GDP would inevitably lead to the absorption of the entire economy by the public sector.[40] Den Uyl's efforts failed nonetheless. Divisions among the spending ministries and within the Socialist Party (PvdA) prevented even a modest restraint on the growth of expenditures.[41]

By the end of the 1970s, public finances in both Belgium and the Netherlands were headed into crisis. Government expenditures accounted for more than half of either country's economic production, and public-sector borrowing requirements were increasing dramatically. Moreover, the rise in public-sector employment and debt service requirements placed growing constraints on either government's ability to make even minor adjustments in public-spending patterns. Government employment grew by an annual average rate of 3.9 percent in Belgium and 2.5 percent in the Netherlands from 1973 to 1979. Government transfers for social security swelled to 20.9 percent of Belgian GDP and 25.5 percent of Dutch GDP by the end of the decade, and it was clear in both countries that national insurance schemes were heading toward insolvency.[42] Public officials in Belgium and the Netherlands began to reconsider the appropriateness of the existing balance between the welfare state and the market economy even before the second oil price shock. In doing so, these officials began to search for means to limit the role of the state in the provision of social welfare, and to stimulate the private sector.

## Value Change and Political Competition

By the end of the 1970s, the combination of inflation, unemployment, and government deficits put the trade unions in an awkward position. In increasing numbers, other actors in society began to turn against what they saw as excessive real wages. Moreover, many analysts outside the labor movement began to accept that real wage cuts would not necessarily lead to full employment. For the trade unions, this meant that they had little to offer their followers in exchange for concerted wage restraint.

Nevertheless, for institutional reasons, trade union leaders retained considerable influence in the parties of the left and center, the Socialists and Christian Democrats. The unions not only brought in the votes, they often distributed social welfare benefits as well. This was particularly the case in Belgium, where the welfare state reforms of the 1960s had increased the role of the trade unions rather than increasing the role of the state. Thus, no matter how elites choose to interact with each other or with society, the interests of the trade unions could not be ignored. Within a consociational formula, the trade unions were a necessary part of any consensus. Within a more competitive political formula, at least part of the trade union movement had to participate in the ruling majority.

Changing the focus of economic policymaking in either Belgium or the Netherlands required a political adjustment running parallel to developments in the economy. Indeed, informed observers of the Belgian and Dutch cases like Göran Therborn and Paulette Kurzer use comparative analysis across European countries to suggest that institutional factors determined the development of Belgian and Dutch neoliberalism. For example, Therborn summarizes his analysis of employment performance in sixteen European countries in the early 1980s with the contention that: "the existence or non-existence of institutional commitment to full employment is the basic explanation for the differential impact of the current crisis." He then goes on to ascribe the political failings of social democracy to the "dominance of finance over industry" (Belgium) and to "the establishment of consistently deflationary policies" (Netherlands). Therborn concludes that a rise in unemployment was unnecessary, and that:

Without the willing or unconscious support...of right-wing politicians and economic advisors and of faint-hearted or weak-willed Social Democrats and, sometimes, of starry-eyed trade unionists, credulously buying the liberal arguments, high unemployment could have been staved off.[43]

Kurzer expands on Therborn's argument through her analysis of central bank independence and financial sectors in Austria, Sweden, Belgium, and the Netherlands. She finds that two factors—the relative independence of central banks and the international orientation of financial sectors—adequately explain the more neoliberal attitudes of Belgium and the Netherlands as compared to either Austria or Sweden. Where the central banks were independent, and the financial sectors were well integrated into international markets, neoliberal economic policies prevailed.[44] For Kurzer, as for Therborn, the rise in unemployment could have been averted without reining in the welfare state. Given a different institutional setting—or perhaps even a strong display of political determination—Belgium and the Netherlands could have had both high employment and generous state provisions for social welfare.

The prior choices made by Belgian and Dutch policymakers during the 1970s made any such accommodation unlikely. The exchange rate pegs adopted to respond to the breakdown of the Bretton Woods system tied monetary policy to the stabilization of the Deutschemark exchange rate. The growing awareness of the relationship between high real wages and unemployment shifted government attention to supply-side policies for economic stabilization. The instability of government finances in combination with the apparent futility of demand stabilization policies reduced enthusiasm for social spending and underscored the potential contradictions between the welfare state and the market economy. Taken together, these three developments gave the Belgians and the Dutch little choice but to cut back on the welfare state and begin transferring resources from wages to profits.

Still nothing explains why trade union leaders would allow themselves to be so "outmaneuvered" (if indeed they were) at the end of the 1970s as compared to during the 1950s or 1960s. If Therborn and Kurzer are correct in emphasizing the role of institutions in the development of neoliberalism (and I believe they are), surely it is reasonable to ask why labor representatives were unable to assert their collective interests during the process of institution-building, or, more correctly, during the process of institutional reform. Put another way, any comprehensive explanation of how the Belgians and the Dutch were going to adjust to global economic change by shifting resources to the market economy must necessarily include some explanation for the declining effectiveness of labor representation in preserving either full employment or labor incomes, if not both at the same time.

At least part of the explanation can be found in the argument about insiders and outsiders. During the 1970s, Belgian and Dutch trade unions placed greater emphasis on the specific needs of their members than on the interests of society at large. Trade union

## The Implications of Change

wage negotiators fought for real pay increases, and often relied on direct action to ensure employer compliance. While this strategy was successful in protecting (and even increasing) the purchasing power of labor income, the conflictive tactics of the trade unions diminished their ability to participate constructively in cooperative efforts at institutional reform. Reform-minded trade union leaders were limited in their actions out of concern that they would not be able to retain control over their followings. At the same time, industry and government representatives were unwilling to negotiate with trade unionists, whom they suspected could not make binding commitments in good faith.

However, neither the insider–outsider dynamic nor the collective action problem can explain the ineffectiveness of labor representatives in promoting their interests at the national political level. Here it is worth repeating that the vertical integration of the Belgian and Dutch societies accords great political influence to the national trade union confederations both within the secular parties of the left and within the confessional parties at the center. Both groups, the left and the center, are closely intertwined with their ideologically affiliated trade union confederations and, indeed, often rely on those confederations to mobilize electoral support. By implication, the social democratic and confessional parties of Belgium and the Netherlands should have emerged as champions of labor interests—as did the Drees–van Schaik cabinet in the Netherlands during the late 1940s and early 1950s or the Lefèvre–Spaak cabinet in Belgium during the 1960s. Therefore, the final piece of the answer lies in the changing relationship between the political parties of the left and center, and their respective trade union confederations. Three lines of analysis are relevant.

To begin with, a rise in political competition among elites created divisions within the progressive parties (whether from the secular left or from the confessional center) between those who would use party organizations as agents of change and those who would use them to defend traditional labor interests. Such divisions were possible because, as the transformation of the Belgian Liberals in the early 1960s and the emergence of a post-materialist Dutch

## The Implications of Change

Liberal Party (Democrats '66) later that same decade had underscored, radical parties need not adhere to traditionally left-wing economic agendas. Indeed, the emergence of so-called "new" political issues like the environment had changed the meaning of terms like "left" and "progressive" to include quality of life as well as equality of income distribution. Where the traditional parties like the PvdA or CVP or PSC sought to accommodate post-materialist concerns, the effect was to create competitive constituencies within the party. Although the results of accommodation were satisfactory in electoral terms—and resulted in an increase of the aggregate votes won by traditional parties—the potential damage to intra-party cohesiveness was considerable.

By 1977, neither the Dutch Socialist Joop Den Uyl nor the Belgian Christian Democrat Leo Tindemans was capable of bridging the conflicts that began to emerge between labor militants and new political activists, but with opposite results: Den Uyl's government lost power to the center-right, and Tindemans was forced to build a new coalition on the center-left. However, neither the Dutch center-right nor the Belgian center-left strengthened unambiguously during the alternation of power. Indeed, the Dutch Christian Democrats accepted a painful (although also successful) fusion of respective Protestant and Catholic political parties even as the Catholic trade union confederation (NKV) merged its Socialist (NVV) counterpart to form the Catholic-Socialist trade union federation (FNV). Meanwhile, the Socialists in Belgium changed in an opposite manner, and finally followed the Liberals and Christian Democrats in accepting a division across regional and linguistic lines—the Socialist Party (SP) for Flanders and the PS for Wallonia.

The conclusion to draw here is that government alternation around the center in Belgium and the Netherlands derived less from left–right divisions over economic policy than it did from relations both between and within the political parties.[45] Those parties willing to strive for consensus among elites formed the government (Christian Democrats and Right Liberals in the Netherlands, and Catholics and Socialists in Belgium) while those parties dominated by more competitive elites moved into the opposition (PvdA in the Netherlands and Liberals in Belgium). The implications for labor representatives were, however, unambiguous. The transformation of the Belgian and Dutch political systems deprived the trade unions of their privileged positions within the left and the center, and thereby diminished their political effectiveness.[46]

The second line of analysis concerning the defense of full employment derives from the responsibilities of trade unions in relation to their constituencies. The institutional role of ideological "pillars" in the provision of social welfare benefits in Belgium and (to a much lesser extent) in the Netherlands significantly transformed the way the trade unions functioned. Where once it might have been possible for trade union leaders to concentrate on their responsibilities as labor representatives per se, the remarkable growth of the Belgian and Dutch welfare states gave the trade unions responsibility for the provision of social services.[47] Although originally encouraged by the trade unions, this division of leadership responsibilities—as labor representatives and as service providers—had the twofold effect of making trade union constituencies more demanding of their leaders, and of making trade union leaders less able to respond to the diverse and often contradictory demands of their constituencies. Inevitably, tension between labor activists and trade union leadership increased with the rate of unemployment and as the continued solvency of the two welfare states came into question. For example, trade union leaders were hard pressed to support higher wage claims coupled with the possibility of direct action when such behavior threatened to run down trade union coffers and to increase the burden of unemployment on social support finances.[48]

The third and final analysis reflects the changing composition of trade union membership. Simply put, the broadening of trade union constituencies away from traditional industrial workers and across a wide array of different service- and public-sector employees complicated the task of "labor" representation. Given the wide disparities between sectoral productivity growth rates, finding a simple formula for making wage demands became increasingly unworkable. The result was to exacerbate the centrifugal tendencies within the national trade union confederations, which shifted the balance of power toward regional groupings in Belgium and toward sectoral or industrial groupings in the Netherlands.[49]

By the end of the 1970s, the political representatives of labor interests found themselves in a three-tier struggle—to influence party agendas, to reconcile their competing responsibilities, and to coordinate the positions of the increasingly powerful and disparate groups of constituents. Finding a simultaneous solution to all three conflicts placed severe constraints on the traditional representative functions of labor leaders. Moreover, the political allies of the trade unions were all too aware of the insider–outsider dynamics, which threatened to make the pursuit of "labor" interests inconsistent with the interests of the work force (and therefore the electorate) at large. In this context, the challenge of institutional reform suggested by Therborn and Kurzer placed the political representatives of labor interests in Belgium and the Netherlands in an untenable situation. Labor leaders had to obtain at least some room for maneuver before they could begin to negotiate with either employers or the government. Thus, labor representatives were forced into a defensive posture, which prevented them from developing a coherent alternative to the reliance on supply-side supports, wage restraint, and fiscal austerity.[50]

## Crisis and the Shift from Labor to Industry

The need for economic adjustment was obvious in Belgium and the Netherlands by the late 1970s and before the second oil price shock. Inflation remained only barely in check, unemployment and government borrowing increased, investment fell off, and current accounts moved into deficit. Moreover, the broad lines of what was required for adjustment were gaining increasing acceptance within policymaking circles: wage restraint, fiscal austerity, and supply-side supports. Nevertheless, consensus on the means of adjustment was lacking. Few elements in either Belgium or the Netherlands were eager to undertake a painful reform of the welfare state, or indeed to transfer income from workers to corporate profits. Rather, the governments of both countries relied on short-term palliative measures in the hopes that an improvement in the world economy would absolve them of the need to make significant adjustments at home. In part, this should be attributed to what Albert Kervijn has described as a breakdown in the political art: incapable of "making possible tomorrow what is impossible today," politicians were thrown back on the worst strategy of relying on decisions which were unwanted and ill-prepared, made inevitable but remaining ineffective.[51] Changes in the nature of political competition in Belgium and the Netherlands had deprived both countries of the facility for consensus building that lay at the heart of their much-vaunted capacity for flexible adjustment.

The failure of the Christian Democrat-Liberal van Agt government's *Blueprint 1981* reform program in the Netherlands provides a striking example of how little consensus could be achieved even with the assistance of a parliamentary majority. Though some authors have suggested that the formation of the first van Agt cabinet marked the transition to neoliberalism in the Netherlands, such an assertion finds little support from the policies which van Agt was able to successfully implement. Indeed, Dutch central banker Nout Wellink argues that *Blueprint 1981* bore strong indications of ambivalence regarding the relative importance of structural and conjunctural measures, and that it failed to bring sufficient force to bear on the need for budgetary consolidation. Wellink also reports that van Agt frequently complained that he never had the opportunity to put forward a coherent adjustment program because of lack of support within the Second Chamber.[52]

The multiple Belgian governments witnessed in the period after 1977 were hardly more successful. Although economic planners argued increasingly in favor of reform, politicians were simply too overwhelmed by the resurgence of interregional tensions to develop a coherent and workable plan for the economy. In spite

## The Implications of Change

of the country's manifestly poor economic health, political analysts gave precedence to constitutional reform. Indeed, a major Belgian political research institute produced an entire volume on the "crisis" of the late 1970s and early 1980s that scarcely mentions economic performance.[53]

However, the second oil price rise and the world recession of the early 1980s meant that economic reform could not be put off indefinitely. And, the four developments outlined in this chapter—the convergence on German inflation norms, the strengthened bargaining position of industry, the emerging contradiction between the welfare state and the market economy, and the diminished effectiveness of labor representatives—supported the adoption of four correctives in order to return to a sustainable equilibrium in the relationship between government and the social partners. First, the government had to reconcile defending the Deutschemark exchange rate with the need for export competitiveness. Second, industry had to find sufficient financial resources to remain solvent and competitive. Third, the government had to stabilize government accounts without simply printing the money. And fourth, labor representatives had to reassert control over their constituencies.

The story ends in both cases with the emergence of narrow center-right majorities that were dedicated to a combination of fiscal austerity, supply-side measures to increase corporate profitability, and participation within the EMS. Labor reluctantly agreed to cooperate with this center-right majority as an (unpleasant but still superior) alternative to devastating and ultimately futile conflict. Accordingly, each of the four correctives came to pass. The government brought inflation under control while relying on the EMS to stabilize effective exchange rates within Europe. Austerity measures stabilized public finances and set in motion a fundamental reorganization of the two welfare states. Industry benefited from an increased share of value added along with a boost in profitability. And labor representatives reasserted control over their constituencies and retained at least some say in national economic policymaking.

## The Implications of Change

The formation of center-right governments under Wilfried Martens and Ruud Lubbers reflected a narrow majority in favor of the adoption of economic adjustment programs centering on wage restraint, price stability, supply-side support measures, and fiscal austerity. However, it is not correct to identify the adjustment measures undertaken in either country with the neoliberalism of Margaret Thatcher or even Ronald Reagan. The Martens and Lubbers majorities had no ambition to marginalize the trade unions. Rather, they hoped to find a new equilibrium in relations between labor and capital, and between the traditional political parties. Doing so, however, first required that they put the economy on a sound footing. Even without a broad-based consensus, the two center-right coalitions were determined to implement their economic programs.

# 4

# "Consensual" Adjustment in Post-Consociational Democracy

Given the policy commitments made by politicians during the 1980s, Belgium and the Netherlands had no choice but to redistribute income from labor to capital in order to bolster international competitiveness, shore up profitability, encourage investment, and, ultimately, create employment. By contrast, the Belgians and the Dutch—elites and electorates—had many choices. They could try to spend their way out of the recession. They could erect barriers to trade and strengthen controls on capital flows. They could restrict working hours, encourage job-sharing, and expel foreign workers. They could do some combination of these things. Or, what is easier and therefore more likely, they could do nothing at all. "Belgium" and "The Netherlands" exist under the moral imperative of statehood. They must serve the national interest in a manner that is consistent with their revealed preferences. The Belgians and the Dutch are unburdened by categorical imperatives. They act only once motivated and in the manner of their own choosing.[1]

This distinction between state agency and human agency is obvious to social scientists. It is so obvious, in fact, that it is easily taken for granted and at times even forgotten. The state has to do what is best. The people and their politicians will do what they want—if they can be motivated to do anything at all. The challenge of statecraft is for politicians to get the people to face the obligations of the state. A real statesperson will get the people to do what is right. It may not always work but it should not always fail either. That is what Keynes meant in the *General Theory* with his famous allusion to the influence of "some defunct economist" on the actions of "practical men."[2] Crisis demands action: as much as possible, it should be correct action.[3]

Both of these challenges were apparent in Belgian and Dutch responses to the crisis of the 1970s. The governments not only had to implement some kind of response to the crisis, but they also had to push through a response that worked for the country as a whole. The difficulty is that cutting back on public expenditure and shifting income from labor to capital goes against the immediate self-interest of much of the electorate. In rapid succession, a number of governments tried and failed to implement such measures in both countries. Sometimes doing nothing is more attractive than doing something that hurts.

In 1981 and 1982, Wilfried Martens in Belgium and Ruud Lubbers in the Netherlands overcame this inertia by invoking their roles as agents of the state. Using the full powers of their offices, they cajoled and even coerced the people into action. Contemporaries expressed concern about this strong self-assertion. Social scientists in Belgium referred to Martens' strategy as "less democracy for a better economy." In the Netherlands, similar voices described the measures introduced by Lubbers as symptomatic of a "neoliberal backlash."[4] For many on the left, the fact that economic adjustment policies were implemented by narrow center-right majorities, rather than broad-based center-left consensus governments, raised the specter of authoritarianism. An "intervention-state," critics believed, had replaced three-way collaboration between the government and the social partners, with the result that social solidarity gave way to the harsh dictates of the market. The combination of fiscal austerity, profit supports, and wage restraint imposed "excessive" burdens on the working classes and they threatened to reverse the progress of social democracy by rolling back the provision of social welfare.[5]

The purpose of this chapter is to explain the origins and functioning of the Belgian and Dutch adjustment strategies during the

1980s. The argument is that these strategies are more similar to the consensual adjustments made by the center-left during the 1950s and 1960s than their critics would like to admit.[6] Much as those earlier strategies, the policies implemented by Martens and Lubbers relied on corporatist bargaining to increase the competitiveness of domestic manufacturing while at the same time using European integration to stabilize trade relations with the outside world. Nevertheless, there are three major differences between the adjustment strategies deployed in the 1950s and 1960s and those pursued in the 1980s.

To begin with, the domestic political context in Belgium and the Netherlands had changed. The depillarization of the late 1960s and 1970s deprived the Belgian and Dutch societies of their self-discipline and encouraged competition among elites. Building a wide-reaching consensus around a particular strategy for adjustment was out of the question because the countries no longer functioned as consociational democracies. Many of the institutional features of consociationalism remained in the form of political parties, trade unions, and employers' associations. Yet elites on all sides had to agree on a new pattern for decision-making before these structures could be used in the interests of economic adjustment.

A second difference was that the government played a stronger leadership role in corporatist bargaining. This resulted because government, industry, and labor all faced severe constraints: the government could not purchase consensus through promises to extend the welfare state; industry could not pay for higher taxes or wages; and trade union leaders had only tenuous control over an increasingly disorganized labor movement. Thus, the government often had to set the terms for acceptable agreements between industry and labor—agreements that could shore up corporate profits and strengthen trade union discipline at the same time.

A third difference lay in the changing function of European integration from opening up foreign markets or attracting foreign investment to stabilizing exchange rates. The breakdown of the Bretton Woods system in the 1970s disrupted trade relations in

## "Consensual" Adjustment in Post-Consociational Democracy

Europe by increasing exchange rate variability. Many countries took advantage of world monetary disorder to reintroduce protectionism through competitive devaluations or, following the American example, through the "benign neglect" of their currencies. Belgium and the Netherlands continued to peg their currencies to the Deutschemark, but also needed some vehicle to impose similar discipline on other European currencies.

Once these differences are taken into account, it is easier to see why many commentators now look back on the Belgian and Dutch adjustments of the early 1980s as further examples of consensus policymaking in small countries.[7] They have a point. The basic thrust of the adjustment strategies was the same in the 1980s as in the 1950s and 1960s. Governments in both countries strove to control manufacturing costs while creating a favorable environment for international trade and investment. And these governments relied on corporatist bargaining and regional integration to achieve the desired results. Nevertheless, the critics are also right. The style of adjustment was more "consensual" than consensual. Not only were the actors representative of a relatively narrow swathe of Belgian and Dutch society, the costs and benefits were unevenly distributed as well.

The chapter has five sections. The first describes how elites were able to convince each other that something had to be done. The second demonstrates that something actually was done. The third examines the use of corporatism in Belgium and the Netherlands as a means to control the development of wages. The fourth explains the role of the EMS. The fifth looks at the winners and losers from this period of adjustment and gives an overview of political developments in the early 1990s.

## Overcoming Inertia

By the end of the 1970s, Belgium and the Netherlands were in the advanced stages of depillarization. Little discipline remained from the old consociational systems of the 1950s and 1960s. Voters turned to nontraditional parties in ever-greater numbers and trade unionists rebelled against one government program after another. Business and labor no longer cooperated meaningfully. And popular satisfaction with the democratic system had reached a historic low for the Eurobarometer public opinion polling series.[8] In the meantime, economic fundamentals, like growth, unemployment, and inflation, continued to deteriorate; the current accounts of both countries moved into deficit; and public-sector borrowing requirements reached unprecedented levels.

Finding a way out of the impending crisis meant recreating links with the past. Belgium and the Netherlands had to reinvigorate the mechanisms for elite-directed politics before they could implement programs for economic adjustment. Reactivating old consociational structures was not the same as recreating the past itself. Neither country became more consociational in the 1980s or early 1990s—if anything, the pluralization of politics in both countries continued apace. Nevertheless, the style of politics in the early 1980s was reminiscent of the 1950s and early 1960s, and, as later sections of this chapter show, the adjustment policies implemented were familiar as well.

## Belgium: Try Everything Else First

The first five Belgian governments formed after 1977 were unable to forge a consensual program for economic and political recovery. Consequently, while negotiations between elites continued, political decision-making virtually ceased, at least with regard to economic matters. Martens dedicated his first four cabinets to the revival of social concentration between the government, industry, and labor.[9] These efforts culminated in March 1981, when Martens sought to convince the trade unions to discuss nominal wage restraint in the context of a general program for economic recovery. However, the national leadership of the Christian-Democratic and Socialist trade unions was both unable and unwilling to give up wage indexation: they were unable because they had little control over their followers who threatened to initiate a series of wildcat strikes; and they were unwilling because the national labor leadership did not believe industry would make sacrifices sufficient to warrant giving up indexation. Martens failed to unite his center-left coalition around the recovery program and subsequently resigned.[10]

Mark Eyskens, son of the famous Prime Minister Gaston Eyskens, was chosen to form a successor government to Martens IV. Because of the implicit threat of labor unrest, however, Eyskens was not allowed to shift coalition partners to the center-right. Neither the business nor the labor constituencies of the Christian Democratic parties would permit a government with the Liberals. Moreover, speculation against the Belgian frank made it impossible for Eyskens to call for early elections. Any further display of political instability, ran the argument, would result in a forced devaluation of the frank.[11]

Within months, Eyskens found he could no longer govern with the support of the Socialist parties. However, the option of shifting to the center-right remained closed. In July 1981, Eyskens began to explore possibilities for cooperation with the Liberals. He succeeded primarily in antagonizing his Socialist coalition partners, and in drawing a stern rebuke from the leadership of his own party. Eyskens' government collapsed in September 1981 and the King called for early legislative elections.[12]

These elections proved disastrous for the Christian Democrats, who lost twenty-one seats, and yielded fifteen new seats for the Liberals. Nevertheless, the leadership of the Christian-Democratic labor movement was at last prepared to make the shift to the center-right. Throughout the course of 1981, the ACW had sponsored a clandestine working group of economists and policymakers to outline an economic recovery package that would be acceptable to labor as well as industry.[13] The resulting JET plan became a centerpiece of the Christian-Democratic electoral platform, and (eventually) set out the framework for Wilfried Martens' negotiations with the Liberal parties.[14]

## "Consensual" Adjustment in Post-Consociational Democracy

The shift to the center-right was not immediate. Instead, it involved a number of intermediate stages as consultations took place between groups within and around the Christian-Democratic institutions. It also was not ideological. It represented a change in the style of politics more than a change in ideology.[15] The decisive actors in the formation of Martens' fifth government were the Christian-Democratic "old guard"—men like P. W. Segers—and the ACW. Segers advised the leadership of the ACW that neither Leo Tindemans nor Mark Eyskens would be a strong enough prime minister to lead the country out of crisis. Therefore, the ACW threw its pivotal support behind Martens. In turn, Martens committed not to betray his backers in the Christian-Democratic labor movement and he received the assurance that ACW discipline would facilitate the implementation of his policies. Where the first four Martens' governments had failed to encourage cooperation between business and labor, the ACW promised (at least in secret) to cooperate in the future. Labor support was critical for the business community as well as for Martens. Once the Flemish business community felt confident that a shift to the center-right would not excite undue labor unrest, they began to initiate contact between key players in the Christian Democratic and Liberal parties.[16]

The shift to the center-right was personal, and it bore many of the hallmarks of elite-directed politics. The ACW economic working group reported to former Prime Minister Martens, but not to the sitting Prime Minister (Eyskens) or to the chairmen of the Christian Democratic parties (Tindemans or Charles-Ferdinand Nothomb). In addition, the initial commitments made between Christian Democrats and Liberals came on the initiative of a business leader, Vaast Leysen, and involved "ordinary" members of parliament (Martens for the CVP and Frans Grootjans for the PVV) rather than party leaders. Finally, Martens refused to form the post-electoral government until the leaders of the Flemish Liberal PVV and Walloon Christian Democratic PSC had tried and failed to do so.[17]

In effect, the Christian Democrats in Belgium revitalized their old consociational structures, primarily in Flanders but in Wallonia as well. Martens could rely on the strength and discipline of the Christian-Democratic labor movement to provide him with ample room for maneuver within both his party and his coalition. This consolidation of the Christian Democrats had a powerful knock-on effect across the political system. Martens' Liberal coalition partners soon found that they too had to enforce party discipline in order to negotiate successfully with a united Christian-Democratic front. The results can be seen in the composition of the Martens V cabinet—which included the chairmen of all four coalition parties: De Clercq (PVV), Jean Gol (PRL), Nothomb (PSC), and Tindemans (CVP)—and also in the ease with which Martens was able to pass a broad enabling act through parliament.[18] Government ministers ceased to canvass important decisions with their parliamentary factions, and politics—at least within the subnational cultures or pillars—returned to the consociational building blocks of deferential followers and compromising elites.[19]

The Socialist parties were the last to reconsolidate around their traditional consociational structures. Although the Flemish and Walloon Socialist parties rely on a very centralized political system, the Socialist labor movement (ABVV-FGTB)—and its vital electoral support—is much more decentralized at the regional and sectoral levels. Thus the Socialists were unable to launch a coherent opposition to Martens' recovery program, just as they had been unable to participate in the implementation of such a program during prior cabinets. So long as the Christian-Democratic trade unions remained in the service of the government, there was little that a disunited Socialist opposition could do.[20]

The return to elite-directed politics within subnational cultures was the essential ingredient for overcoming political inertia. However, relations between elites from different subnational groups remained more competitive than coalescent. No one believed that they could turn back the clock and recreate the political system of the 1960s, and few would have desired such a regression. At the same time, elites—particularly in the Christian-Democratic labor movement—were well aware of the dangers implied by a swift transition to open competition between vested interests. Nevertheless, elites finally accepted that something must be done. If this meant "less democracy for a better economy," then impending economic crisis offered more than sufficient justification.[21]

## The Netherlands: Threaten Direct Intervention

The situation in the Netherlands was very different. Depillarization changed the Dutch political landscape to make it less like the political scene in Belgium than before. To begin with, the fusion of the Catholic and Socialist trade unions deprived the Christian Democratic parties of an "organic" labor movement, although these parties still enjoyed widespread support from working-class voters.[22] Second, the merger of the Protestant and Catholic "pillars" complicated the political dynamics of the newly formed Christian Democratic Appeal (CDA).[23] And third, the strength of New Left sentiments in the Socialist Party (PvdA) and in the Left-Liberal Party (D66) blurred the ideological distinctions necessary for traditional coalition forming and threatened to polarize the Dutch political systems along the left–right dimension.[24] No secret arrangements among the reigning powers in the Christian-Democratic pillar could ensure smooth cooperation between government, industry, and labor, and so the formation of Lubbers' center-right coalition relied more on interparty dynamics than on developments within the CDA itself.

The Dutch turn to the center-right is a story of elections and coalition-forming. The 1981 elections deprived the center-right government under Christian Democrat Dries Van Agt of its parliamentary majority, and forced the CDA to form a broad coalition on the center-left. However, the relationship between Minister-President Van Agt and his PvdA counterpart, Joop Den Uyl, was poor and so the socialist Labour Party soon left the government.[25] The CDA and D66 remained in a caretaker government until early elections could be held, and the electorate gave a strong boost to the Liberal VVD. Van Agt unexpectedly withdrew from public life, and CDA parliamentary leader Ruud Lubbers was allowed to form the coalition of Christian Democrats and Liberals.[26]

The success of this turn to the center-right hinged on a change in the style of government as well as on a change in the texture of interparty relations. The Lubbers' cabinet had to be more decisive in its policymaking, and the opposition Socialist and Left-Liberal parties had to cease trying to change the Dutch party system. Both of these developments relied on the ability of elites to negotiate with each other and be supported by deferential followers.

Two factors eased the return to elite-directed politics: the personality of Ruud Lubbers as a "manager in politics," and the shock of the failed Van Agt center-left coalition. Lubbers provided the necessary "decisiveness" in Dutch policymaking during the early part of the 1980s. Although his sympathies lay with the political left, Lubbers' direct managerial style enabled him to work effectively with his Liberal coalition partners in implementing a coherent package of reform legislation.[27] Conflict was not uncommon within the Lubbers' cabinet, but was more likely to be solved through compromise than during the cabinets headed by Den Uyl or Van Agt.[28]

It was, however, the shock of the failed center-left Van Agt cabinet that had the greatest impact. Within the CDA, the collapse of the center-left coalition decisively shifted the balance away from the left and toward the right wing of the party, thereby mitigating some of the confusion caused by the merger of Protestant and Catholic groups.[29] The Left-Liberal D66 party suffered a crushing defeat at the polls in 1982, and so ceased its attempts to reform the Dutch political system and attempted to broker between the PvdA and the CDA.[30] Only the Socialist PvdA failed to reform, and consequently it came to be regarded as "a radical and populist party prone to flaunting socialist symbols and defending a potpourri of causes."[31]

The negotiation and content of the cabinet agreement demonstrates how much the Lubbers' cabinet was directed by elites. As Ilja Scholten points out: "the 'governing contract' was hammered out in total secrecy by a very small number of participants."[32]

However, the content of the Lubbers' economic adjustment program was largely consistent with the plan supported by the then Finance Minister Frans Andriessen in 1980. The difference was that in 1980 Lubbers, as party faction leader, undermined Andriessen's plan by offering only lukewarm support. By 1982, Lubbers, as minister-president, was determined to impose his will on diverse factions within the CDA. He was determined to impose his will on the social partners as well. Should they fail to come to agreement on price–wage moderation, he would use the state to intervene directly in the labor market.[33] Governments had intervened in wage bargaining repeatedly in the 1970s, but without positive effect. Wage costs continued to rise and both labor and industry grew wary of the distortions created by government action.[34] This time the threat of direct involvement provoked a disciplined response. Elites directed their own followers in consociational fashion, while they negotiated with elites from other groups to form majorities instead of consensus. More effective policy implementation was the result.[35]

## Fiscal Consolidation and Wage Restraint

The argument so far is that center-right governments in Belgium and the Netherlands finally built up the momentum to do something. And the "something" they chose to do is stabilize fiscal accounts while at the same time shifting income from labor to industry. Before describing how this came about, it is useful to look to the data to see whether anything actually happened. The point is not to compare the consequences for profitability, investment, growth, and employment. These macroeconomic outcomes are important, but they are also affected by a wide range of variables, most of which are beyond the control of any government. The first priority is to focus on what the government can influence and to see if that influence was used.

The two major instruments for economic adjustment in Belgium and the Netherlands were fiscal consolidation and wage restraint.

Fiscal consolidation gradually brought the growth of government debt under control, and wage restraint shifted value added from labor to industry while providing the international competitiveness necessary for export-led growth. The aggregate data suggest that the Martens and Lubbers coalitions were successful on both counts.[36]

Figure 4.1 shows the primary balance on government accounts, meaning the balance of receipts and expenditures less interest payments.[37] The turning points for Belgium and the Netherlands correspond to the formation of the Martens and Lubbers cabinets.[38] Belgium's primary deficit narrowed from 7.4 percent of GDP to 3.1 percent in 1981–2, while the Netherlands' primary balance moved from a deficit of 1 percent to a surplus of 0.2 percent in 1982–3. Belgium achieved a primary surplus after three years of austerity, and both countries retained their surpluses through the end of the 1980s. Clearly, the effort at fiscal consolidation was greater in Belgium than in the Netherlands, but so too was the mountain of outstanding public debt—which was 89 percent of GDP in Belgium at the end of 1981, and 48 percent of GDP in the Netherlands at the end of 1982. By 1989, the debt-to-GDP ratios for Belgium and the Netherlands had stabilized at 122 percent and 74 percent, respectively.[39]

The formation of the Martens and Lubbers cabinets also marks a turning point in the development of wages. Figure 4.2 displays the wage share of value added in manufacturing.[40] The peak for both countries is in 1981—at 72.3 percent in Belgium and 74.4 percent in the Netherlands. The subsequent decline is precipitous, first in Belgium and later in the Netherlands. Moreover, the effects were not limited to the manufacturing sector. Service-sector wages were compressed as well. By the end of the decade, the two governments redistributed between 5 and 7 percent of GDP from labor to industry across the economy as a whole.

Wage restraint also had considerable impact in terms of international competitiveness—meaning the relative cost of labor inputs to manufacturing across countries. Figures 4.3 and 4.4 show the evolution of real Deutschemark exchange rates measured in terms

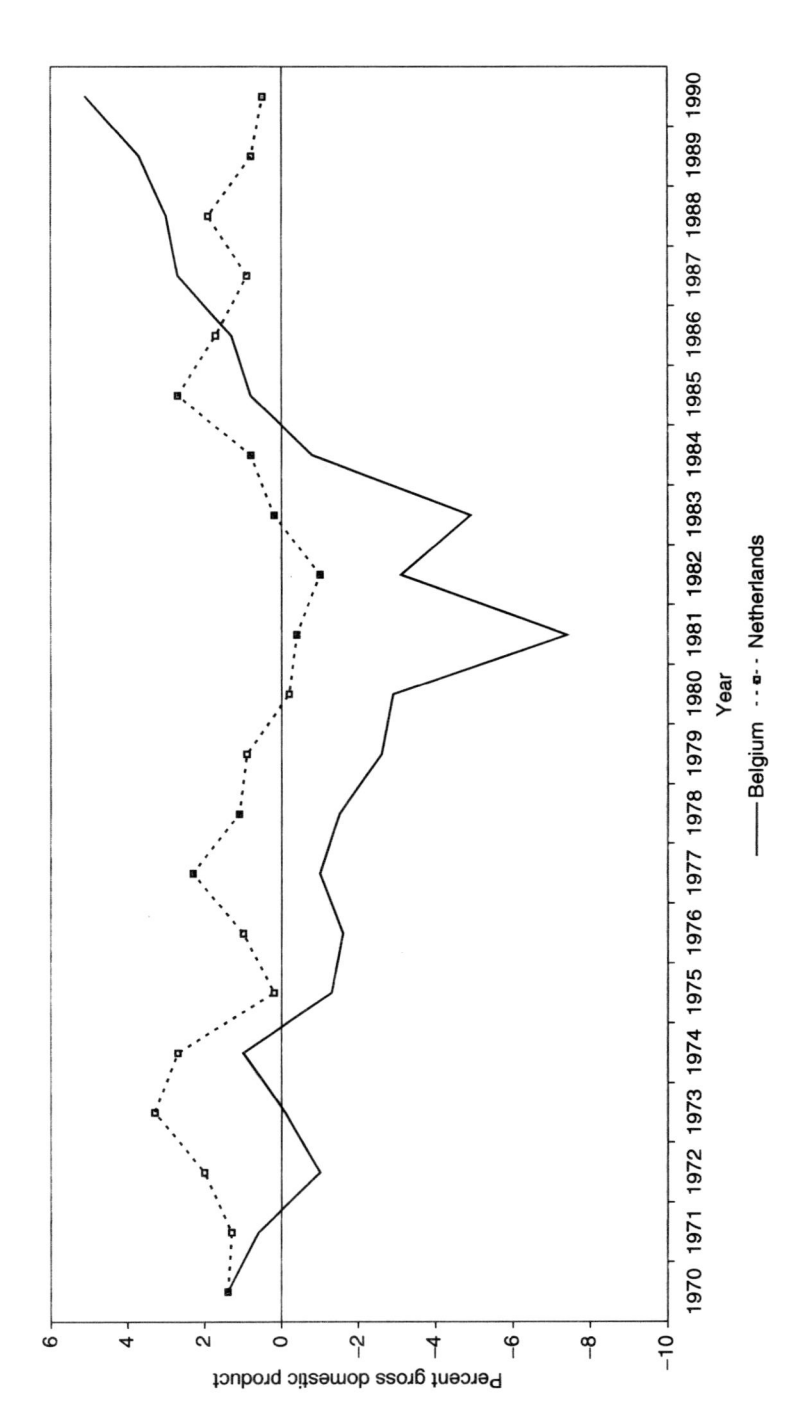

**Figure 4.1.** Primary fiscal balances

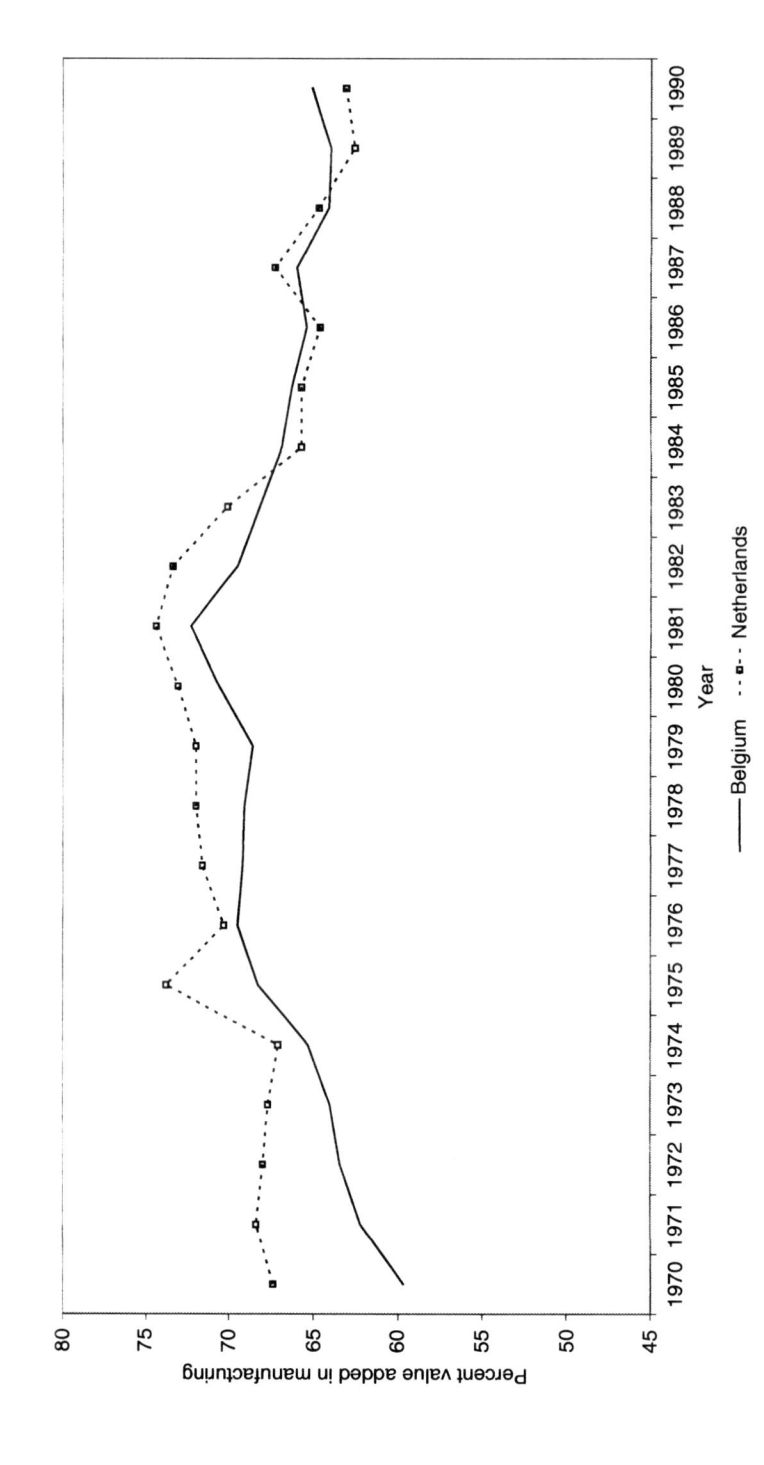

**Figure 4.2.** Adjusted wage share in manufacturing

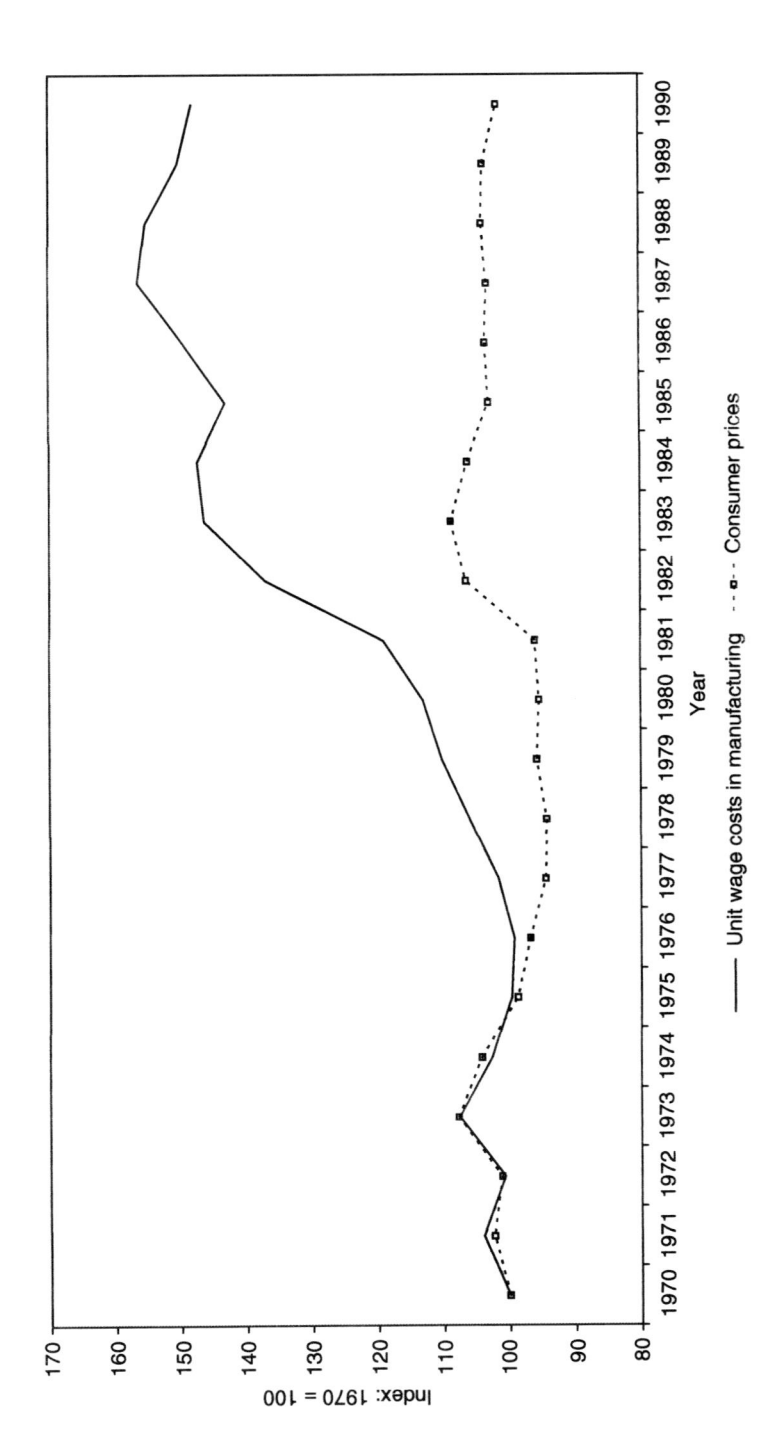

**Figure 4.3.** Belgian real Deutschemark exchange rates

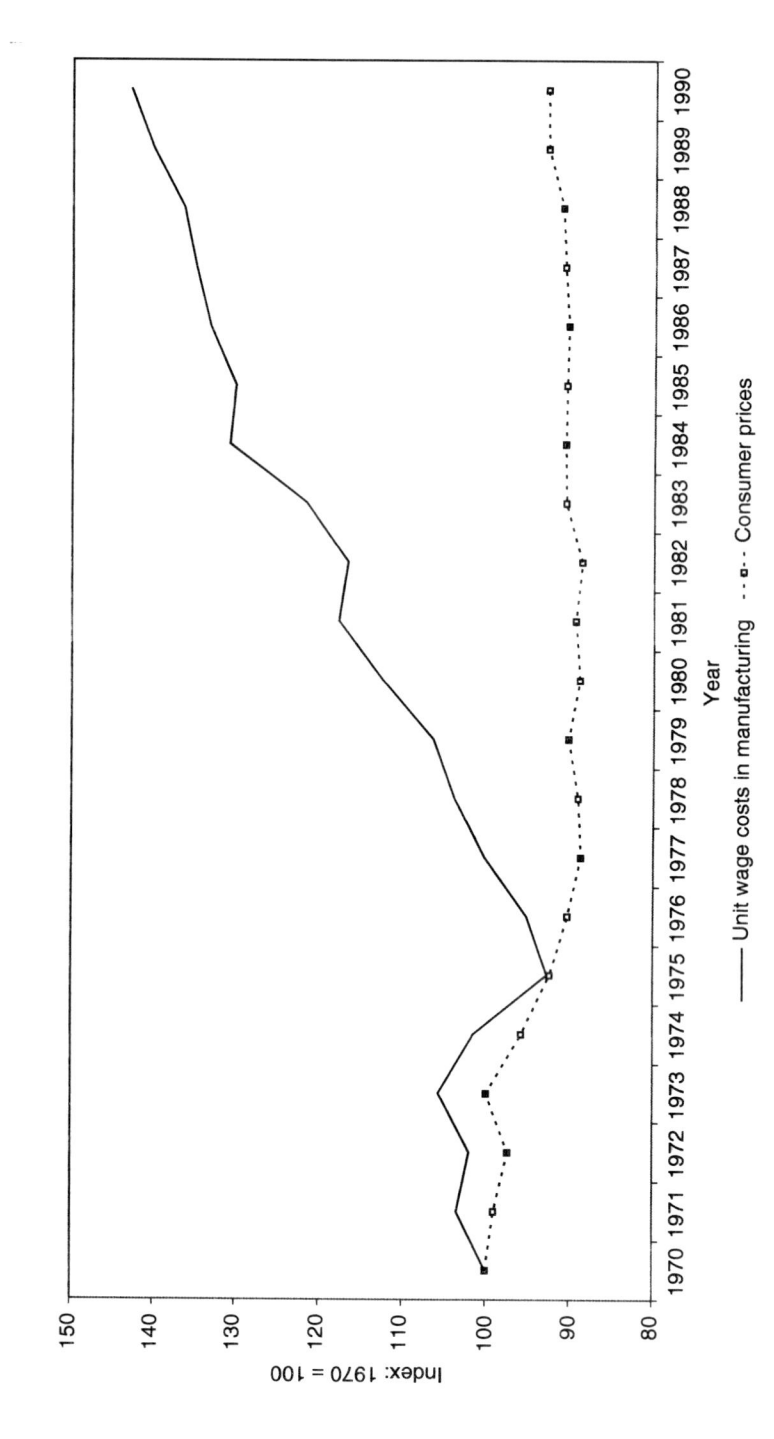

Figure 4.4. Dutch real Deutschemark exchange rates

of unit wage costs and consumer prices. Belgian and Dutch unit labor costs depreciate relative to Germany, starting in the late 1970s and accelerating in the early 1980s. However, this depreciation in unit wage costs is not reflected in relative consumer price movements between Belgium, the Netherlands, and Germany, which are more stable across the period depicted in the figure. These relative movements in unit wage costs and consumer prices suggest, first, that Belgian and Dutch export competitiveness increased in German markets during the 1980s, and second, that the increase in competitiveness resulted from wage restraint and not from changes in the nominal exchange rate.[41]

The claim that Martens and Lubbers succeeded in engineering nationwide wage restraint relies on a somewhat technical understanding of the exchange rates depicted in Figures 4.3 and 4.4. "Real" exchange rates are the product of nominal exchange rate indexes and the ratio of national price indexes using a common base year. For example, Belgian unit wage costs relative to Germany are the product of the nominal exchange rate, frank/Deutschemark, and the ratio of the German index for unit wage costs in manufacturing to the Belgian one. These indexes are constructed setting 1970 equal to 100. An upward movement in the figures indicates a real depreciation of the Belgian and Dutch exchange rates vis-à-vis Germany, while a downward movement indicates a real appreciation of those exchange rates. When Belgian or Dutch unit wage costs depreciate relative to Germany, the competitiveness of Belgian and Dutch exports to German markets increases.

How much wage restraint did Belgian and Dutch workers show relative to each other? Figure 4.5 makes it possible to compare wage restraint across the two countries by showing the development of real exchange rates between Belgium and the Netherlands. An upward movement implies a real depreciation of Belgian versus Dutch costs, while a downward movement shows an appreciation of Belgian versus Dutch costs. Moreover, the positioning of the two real exchange rates reveals the relative change in goods prices as opposed to labor costs across the two countries. When the unit

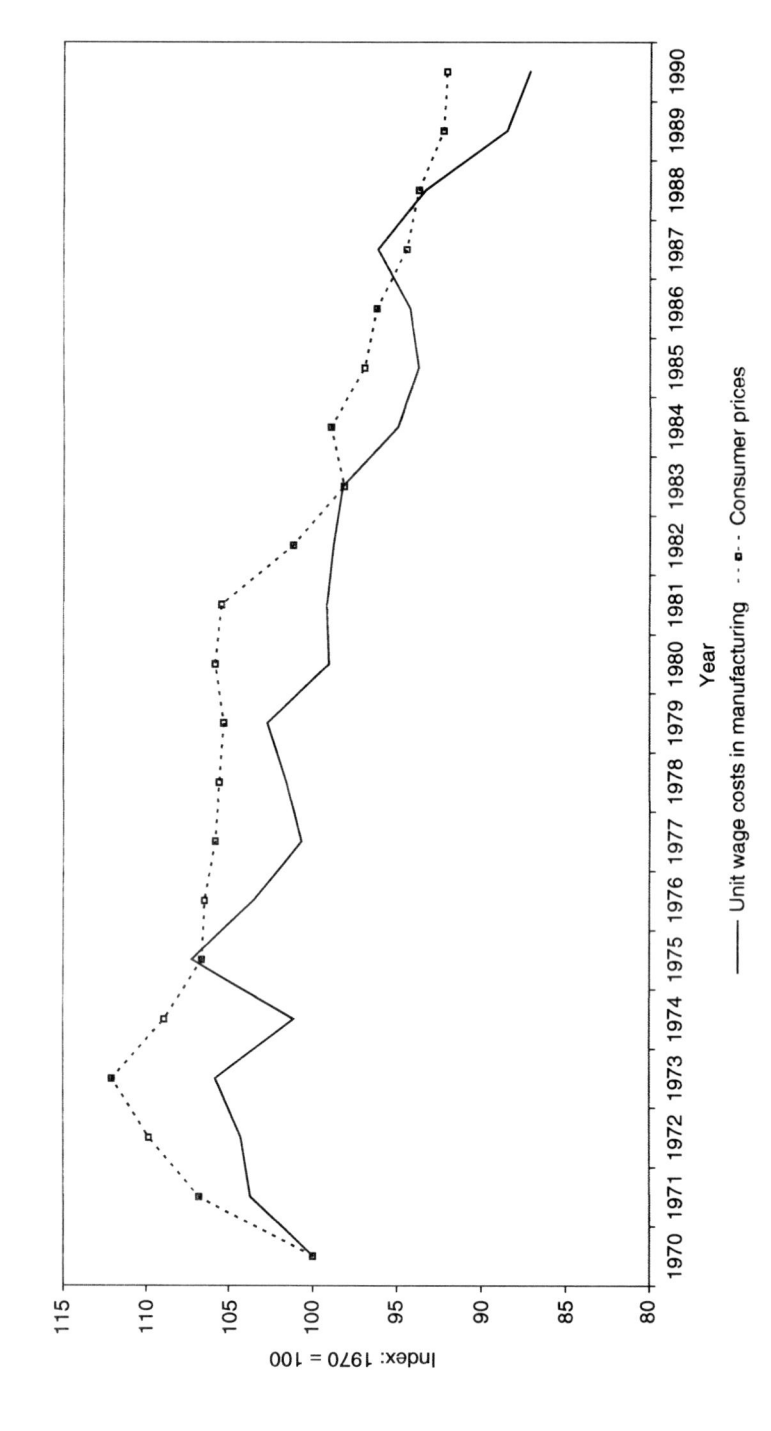

**Figure 4.5.** Belgian real guilder exchange rates

## "Consensual" Adjustment in Post-Consociational Democracy

Table 4.1. Average annual productivity growth (percent)

|  | 1975–82 | 1982–89 |
|---|---|---|
| Belgium | 2.61 | 1.65 |
| Netherlands | 1.70 | 1.61 |
| West Germany | 1.84 | 1.40 |

Note: Productivity is real GDP per employee.
Source: European Commission.

wage cost exchange rate lies below the consumer price exchange rate, as during the late 1970s, the relative price of goods versus labor is lower in Belgium than in the Netherlands. This suggests that Belgian labor showed less discipline in wage setting than Dutch labor before Martens came to power. After the Martens' coalition came to power, relative wage costs stabilized and in time even improved. Nevertheless, the impact of wage restraint was greater for the Netherlands than for Belgium across the 1980s, and the tendency of both Belgian real exchange rates has been to appreciate against the guilder over time.

A final question concerns the influence of productivity growth as opposed to wage bargaining. As Table 4.1 demonstrates, during the period from 1975 to 1982, Belgian average annual productivity growth outstripped performance in either Germany or the Netherlands by almost a full percentage point. This explains much of the marginal depreciation of Belgian unit labor costs relative to Germany. During the 1980s, however, productivity growth is almost the same in Belgium and the Netherlands, and only marginally greater than in Germany. Thus the post-1982 depreciation of Belgian and Dutch unit labor costs relative to Germany should be attributed to wage restraint and not to superior productivity growth.

The data so far reveal a clear division between the period before the formation of the Martens V cabinet in Belgium (December 1981) and the Lubbers I cabinet in the Netherlands (November 1982), and the period after those governments began to implement their adjustment strategies. The same data also reveal that both governments combined domestic austerity measures with wage restraint. The results of these policies are less clear cut. Nevertheless, they are suggestive. Consider, for example, the composition of GDP growth. The period to 1985 is marked by the relatively rapid growth of exports, with little improvement in domestic consumption or investment. The development is consistent with increased international competitiveness in combination with domestic austerity measures—so-called "export-led" growth. Starting in 1986, domestic investment and consumption have a more consistently positive influence on the growth of "final uses" (GDP before subtracting for imports of goods and services). And, in the period from 1988 to 1989, final uses in both countries benefit from strong performance in all three categories: exports, investment, and consumption.[42]

Unemployment is another consideration. Unemployment continued to rise in both countries until 1984, when it peaked at 12.3 percent in Belgium and 13.3 percent in the Netherlands. Thereafter, both countries benefited from gradually accelerating job creation and falling levels of unemployment through the end of the 1980s. The delay between the introduction of wage restraint and improvements in the labor market results from the impact of lower wages on domestic demand and from the difficulties of job creation in the presence of high levels of structural unemployment. A change in the relative price of labor coupled with the transfer of value added from labor to industry can result in capital broadening and job creation only over the medium-to-long term. Initially, employers tend to capture profits in order to improve corporate balance sheets rather than to invest in larger production facilities.

The pattern of Belgian and Dutch recovery shows an early growth in exports, with a more gradual increase in consumption, investment, and employment. How much of the performance of the two economies should be attributed to the upturn in the world economic climate is an open question. It is widely accepted that the dependence of Belgium and the Netherlands on world market conditions is considerable. However, the statistical evidence presented here reveals an important changeover in the economic behavior of both countries. This changeover resulted in a substantial redistribution of economic resources from the government to the market and from wages to profits. Whether or not it proved decisive in changing overall performance, this adjustment of economic resources enabled the Belgian and Dutch economies to take advantage of the upturn in world economic activity.

## Corporatism and the Intervention State

How did the Belgian and Dutch governments rely on corporatism for the implementation of wage restraint and why did the representatives of labor participate? This two-part question is the first key to understanding the Belgian and Dutch adjustment policies of the 1980s. And, at least to a certain extent, the answer has already been anticipated. Corporatist intermediation is more likely in the presence of high (rather than low) unemployment for three reasons. First, the government has a strong mandate for the implementation of an adjustment program—at least once political elites can put forward the argument that something must be done.[43] In turn, this means that the government can impose a clear agenda for trilateral negotiations. Second, industry prefers cooperation with labor representatives to social unrest. Third, labor favors centralized negotiations as a means to strengthen its bargaining position relative to industry.

Each of these three arguments applied in Belgium and the Netherlands during the early part of the 1980s. To begin with, the crisis in government finances and the rapid rise in unemployment made economic adjustment a political imperative that could be easily explained. Second, the poor state of corporate balances strengthened the bargaining position of industry even at the most centralized level, at the same time as it also increased the industry's desire to avoid social unrest. Finally, national labor representatives had to cooperate in order to retain (and reassert) central control over the trade union movement.

Of these three arguments, the claim that labor leaders resorted to corporatism as a means to increase their national effectiveness is the most open to question. Why should national labor representatives reassert control over their trade unions only to sell out the interests of labor to industry and government? The answer lies in a combination of realism and desperation: trade union leaders were realistic enough to recognize that firms had to be competitive and profitable to survive. And they were desperate to do something to stop the explosion of unemployment. Finally, national trade union leaders were able (at least partially) to escape the detrimental effects of wage restraint by leaving the predominant role in the implementation of corporatist bargaining to government. Once having distanced themselves from the decision to impose wage restraint, trade union leaders could discipline wage setting without accepting blame for the government's policies.

The statistical evidence in support of this argument has already been presented in terms of the development of unit labor costs in Belgium and the Netherlands relative to Germany as well as to each other. The argument can be generalized on the basis of calculations by C. De Neubourg, who points out that unit labor costs grew more slowly in Belgium and the Netherlands during the 1980s than elsewhere in Europe.[44] Soon after the formation of the Martens and Lubbers cabinets, Belgian and Dutch labor began to exhibit impressive restraint in wage bargaining. Moreover, this restraint was an important change in trade union behavior from the 1970s. The question that remains to be answered is how this change in trade union behavior came about.

The pattern of events in Belgium and the Netherlands was similar during the early 1980s. The Martens and Lubbers coalitions negotiated major "crisis-averting" agreements with the heads of labor and industry soon after coming to power. The terms of these agreements traded wage restraint for capital broadening and job creation. However, labor leaders proved to be difficult negotiating partners in both Belgium and the Netherlands, and there were important strikes concerning the degree of wage restraint and the extent of concessions accorded to the trade unions. Ultimately, both governments publicly abandoned trilateral bargaining over prices and wages and imposed statutory limitations on nominal wage growth.

At first glance, this pattern looks more like direct government intervention than corporatism. However, a closer look at the process of policy formation and implementation in both countries reveals that corporatism was an important part of the adjustment process. The trade unions were not excluded by the center-right majority. Rather they chose (or at least accepted) to participate as a minority opposition, abiding by and in some senses even enforcing government policies that they did not openly accept. The case for this claim is made most easily in Belgium, where Wilfried Martens came to power with the backing of the Christian-Democratic labor movement. Both industry and labor had resisted a shift to the center-right under Mark Eyskens in April 1981, and both industry and labor had a hand in forging the center-right Martens' coalition in December 1981. The Christian-Democratic labor movement designed the JET plan at the center of Martens' economic strategy, and industry played an important role in the plan's implementation.

Once in power, Martens continued to rely on the expertise and influence of the Christian-Democratic labor movement. Martens met regularly with Christian trade union leader Jef Houthuys, Hubert Detremmerie (who headed the financial arm of the Christian-Democratic labor movement), and Fons Verplaetse (a former economic-adviser-cum-trade-unionist at the Belgian National Bank, and Martens' economic cabinet chief) during the period from 1982 to 1987. The series of meetings started when Martens first called for a nominal wage freeze in 1982 and ended when Martens formed a government on the center-left. Houthuys' contribution to the group was to provide assurance that the ACV would support the government's policies, including particularly the restraint of real wage growth.[45] And it was this support which ensured that labor opposition to wage restraint would be divided and ineffective.

## "Consensual" Adjustment in Post-Consociational Democracy

With the benefit of hindsight, the fact that Martens continued to rely on the support of the Christian-Democratic labor movement is not surprising, even in spite of the center-right coloration of his government. What is surprising is the fact that only a small group of people was ever aware of the extent of collusion between Martens and the ACW. The meetings between Martens and Houthuys only became known in 1991, through an interview with Houthuys by Flemish journalist Hugo De Ridder.[46] Popular outrage over the complicity of the ACV in Martens' adjustment strategy offers stark testimony to the silent nature of the trade union's involvement.

Even without De Ridder's investigative journalism, it would still be possible to demonstrate the participation of labor in the center-right adjustment strategy. The pattern of corporatism in Belgium is simply too diffuse for the trade unions to withdraw with every change in the composition of the government. Labor can play a combative role, as during the 1970s, but it cannot cease to play any role at all. Thus the special powers claimed by the Martens' government served more to preserve the dialog between industry and labor than to replace it. As A. Van den Brande explains:

> The fact that since 1982 the cabinet governs by decree powers which bypass the parliament, may be interpreted as a method to forestall the chances of policization of this delicate concertation (between employers and trade unions), and as an indication that the leading actors do not see a real alternative for neo-corporatism at the moment.[47]

By governing with the use of enabling legislation, Martens shielded the national trade union leadership from the adverse effects of his policies, and thereby freed labor leaders to ensure that his policies would have their desired result.[48]

The case for the silent company complicity of national trade union leadership is more difficult to make with the Netherlands. Initially, there were indications that the head of the combined Catholic and Socialist trade unions (FNV) was prepared to cooperate openly with industry and with Lubbers' center-right cabinet. The chairman of the FNV, Wim Kok, asked to meet with the (then future) minister-president and with the chairman of the largest employers' federation *Verbond van Nederlandse Ondernemingen* (VNO), Chris van Veen. Kok hoped to use this meeting in order to stave off the threat by Lubbers to intervene directly in wage bargaining. The result was only a partial success. Kok and van Veen traded wage restraint for working-time reductions. The "Wassenaar Accord" was the first agreement of its kind in more than a decade, and many hoped that it would lead to a new era of corporatist wage concertation. Lubbers warmly received the agreement, but Wim Duisenberg, chairman of the Dutch National Bank, did not. Duisenberg claimed that the wage-cost concessions made by Kok on behalf of the trade unions were insufficient to stabilize corporate profits or to promote an export-led recovery. Moreover, Duisenberg insisted, the Wassenaar Accord did little to address the fundamental problems of public-sector borrowing.[49]

The 1982 national agreement between Kok and van Veen was not repeated during either of Lubbers' center-right governments. Moreover, as Lubbers began to bring pressure to bear on public-sector wage costs, the relationship between his cabinet and the FNV deteriorated. The trade unions struck against public-sector wage reforms and forced the government to moderate its policy. Despite such disagreements, however, labor did not abandon the government and began even to cooperate more closely with industry. As Steven Wolinetz explains:

Ironically, the government's posture led to limited rapprochement between trade union federations and employers' associations... (This) should not be interrupted as a return to earlier patterns of social partnership. Trade unions, faced with rising unemployment and declining membership... were in no position to engage in militant actions. Agreements with employers were one avenue to achieve a desired goal, the preservation of employment.[50]

Even this partial success was able to deliver considerable wage restraint. Wolinetz concludes his analysis with the argument that the policymaking under Lubbers revealed "traits of corporatism but also substantial scope for other forms of decision making."[51]

As was the case with Belgium, the interventionist posture of the government prevented the collapse of the social partnership, while leaving space for the national leadership of the FNV to safeguard the general interests of labor.

But was it really corporatism that was responsible for wage restraint, or were the Dutch unions simply coerced into making wage claims? Three pieces of evidence suggest that the willingness of labor leaders to cooperate with the Lubbers recovery program played a crucial role in its effectiveness in holding down labor costs. First, the lines of discipline within the FNV strengthened from the top down under the leadership of Wim Kok. Second, the public break between Kok's FNV and the Lubbers government occurred because of a dispute over public-sector employment, and not because of trade union objections to price–wage restraint per se. Kok worked energetically to support the government's efforts at economic adjustment through his collaboration with van Veen's VNO. And third, econometric analysis of wage bargaining in the Netherlands reveals that Dutch trade unions began to set wages in the interests of the unemployed (outsiders) rather than in the interests of dues-paying members (insiders) during the 1980s.[52] Given the relatively small percentage of unionized workers in the Dutch labor force (equal to about 26 percent), this "large" union behavior contradicts conventional wisdom about union centralization and wage bargaining, even in the presence of high unemployment.[53] Thus, the traits of corporatism identified by Wolinetz are at least as important to understanding the Dutch recovery during the 1980s as "other forms of policymaking" during the same period.[54]

Trade unions in Belgium and the Netherlands certainly did not agree with all aspects of the economic adjustment policies implemented by Martens and Lubbers. Nevertheless, they recognized that something had to be done to stop the growth of unemployment, and they feared the consequences of open social unrest. Labor leaders in both countries tacitly accepted the economic remedies imposed by the government and helped to enforce restraints on wage growth.

## The "Europeanization" of Exchange Rate Pegs

European integration played both passive and active roles in the adjustment process for Belgium and the Netherlands. The passive role was to ensure access to European markets. Intra-European trade had an important stabilizing influence on aggregate demand for Belgian and Dutch production during the early 1980s as well as during the period of export-led growth. Moreover, the advantages of free trade within Europe were obvious to most if not all members of the community, and few if any desired a return to the competitive mercantilism of the 1930s. Thus, while the Dutch Central Planning Bureau noted a rise of protectionism during the latter part of 1982, for example, there was little real fear of protectionism inside the Community.[55]

The active contribution of European integration to the economic performance of the Low Countries came in the form of exchange rate coordination—specifically in the functioning of the EMS. The EMS provided a supportive exchange rate environment for the pursuit of export competitiveness via concerted wage restraint. Had there been no institution for binding exchange rates to the Deutschemark, Belgian and Dutch wage restraint might not have resulted in greater export competitiveness. Either Belgium and the Netherlands would have seen their relative wage cuts dissipate in a rush of competitive nominal exchange rate devaluations by the weaker currency countries of Europe, or Belgium and the Netherlands would have had to resort to ever greater reductions in employee compensation in order to offset the nominal depreciations of their non-German trading partners.

This interpretation of the EMS draws on the statistical record for medium-term nominal exchange rate variability between Belgium and the Netherlands, on the one hand, and Germany and France on the other. Table 4.2 shows the variability of nominal exchange rates against the French franc, the Deutschemark, and a weighted basket of the twelve members of the EC (nominal effective exchange rates). The Belgian frank and the Dutch guilder stabilized against the French franc after the introduction of the

Table 4.2. Medium-term exchange rate variability (1961–89)

| Currency | Country | 1961–72 | 1972–80 | 1980–9 | 1983–9 |
|---|---|---|---|---|---|
| Deutschmark | Belgium | 2.0 | 1.9 | 4.0 | 2.1 |
|  | Netherlands | 2.0 | 1.5 | 0.6 | 0.6 |
| French Franc | Belgium | 2.2 | 4.6 | 1.7 | 1.5 |
|  | Netherlands | 2.2 | 5.1 | 3.8 | 2.9 |
| ECU (EU 12) | Belgium | 1.0 | 2.0 | 2.9 | 1.4 |
|  | Netherlands | 1.2 | 2.1 | 2.4 | 2.0 |

Note: Variability is the standard deviation of first-order (year-to-year) log changes ($t - [t-1]$).
Source: European Commission.

EMS in 1979 and particularly after the renewal of French commitment to the EMS in 1983. The Netherlands used the EMS to further its convergence on the Deutschemark, and Belgium relied on the EMS to balance between the Deutschemark and the French franc. This stabilization is medium term because the calculated variability relies on average annual exchange rates.

The medium-term stabilization of nominal effective exchange rates between Belgium or the Netherlands and the rest of the EU is less clear cut. After 1983, there is some improvement for the Netherlands and more for Belgium. However, the first ten years of the EMS look worse than the ten years prior rather than better. Therefore, much of the argument that the EMS broadened the zone of monetary stability depends on guesswork about what would have happened without a European monetary system. Would Belgian and Dutch exchange rates have fluctuated more against their trading partners without the EMS? The answer is probably yes.

Concern for exchange-rate stability was the principal motivation behind the creation of the EMS during the mid-to-late 1970s. When it became obvious that the European snake system did not work, the member states of the EC began to discuss alternative forms for exchange rate coordination. The snake had two principal shortcomings: to begin with, it was dependent upon the dollar as a central pivot, a fact which made the snake vulnerable to the dollar's wide fluctuations.[56] Second, it placed the burden of exchange-rate stabilization on the "weaker" currency, which is to say the country running a current account deficit and therefore losing foreign exchange reserves.[57] The combination of these shortcomings gave the Deutschemark a predominant role in the snake system, and at the same time forced all other participating countries to defend the value of their Deutschemark exchange rates. Within the first year of its existence, the snake virtually ceased to function as a Europe-wide mechanism for exchange rate stabilization.

The institutional structure negotiated for the EMS sought to alleviate the shortcomings of the snake by creating a new pivot, and by making the intervention requirements more symmetrical. The new pivot emerged as a "basket currency," the European currency unit (ECU), which was a GDP-weighted combination of the European countries participating in the EMS. The greater symmetry of intervention requirements arose from the use of "divergence indicators" based on the ECU, and from the availability of larger short-term financial resources to use in support of central bank interventions. Although neither the ECU nor the peculiarities of intervention rules in the exchange rate mechanism (ERM) had a huge (or decisive) impact on the functioning of the EMS, the history of the negotiations indicates that both correctives were essential to forging an agreement on the use of the EMS for the promotion of a "broader zone of monetary stability in Europe."[58]

The argument that monetary stability was the greatest contribution of the EMS to Belgian and Dutch adjustment policies may seem simple-minded to many students of European monetary integration. These analysts tend to regard the EMS as a highly visible commitment to "responsible" monetary policy or, more negatively, as an institutional cloak behind which policymakers could impose overly harsh or politically unpalatable austerity measures.[59] Perhaps this interpretation is accurate for many of the traditional weak-currency countries like Italy or even France. Three observations suggest that it is less plausible for Belgium and the Netherlands. To begin with, unlike other Community member states, Belgium and the Netherlands had succeeded in converging on German inflation norms by the late 1970s. Second, the introduction of the EMS did not change the short-tem variability

## "Consensual" Adjustment in Post-Consociational Democracy

of nominal Deutschemark exchange rates for Belgium and the Netherlands, except for the 1982 devaluation of the Belgian frank. Third, the European Council at times refused to allow Belgium and the Netherlands to follow the Deutschemark in an upward realignment, and thereby insisted that the Belgians and the Dutch accept some leeway in their hard-currency policies.

As mentioned throughout this book, Belgium and the Netherlands have long "hard currency" traditions. Both countries were reluctant to devalue against the dollar during the Bretton Woods system, and both had targeted their currencies on the Deutschemark during the 1970s. Therefore, it is difficult to argue that Belgian or Dutch monetary authorities needed the EMS in order to do what they had already been doing. Data for inflation performance in the EC reveal the extent of Belgian and Dutch convergence on German inflation norms prior to the formation of the EMS (Table 4.3). At the same time, however, countries like Denmark, France, Ireland, and Italy show a marked change in price inflation after 1983, which suggests that the EMS may have played a role in their convergence on German inflation norms. Thus while the EMS may have lent policy credibility to some members of the EC, there is little evidence that enhanced credibility was important to Belgium or the Netherlands.[60]

This data for inflation convergence is consistent with the argument that convergence on German inflation norms was necessary

Table 4.3. Inflation performance (1972–89)

|             | 1972–6 | 1976–9 | 1979–83 | 1983–9 |
|-------------|--------|--------|---------|--------|
| West Germany | 5.8    | 3.6    | 4.7     | 1.7    |
| Belgium     | 8.5    | 5.6    | 6.5     | 3.7    |
| Netherlands | 8.7    | 5.8    | 5.0     | 1.4    |
| Denmark     | 10.3   | 9.6    | 9.6     | 4.6    |
| France      | 9.5    | 9.3    | 11.0    | 4.8    |
| Italy       | 13.9   | 13.3   | 14.3    | 4.9    |
| Ireland     | 14.1   | 14.6   | 15.6    | 8.2    |

*Note*: Inflation is the average annual percentage change in the private consumption deflator.

*Source*: European Commission.

## "Consensual" Adjustment in Post-Consociational Democracy

for Belgium and the Netherlands to support Deutschemark exchange rate targets during the 1970s. The closer the convergence on German inflation performance, the easier the task of maintaining the exchange rate target becomes.[61] Here it is possible to reverse the analysis and suggest that, having achieved considerable convergence by the late 1970s, short-term exchange rate fluctuations between the Deutschemark and the frank or guilder should have stabilized at a relatively low level. If inflation convergence preceded the start of the EMS, so would the stabilization of short-term nominal exchange rates.

Data for short-term exchange rate variability reveal that the relationship between the Belgian frank or Dutch guilder and the Deutschemark changed very little after the introduction of the EMS, except during the period of multiple realignments at the start of the 1980s. Thus, here again there is little support for assertions that the EMS somehow changed exchange rate policy in either country. Moreover, in contrast to exchange rate stability over the medium term, the Belgian-German exchange rate appears more stable over the short term than the Dutch-German. This can be seen in Table 4.4, which summarizes the data for Deutschemark exchange rate variability across different time periods and during the EMS for Belgium and the Netherlands, as well as for Denmark, France, Ireland, and Italy. A comparison across countries reveals the relatively small impact of the EMS on the hard-currency policies of Belgium and the Netherlands, in relation

Table 4.4. Deutschemark exchange rate variability (1975–93)

|  | February 1975 to August 1979 | September 1979 to March 1983 | April 1983 to January 1987 | February 1987 to December 1993 |
|---|---|---|---|---|
| Belgium | 0.52 | 1.34 | 0.39 | 0.55 |
| Netherlands | 0.66 | 0.72 | 0.40 | 0.47 |
| Denmark | 1.03 | 1.00 | 0.59 | 0.89 |
| France | 1.71 | 1.57 | 0.91 | 0.63 |
| Ireland | 2.68 | 1.09 | 1.25 | 1.03 |
| Italy | 2.97 | 1.27 | 0.99 | 1.93 |

Note: Variability is the standard deviation of first-order (month-to-month) log changes ($t - [t-1]$).
Source: International Monetary Fund.

to countries having weaker currencies prior to 1979 (Denmark), or 1983 (France, Ireland, and Italy). In addition, a comparison of the first three columns of Table 4.4 with the last three columns of Table 4.3 suggests a rough correlation between inflation convergence and nominal exchange rate stability. Thus it is possible to argue that exchange-rate stabilization occurred prior to the EMS for Belgium and the Netherlands, and after the EMS started for other countries.

The time periods used in Table 4.4 reflect changes in political support for the EMS among the EC member states. The EMS existed outside the institutional framework of the EC, but nevertheless formed part of the larger process of European integration. Realignments within the ERM were not imposed unilaterally as they would be in an ad hoc system of bilateral exchange rate targeting, and exchange rate realignments were negotiated in meetings between national finance ministers and central bank governors of the participating countries. As a result, the realignments reflected a compromise between the economic and political needs of the member state seeking to change its nominal exchange rate, the needs of the other member states, and the objectives of the EMS as a currency regime. Between September 1979 (the date of the first exchange rate realignment) and March 1983 (the realignment that marked France's commitment to rigueur), participants in the European ERM accorded greater emphasis to the needs of countries that wanted to change their exchange rates. Consequently, realignments were common and exchange rate policy was regarded as a legitimate instrument for macroeconomic stabilization. After March 1983, realignments became less common as the member states began to place more emphasis on exchange-rate stability. And, after January 1987, realignments within the ERM virtually ceased.[62]

The record of exchange rate realignments provides additional evidence that the EMS served primarily to broaden the area of exchange-rate stability for Belgium and the Netherlands. What it does not reveal, however, is a single-minded emphasis on disinflation within the councils of the EMS. Sometimes, it is true, countries were not allowed to devalue as much as they sought. Other times, however, countries were not allowed to revalue.

Belgium experienced both sides of the institutional constraint. When the first realignment of the ERM took place in September 1979, the ERM countries resisted a Belgian request to maintain parity between the frank and the Deutschemark. And, when the Belgian government sought a 12 percent devaluation of its currency in February 1982, the other countries permitted only an 8.5 percent realignment. In the first instance, September 1979, the European finance ministers and central bankers reasoned that a revaluation of the Belgian frank would exacerbate Belgium's lack of international competitiveness. In the second, February 1982, concern was expressed—particularly by Germany—that a full 12 percent devaluation of the Belgian frank would undermine the stability of the currency grid.[63]

The Netherlands felt only the upward barrier in making realignments. When the ERM countries prevented the Belgian frank following the Deutschemark upward in September 1979, the Netherlands held the guilder back as well. The Dutch reasoned that it was more important to retain the link between the frank and the guilder rather than that between the guilder and the Deutschemark. A similar event transpired in March 1983, when Dutch Finance Minister Onno Ruding resisted pressure from the Dutch central bank to follow the Deutschemark in its 4 percent revaluation.[64]

Thus the history of exchange-rate realignments does not support the hypothesis that EMS participation was a political support (or cover) for excessive austerity in Belgium and the Netherlands. Moreover, statistical data for short-term exchange-rate variability casts doubt on assertions that EMS participation somehow changed the behavior of the Belgian and Dutch central banks. One thing is, however, certain. The Belgians and the Dutch were able to use the EMS as a relatively stable nominal exchange-rate grid within which to engineer a real depreciation of labor costs. In this sense, the relationship between the EMS and economic adjustment is different for Belgium and the Netherlands from elsewhere. The EMS increased the authority of the French and Italian governments in their disinflation, but it decreased the need for austerity and wage restraint in Belgium and the Netherlands. Where, during the 1970s, the Low Countries had been virtually alone in following the Deutschemark in its appreciation, during the 1980s the EMS ensured that other countries would follow the Deutschemark as well. This way, the EMS did as much to stabilize currency relations as the Economic Community did to stabilize trade relations. On both counts, economic adjustment in Belgium and the Netherlands relied on European integration for valuable support.

## Distribution and Disaffection

A temporary stabilization of Belgian and Dutch political life paralleled the economic adjustment measures introduced by Martens and Lubbers. In part this resulted from the reactivation of consociational and corporatist relationships, such as the links between the ACW and the CVP in Belgium, or between Wim Kok's FNV and Chris van Veen's national employer federation (VNO) in the Netherlands. Another part of the new-found stability arose from the assertiveness and decisiveness of the two prime ministers—Martens with his enabling legislation or Lubbers and his "managerial style."

The most important reason for this restabilization of Belgian and Dutch politics came from the growing acceptance, first, that something had to be done, and later that something was being done. The argument here is somewhat akin to the notion of "extraordinary politics" that is popular among students of democratic and market transitions.[65] Although the economic adjustment measures introduced by Martens and Lubbers were never widely popular, the electorate did respect the fact that Martens and Lubbers had comprehensive policy programs. Consequently voters were willing to wait and see if the economic adjustment measures would yield positive results, even though "waiting and seeing" entailed making sacrifices out of personal incomes and public services.[66]

Here, it is interesting to return to the claim made by critics of the Martens and Lubbers cabinets that the two leaders were offering "less democracy for a better economy" and trading consensual government for an "intervention state." Certainly it is true that both prime ministers ruled with a strong hand, relying on enabling legislation and even secret deals with elites from business and labor. However, public opinion polling data reveals a growing sense of satisfaction with the democratic systems of Belgium and the Netherlands once Martens and Lubbers came to power. This can be seen in Figure 4.6, which provides the results of Eurobarometer surveys through the 1980s and into the early 1990s.[67] Such evidence places critics of the two prime ministers in the unenviable position of accepting that—from the popular standpoint—less democracy is better democracy, and that an effective "intervention state" is preferable to ineffective attempts at consensus building.

Voters re-elected first the Martens and then the Lubbers center-right cabinets after almost four years of austerity measures and wage restraint. In October 1985, the center-right Martens' coalition increased its parliamentary majority from 7 to 9 seats in the 212-seat Chamber of Representatives. And in May 1986, the center-right Lubbers coalition held onto its 11-seat majority in the 150-seat Second Chamber. In both cases, the ruling center-right coalition announced its intention to continue austerity before the elections, and also in both cases the right-wing Liberals lost seats to the centrist Christian Democrats—six in Belgium and nine in the Netherlands. When surveyed about the results after the election, voters in Belgium expressed reluctance to "change horses in midstream" and voters in the Netherlands felt that the policies implemented by Lubbers would yield positive results if given enough time.[68]

As it happened, it was the politicians and not the voters who changed coalitions. Both Martens (1987) and Lubbers (1989) made the transition from the center-right to the center-left even though the electoral results in both cases were not fatal to the coalition

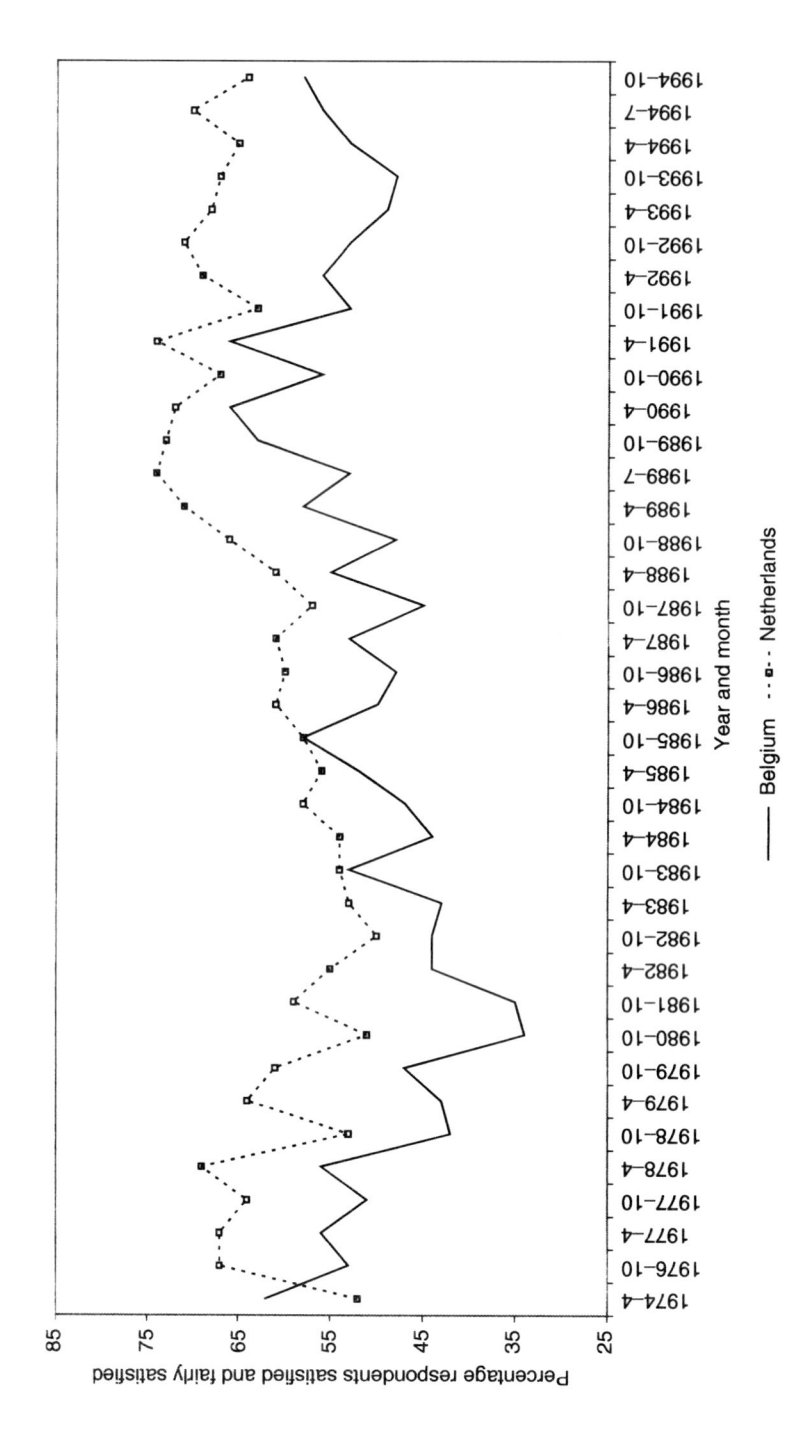

Figure 4.6. Satisfaction with democracy

of Christian Democrats and Liberals. Martens could have governed on the center-right with 110 seats out of 212, and Lubbers could have remained with 76 out of 150. These majorities are small but sufficient. Moreover, both Martens and Lubbers had expressed reluctance to change coalition partners prior to the elections—and Martens had even gone further to claim that the Socialists were simply untrustworthy.[69] Nevertheless, Martens and Lubbers claimed to be working toward a more consensual style of government, and that close cooperation with the Socialist parties was necessary to return to consensual politics.[70]

This shift to the center-left is in contrast with developments in Germany or the UK, where the conservative parties remained in control throughout the 1980s and well into the 1990s. Yet it is consistent with the hypothesis that narrow center-right majorities were necessary to implement economic adjustment policies and therefore dispensable once the adjustments were largely completed. The basic policies for wage moderation and regional integration remained in place. But the focus for attention moved to more complicated matters of welfare-state and market-institutional reform.

The irony is that the electorates of Belgium and the Netherlands showed little ambition to retain—and certainly not to strengthen—the structures for consensual decision-making. And if Martens and Lubbers did benefit from a period of extraordinary politics, it was long over by the time they made the transition to the center-left. Even before the start of the 1990s, voters began to express their disaffection with the pace of corporatist bargaining, they grew tired of the discipline required for continuous wage moderation and fiscal austerity, and they sought new forms of political participation beyond the direction of elites.

At least part of this frustration was due to the inequitable distribution of adjustment costs. Here it is important to be careful with the data. Belgium and the Netherlands have two of the most equitable post-tax and transfer income distribution profiles in Europe.[71] Even so, it is possible to demonstrate that income inequality increased during the period of adjustment. For the

Netherlands, the evidence is straightforward. The distribution of income worsened by almost 12 percent in the late 1980s and a further 5 percent in the early 1990s.[72] Poverty rates increased by 3.7 percent during the period from 1977 to 1994, while they declined in countries such as France, Finland, Canada, Denmark, and Australia over the same period. Of course the starting point was much lower in the Netherlands than elsewhere (apart from Finland). But the movement is clearly in the wrong direction. Moreover, the groups hardest hit include the young, the elderly, and single-parent households. Those who benefited were in the prime of life, living in two-income households, and preferably did not have children.[73] As distributive coalitions go, this one is very narrowly drawn.

The situation in Belgium is more complicated. Social inequality is as important in Belgium as in the Netherlands. But regional inequality has a much greater political salience. Throughout the 1980s, regional politicians struggled to increase their autonomy within the Belgian state. For much of the decade, those struggles eclipsed the economic adjustment process in importance—much as they had during the late 1970s as well. The skewed distribution of adjustment burdens made matters worse. Here it is useful to update the regional structure of Belgium with data from the 1990s (in contrast to the data for the 1940s provided in Table 2.1 of this book) (Table 4.5). The two points to note in the data are the relative importance of manufacturing in Flanders and the relative dominance of the Socialists in Wallonia. The policy of wage moderation was more beneficial to Flanders than Wallonia, and the Walloon Socialists—and the Walloon socialist trade unions—had little or no input on the policy. Once the Socialists joined the coalition, the implications of wage moderation for incomes in Wallonia had to be taken into account. Such subtlety in wage policy is difficult, if not impossible, to engineer. As a result, wage discipline faltered and the country began to lose its competitiveness in Europe.[74]

The distribution of costs was not the only problem. The structure and distribution of benefits was problematic as well. Here the focus is on employment and unemployment. From the standpoint of the trade unionists who argued in favor of wage moderation,

## "Consensual" Adjustment in Post-Consociational Democracy

**Table 4.5.** The regional structure of Belgium (1993–5)

|  | Belgium | Brussels | Flanders | Wallonia |
| --- | --- | --- | --- | --- |
| *Production* (percent total output) | | | | |
| Agriculture | 1.7 | 0.0 | 1.9 | 2.2 |
| Manufacturing | 29.2 | 19.2 | 32.6 | 27.6 |
| Services | 69.1 | 80.8 | 65.5 | 70.2 |
| *Political alignment* (percent of national vote in 1995 elections) | | | | |
| Catholics | 24.9 | 18.5 | 27.6 | 22.5 |
| Liberals | 23.4 | 33.5 | 20.9 | 23.9 |
| Socialists | 24.4 | 18.2 | 20.7 | 33.7 |
| *Relative wealth and size* | | | | |
| GDP per capita (Index Belgium = 100) | 100 | 161 | 101 | 80 |
| Population share (percent) | 100 | 9.4 | 57.9 | 32.7 |

*Source*: European Commission.

the goal was to maintain or even increase full-time employment in manufacturing. Full-time manufacturing workers constituted the rank and file of the trade unions at the start of the 1980s, and most of these members were sole breadwinners and heads of household. They did not get what they bargained for. From 1983 to 1991, the level of total employment increased by 21 percent in the Netherlands and 5 percent in Belgium. However, the level of manufacturing employment increased by only 5 percent in the Netherlands and it declined by 5 percent in Belgium. Moreover, while Belgian participation rates remained constant, Dutch participation rates increased by 6 percent and the working age population increased by 7 percent. For any given worker in either country, the number of jobs in manufacturing declined. Unsurprisingly, the Dutch trade unions hemorrhaged membership.[75]

The open secret about the Dutch miracle is that the jobs that were created offered part-time employment in the service sector, mostly to women.[76] This explains why two-income households got richer despite the wage moderation. Meanwhile, single-income households—meaning the male breadwinners who made up the union rank and file in the early 1980s—lost out. This pattern of part-time employment did not emerge in Belgium. Hence, while employment there stagnated, relative incomes declined. Wage discipline was harder to maintain as a result, and disaffection with corporatist wage bargaining was rife.

Populist challengers in the political system were eager to inflame public sentiment. During the late 1980s and early 1990s, this is easier to illustrate in Belgium than in the Netherlands. On the francophone left, José Happart played an important role in raising the profile of Walloon nationalism and agitating for greater economic autonomy. And on the Flemish right, Filip Dewinter and the Flemish Bloc (VB) dreamed of an economy with no trade unions. Both sides built on a critique of Martens' style of managing the economy and both sought to capitalize on the revelation that the Christian-Democratic trade unions were somehow complicit in the bargain.[77]

Populist extremists had an important impact on the margins and they played a critical role in the federalization of the Belgian state. Nevertheless, it was the underlying pluralization of Belgian and Dutch society that had the predominant influence on political stability in the two countries. Although Martens and Lubbers had succeeded in revitalizing consociational institutions, they did not succeed in bringing consociationalism back into being. On the contrary, demands for political renewal only gained momentum once the economic crisis had passed. Moreover, such demands found important conduits within the liberal parties—particularly the Flemish liberals under Guy Verhofstadt and the progressive liberal D66 under Hans van Mierlo. Both Verhofstadt and van Mierlo promised to strengthen the direct connections between politicians and voters. They offered a model of politics that was more elite-challenging than elite-directed. And they carried a grudge against the center-left coalitions in power—the Christian Democrats in particular.

Two electoral contests provide the capstones for this narrative of adjustment—the 1991 parliamentary elections in Belgium, and the 1994 elections in the Netherlands. Both are dramatic and both can be interpreted as popular rejections of government policy in terms of people, style, and substance. The 1991 contest in Belgium is known as "Black Sunday" because the major winner in Flanders was the right-wing extremist VB. The VB won 16.7 percent of the vote in Antwerp, where it became the third-largest party ahead of the Flemish Liberal PVV. Across Flanders as a whole, it scored just over 10 percent. Meanwhile, the coalition partners—the CVP and the SP—both dropped to historic lows. The coalition partners in Wallonia also lost votes (PSC and PS), though to the greens rather than to the extreme right. Liberals, who were widely tipped to benefit in the election, achieved only modest gains. Importantly, though, Verhofstadt outpolled Martens in their shared constituency of Ghent. Martens resigned from national politics and positioned himself to take up a career in the European Parliament.

The Christian Democrats and Socialists formed a new coalition under Martens' old cabinet chief, Jean-Luc Dehaene. Nevertheless, the 1991 elections had a profound effect on the structure of Belgian politics and on the Flemish Liberal Party in particular. Verhofstadt re-branded the Flemish Liberals with strong nationalist and populist overtones—the "Flemish" Liberals and Democrats (VLD). He democratized the party's internal structure and he focused his political ambitions on becoming the largest force in the Flemish-speaking part of the country.[78] In doing so, Verhofstadt set a strong example for the rest of the political system, particularly the Christian Democrats.[79] He also anticipated the changed structure of political competition in an explicitly federal Belgium.[80] From 1991 onward, the prospects for nationwide corporatist bargaining diminished greatly as a result. Looking back on the 1991 elections and the political transformation that followed, Belgian sociologist Luc Huyse—the dean of Belgian consociationalism—argued that his country had moved *Beyond Politics*.[81]

The 1994 elections in the Netherlands were similarly dramatic, if not more so. Popular resentment toward the coalition partners was widely evident in the polling data. Nevertheless, the prime minister remained the most popular politician in the country. When Lubbers announced that he would stand down from politics before the campaign, he inadvertently made it easier for critics of the government to mobilize support. The result was substantial losses for both coalition partners, the greater share of which fell on the Christian Democrats. A few parliamentary seats also leaked out of the mainstream parties to fringe movements. The right-wing extremist Center Democrats gained two seats and a newly formed "General Union for the Elderly" gained six. But the biggest winners were the liberal parties. The VVD picked up nine seats and D66 picked up twelve. As a result, parliamentary seats were distributed across four parties of roughly equal size. And the only coalition possibilities required any three parties to join without the fourth. D66 emerged as the pivotal group in the formation of the new government. The demand that they made was that the Christian Democrats be kept out of power—for the first time in seven decades.[82]

# Conclusion

The electoral turmoil of the early 1990s signaled a deepening demand for political reform in Belgium and the Netherlands. Politicians and voters in both countries began to emphasize "renewal" as an important break with their consociational past. They also talked about escaping from the "viscosity" of consensus politics.[1] Decisions took too long, involved too many powerful interest groups, and were too often watered down along the way. Surprisingly, however, this insistence on political reform did not spark a dramatic change in policy. On the contrary, both Belgium and the Netherlands continued to follow along much the same path they started in the early 1980s, combining fiscal consolidation with wage restraint while using European integration to open up markets and stabilize exchange rates. Progress was not uniform but the results were striking, at least by some measures. Not only did Belgium and the Netherlands succeed in running consistent current account surpluses, but they also managed to pay down a substantial amount of their national debt. If Belgium and the Netherlands were globally uncompetitive and risking insolvency at the end of the 1970s, those problems were no longer evident as they moved into the twenty-first century.[2]

The question is how long the efforts of the past two decades can continue and whether the strategy itself can be repeated. My argument in this book is that it will be difficult for the Belgians and the Dutch to forge a consensual adjustment strategy in the

# Conclusion

future—even along relatively majoritarian lines. Should the two countries suffer a sudden loss of competitiveness in foreign markets or should they find themselves producing things that the rest of the world does not want to buy, they will be unable to engineer a movement in relative labor costs to solve the problem. If wages have to fall, they will have to do so under the weight of unemployment rather than via concerted action. This means that future adjustments will be painful even with the provision of generous welfare-state support. In addition, the Belgians and the Dutch may be unable to rely on the process of European integration in order to offset or shield themselves from the impact of globalization. Of course the static advantages of the EU will remain, but initiatives on the scale of the common market or the EMS are unlikely. Indeed, it is an open question whether the Belgians and the Dutch would support such initiatives in the first place.

My pessimistic view of the future of consensual adjustment in Belgium and the Netherlands stems in part from the processes of political transformation underway in both countries and in part from the implications of past adjustments. Going into the twenty-first century, neither Belgium nor the Netherlands can be described as consociational democracies. Political renewal has progressed too far. The electorates of both countries no longer show much deference to their elites and instead are more likely to challenge elite behavior. As a result, politicians must compete with each other actively in order to win elections, and once the elections are over, they find that they no longer have the flexibility to engage in negotiated consensus building with the whole range of possible coalition partners.

This change in political behavior from consociational democracy to a more pluralist style is the major reason that Belgium and the Netherlands will find it difficult to build consensus around a strategy for adjustment in the future. When elites would rather compete with one another than work together, the prospects for consensus are slim. Extensive reliance on consensual adjustment strategies over the past two decades plays a role as well. Because consensus building requires compromise and self-discipline, it grows wearisome over time. Voters no longer see the need; they only see the costs. As a result, voters challenge elites to break with consensus and to pursue an ever wider array of competing objectives instead.

These two factors—the long-term process of political transformation and the shorter-term frustration that emerges in response to prolonged consensus building—are not fatal in themselves. It could be possible that a real crisis in the future will bring the Dutch and Belgians together in common cause. But coming together relies on more than just opportunity, awareness, or determination. Consensus building was never easy or automatic. Both countries went through periods of intense domestic conflict and both struggled to find a way to bring that conflict to an end.

The solution they found lay in institutions as well as practices. Effective policymaking and implementation depends on the existence of institutions for negotiation, decision-making, and enforcement. In the general example of small states, these institutions support corporatism at home and integration abroad. They range from trade unions and employers' associations to labor foundations, planning bureaus, supranational commissions, and independent central banks. Hence the danger arises when the Belgians and the Dutch begin to politicize or dismantle key institutions for consensus building. When the goal for many actors is to do away with corporatism or to limit European integration, it is hard for these instruments to support consensus. Recent evidence suggests that this is the case. The Belgians and the Dutch are well on their way to politicizing and dismantling the institutions necessary to build consensus. They may even be preparing to abandon the practice of consensus building altogether. If they succeed, the period of their remarkable adaptability to world markets will come to an end.

This conclusion has three parts. The first discusses the continuity in policymaking and the success of the 1990s and beyond. The second explores the process of political transformation. The third suggests how we might apply this argument to other cases.

# Conclusion

## Economic Adjustment

When they celebrated the fifteenth anniversary of the Wassenaar Accord in the Netherlands, probably no one was more surprised than former Minister President Ruud Lubbers. The Dutch Social and Economic Council organized a special issue of its monthly bulletin and Lubbers gave an interview. In it, he admitted that it was very "gratifying" (using the English word) to hear a story where the new government was not doing everything better than he had. On the contrary, Lubbers noted, the coalition that followed his consciously acknowledged the roots of their policies in his own.[3] They had good reason to do so. Although the new coalition of social democrats (PvdA), right- (VVD), and left-liberals (D66) had campaigned on different agendas, the coalition agreement they forged held some basic issues in common—competitive wage restraint, fiscal consolidation, and monetary integration chief among them. Indeed, few people really challenged these commitments at the time, even outside the coalition. When the German economist Alfred Kleinknecht suggested that the Dutch might benefit from faster wage growth, his arguments were broadly rejected.[4]

Belgian Prime Minister Jean-Luc Dehaene found himself in much the same position as his Dutch counterparts. Although the scandal surrounding Wilfried Martens' collusion with the trade unions in the 1980s remained acute, Dehaene saw little choice but to continue with the broad outlines of the policy—again, competitive wage restraint, fiscal consolidation, and monetary integration. Moreover, Dehaene was armed with a 1989 law on competitiveness that allowed him to intervene in wage bargains that went beyond a weighted average of Belgium's major trading partners. When the trade unions tested this law in 1993, Dehaene not only refused to yield but he succeeded in breaking strikes led by his own Christian-Democratic trade unions.[5] Going into the 1995 elections, Dehaene placed this policy triptych as a prominent part of his campaign: only the Christian Democrats, he argued, could maintain competitiveness while paying down the debt and paving the way for Belgium's entry into Europe's economic and monetary union.[6]

## Conclusion

The policy continuity extended beyond Dehaene's tenure as prime minister and well into the twenty-first century. The same is true in the Netherlands as well. Indeed, governments in both countries have consistently worked to hold down wages and to pay down the public debt even after symptoms of the crisis were long past. The evidence is manifest in the data. For example, Figure C.1 shows the evolution of real unit labor costs relative to the fifteen EU member states of Western Europe (EU 15). The base year is 1992, which means that upward movements show a relative increase in labor costs compared to that year while downward movements show a decrease. Data for Germany are included as well for comparison. What the figure shows is that Belgium was broadly able to track German movements in relative unit labor costs and the Netherlands did slightly better. Although the differences look dramatic in the figure as drawn, the scale (given in the left-hand axis) is a range of less than 6 percent. The results can be seen in terms of net exports (Figure C.2). Belgium manages to maintain a trade surplus throughout the period. Meanwhile, the Netherlands moves from strength to strength.

The data for fiscal performance show a greater effort by the Belgians than by the Dutch, and with good reason. As Figure C.3 reveals, Belgium started with a much greater problem. Gross public debt accounted for well over 130 percent of GDP in the early 1990s. By contrast, it amounted to around 78 percent of GDP in the Netherlands. Fifteen years later, both countries were much improved. Belgian debt had fallen to 85 percent of GDP and Dutch debt was much lower at below 50 percent. The effort can be seen in the primary balances, meaning the level of expenditures less revenues net of service charges on the existing debt (Figure C.4). These balances show the extent to which governments are willing to use money to pay off the debt rather than to finance other expenditures (or to pay off their supporters). The surpluses are impressive in both countries, but particularly in Belgium where the primary surplus routinely exceeded 4 percent of GDP.

The commitment to monetary integration is present in the data as well. Specifically, it can be seen in the convergence of long-term

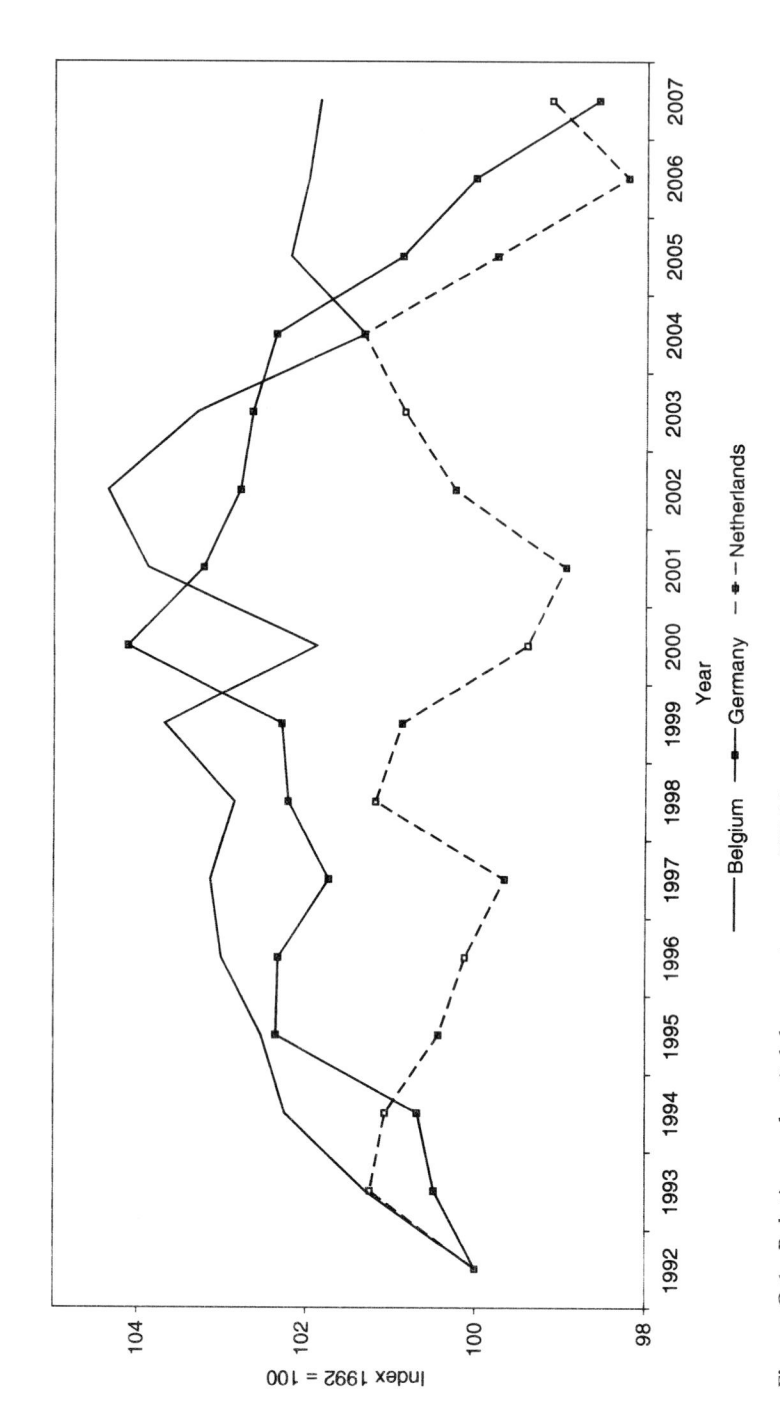

**Figure C.1.** Relative real unit labor costs versus EU 15

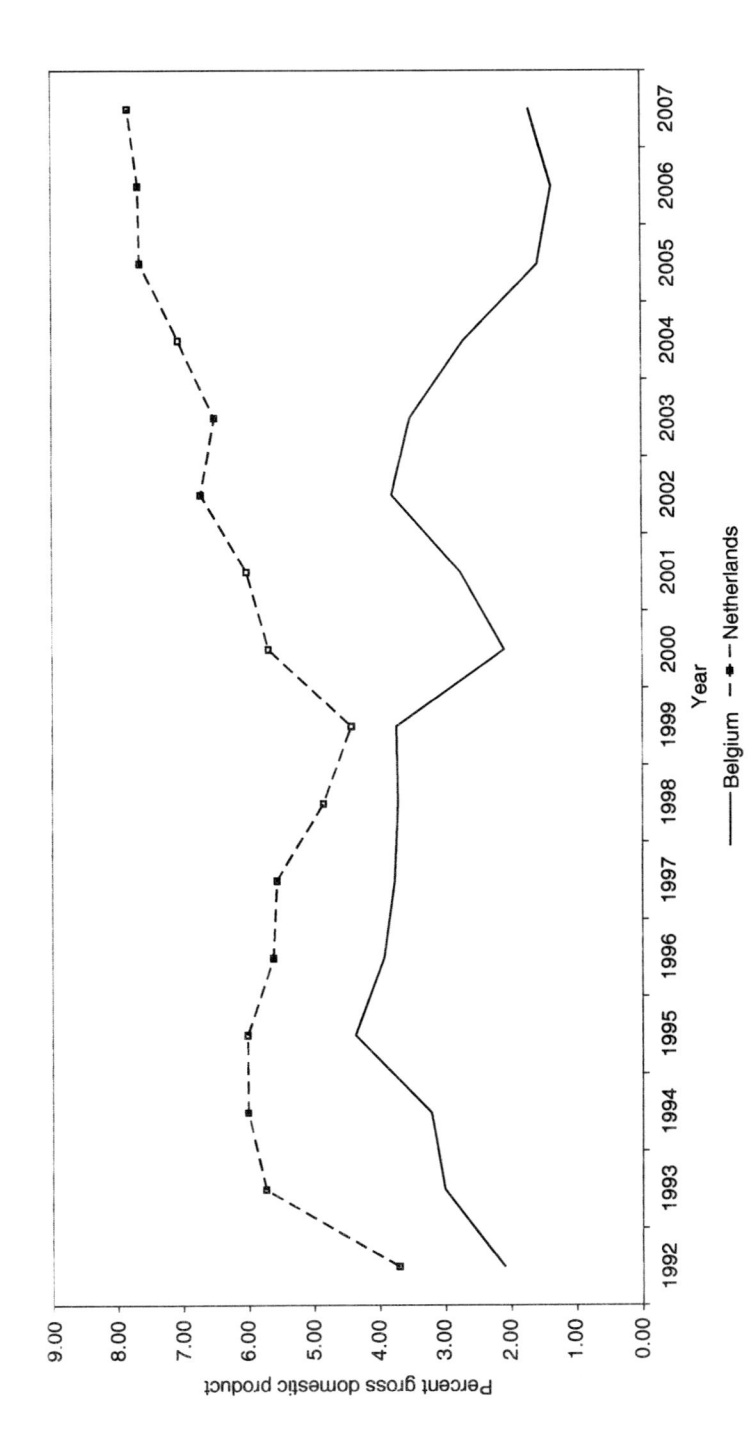

**Figure C.2.** Net exports

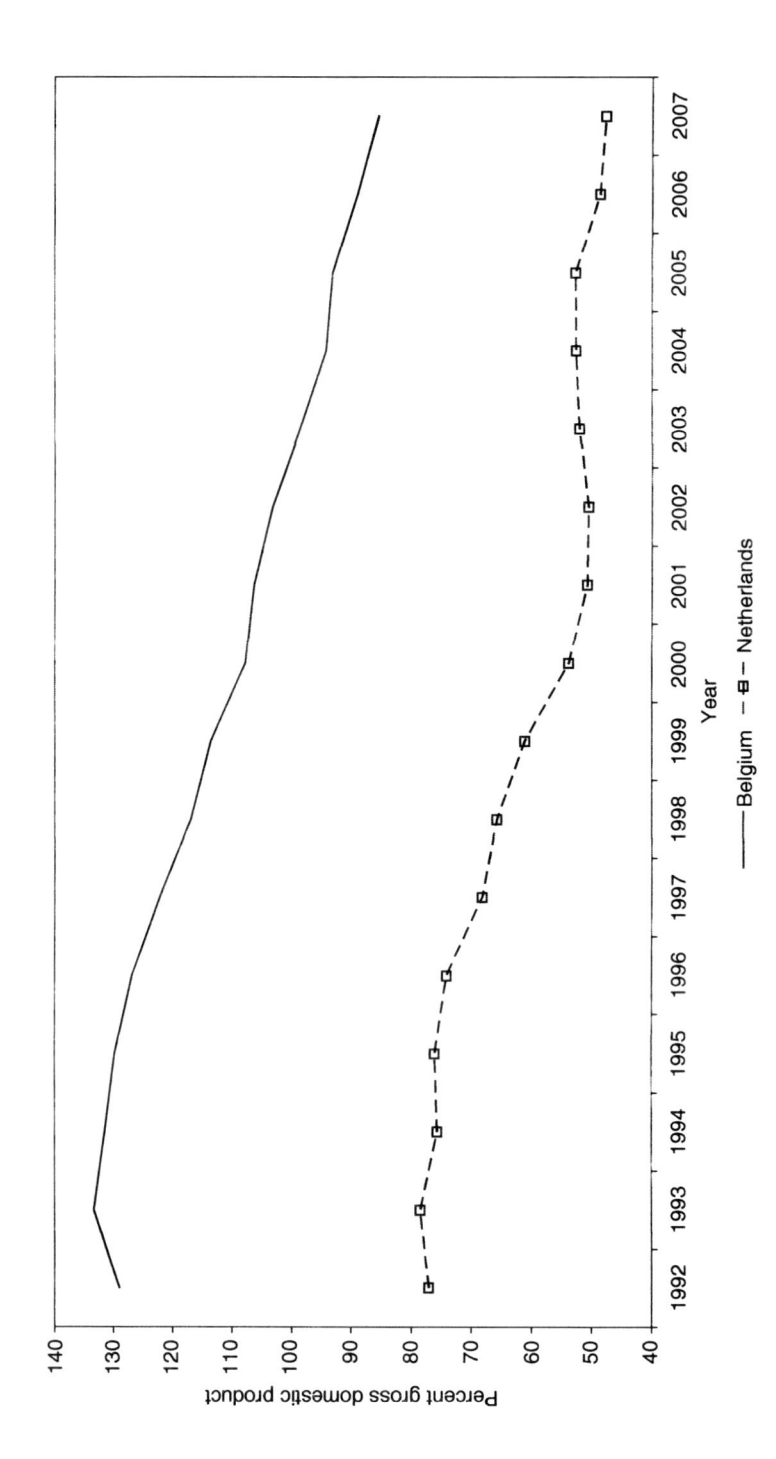

**Figure C.3.** Gross public debt

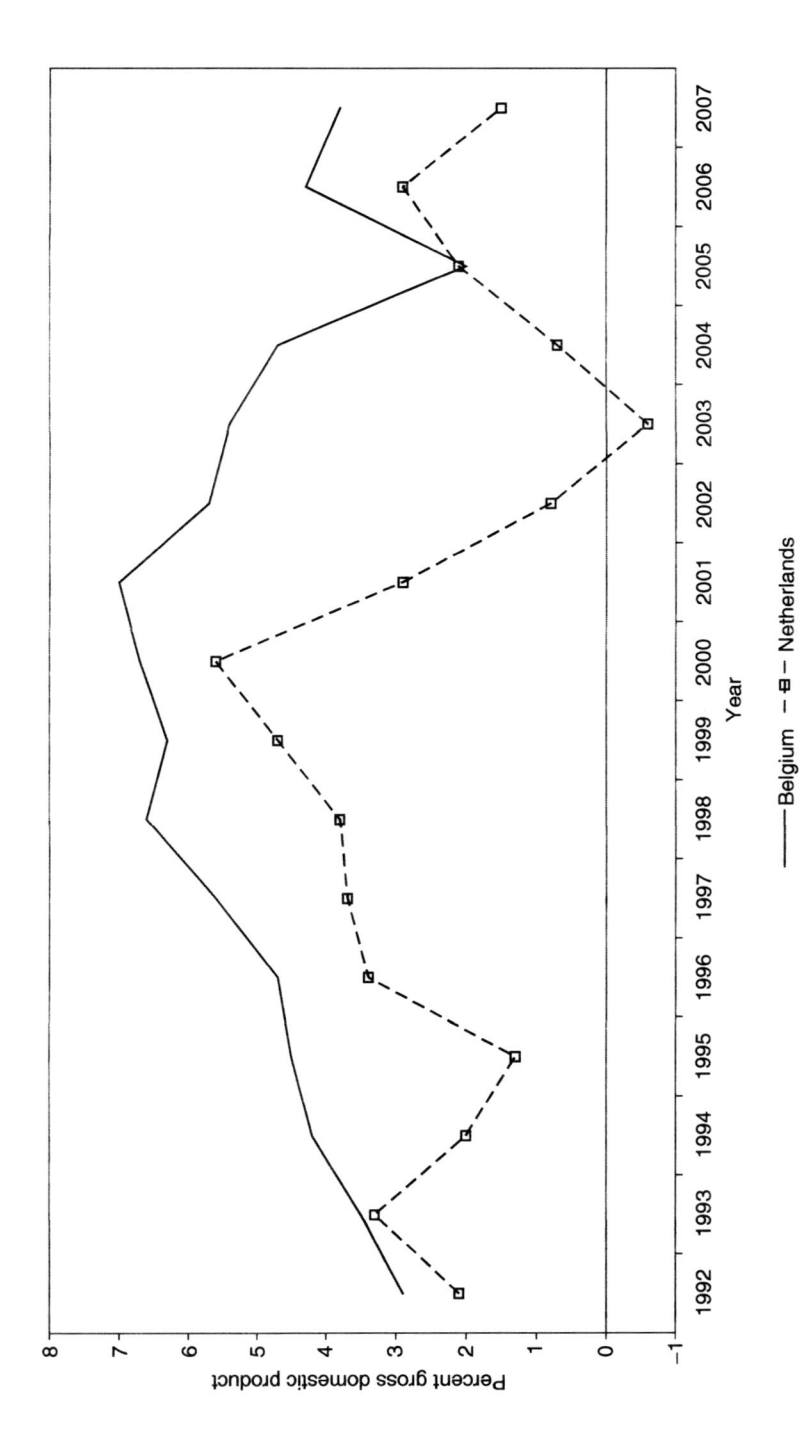

**Figure C.4.** Primary fiscal balances

## Conclusion

interest rates on German norms. When market participants are willing to pay as much for Belgian or Dutch bonds as for German ones, it means that they do not expect any change in the exchange rates between these countries and that they are confident of being able to find a buyer for the bonds should they choose to sell. More important, bond traders are well aware of the fact that yield differences are small once a country is credibly committed to its exchange rate peg with another and so they buy the bonds of the higher-yielding country in order to take advantage of the expected price rise. As the data in Figure C.5 reveal, this convergence in long-term interest rates took place earlier for the Netherlands than for Belgium. At times, indeed, Dutch interest rates fell below German norms. Nevertheless, the important point is that convergence was largely accomplished by 1996, three years before monetary union came about.

The convergence in long-term interest rates shows one of the important complementarities between the different policy measures: lower long-term interest rate differentials mean lower relative interest charges to pay on the national debt and the existence of a single currency means a deeper and more liquid market for government borrowers—which again translates into lower debt servicing costs. Hence by joining the single currency, the Belgians and the Dutch made it easier to control their public spending.

The complementarities are not limited to interest rates. The single currency also makes it possible for Belgium and the Netherlands to run consistent trade surpluses. Since they do not have a domestic currency, they do not have to worry that such strong trade performance will undermine competitiveness by causing the domestic currency to appreciate.[7] The only trick is to make sure that domestic costs remain under control relative to major trading partners. So long as they can depend on maintaining wage restraint, relative cost movements should not create a competitive problem.

The connections between the policies are not accidental. On the contrary, they were evident to analysts and policymakers in both countries from the start. Belgian and Dutch politicians knew

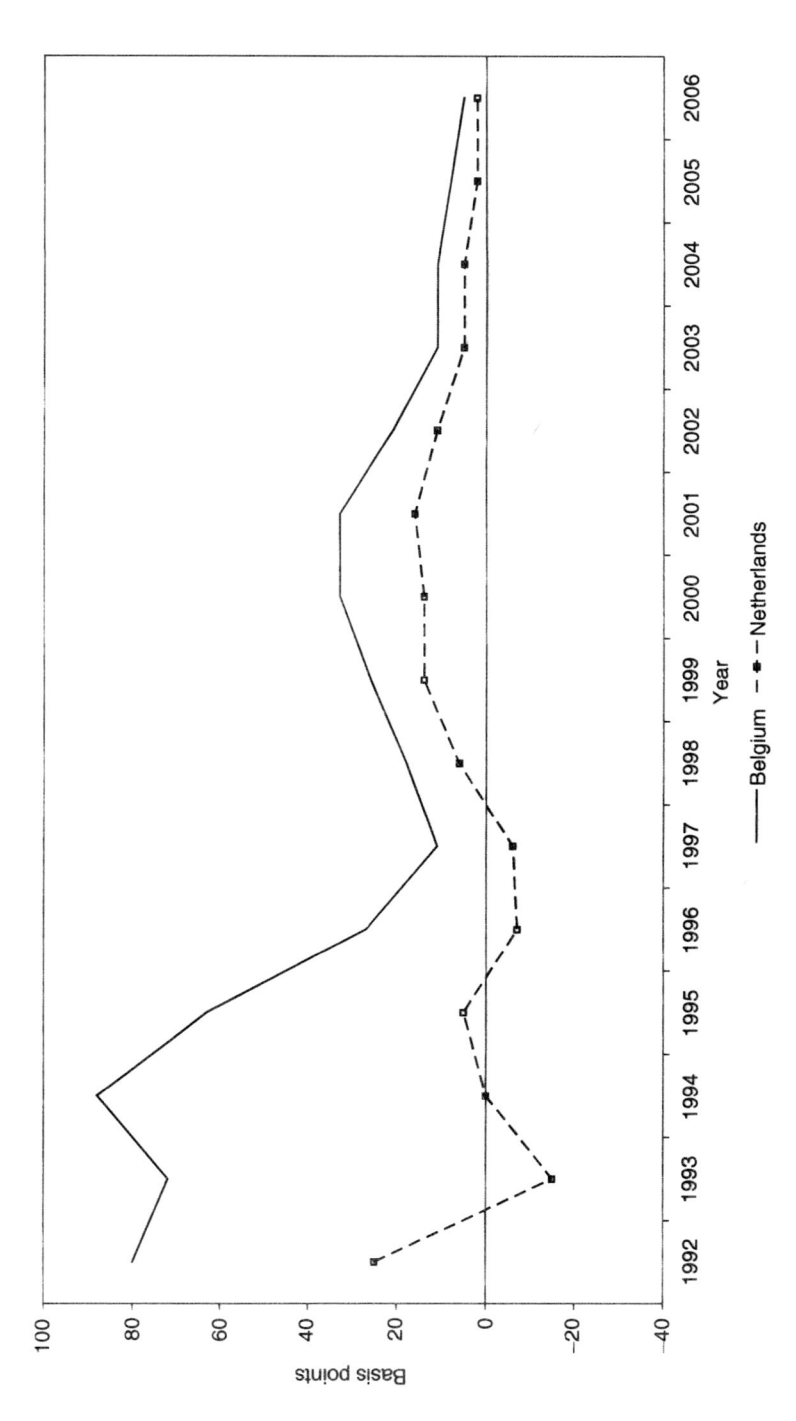

**Figure C.5.** Long-term interest rate differentials with Germany

## Conclusion

already in the early 1990s that monetary integration would provide these reinforcing benefits. They also recognized that there are important weaknesses in the policy mix. If they fail to control relative real wage costs, they could suffer a permanent loss of competitiveness. And if they fail to promote European integration, they could lose the arena within which their particular formula for maintaining competitiveness actually works.[8] Indeed Jean-Luc Dehaene made this point explicitly in his 1995 election manifesto.[9] There was no secret to small country success—just a broad policy consensus.

### Political Transformation

What Belgian and Dutch policymakers did not foresee at the start of the 1990s was the extent of political transformation underway in their countries. Although the elections of the early part of the decade were dramatic, they were only a taste of what was to come. The early twenty-first century provided a string of hotly contested elections, often against a background of relatively strong economic performance. Indeed, that may have been part of the problem. In the absence of an economic crisis, politicians and voters were free to pursue a variety of causes ranging from nationwide monoculturalism in the Netherlands to greater regional autonomy in Belgium.[10]

The broad narratives in both countries were oddly similar. First in the Netherlands and then in Belgium, the Christian Democrats were pushed from power and replaced with "purple"—meaning red (social-democrat)–blue (liberal)—coalitions. These purple coalitions each survived for two parliaments, losing increasing support from one election to the next. Meanwhile, those governing parties most committed to the process of political renewal and to the rejection of institutionalized consensus, like D66 in the Netherlands or the Flemish green party, *Agalev*, in Belgium, suffered worst while in office. When the purple coalition finally collapsed, the Christian Democrats proved to be the big winners.

# Conclusion

The Christian Democrats reaped the whirlwind. In the Netherlands, the Christian Democratic Appeal (CDA) ruled over a series of weak coalition governments punctuated by a succession of early parliamentary elections. In Belgium, the Christian Democrats struggled to form a government and faced an increasingly real prospect that Belgium would break apart. The old purple coalition partners suffered in opposition as well: the Liberals experienced defections to form more openly xenophobic right-wing groups, like Geert Wilders' Freedom Party (PVV) in the Netherlands or Jean-Marie Dedecker's eponymous list in Belgium; meanwhile, the Social Democrats faced vigorous challengers from both the left, like the Dutch Socialist Party (SP) and the right, like the Walloon Reform Movement (MR).

Despite the similarity in the broad narrative, however, the issues were different from one country to the next and so was the structure of electoral competition. Vestiges of the old consociational systems remained, but they were overshadowed by new developments. In Belgium, for example, the evolution of the party system splits decisively with the federalization of the country in 1993. From that point, relations between the Christian Democrats, Liberals, and Socialists in different language communities and geographic regions deteriorated. The reason had much to do with the changing incentive structures facing politicians in the North and South of the country. Flemish politicians were more concerned with containing the far right and perhaps also limiting the gains made by the greens than in nurturing relations with their sister parties in Wallonia. Meanwhile, the Walloon parties struggled to overcome a succession of corruption scandals and to assert the interests of their region at the federal level. The old Belgian consociational parties retained influence through their institutionalized role in the provision of social welfare but their interests diverged sharply. The Christian Democrats are a good example: in the North, the Christian People's Party (CVP) changed names to replace the generic reference to the "people" and add a specific reference to Flanders—becoming the Christian Democratic and Flemish Party (CD&V). Meanwhile, the Christian Democrats

## Conclusion

in the south changed the name of their party to drop any allusion to Christian Democracy, instead opting to form a Humanist and Democratic Center (CDH).[11]

The changes in the Netherlands were no less sweeping. The process started with the emergence of small protest parties in the 1994 election and continued with a succession of new political movements appearing and disappearing from one election to the next. Then in 2002 a populist succeeded in catapulting one of these groups into the public's attention. Pim Fortuyn used his leadership of a grassroots movement called "Livable Netherlands" to attack the politics of consensus head on. His appeal had much to do with problems of immigration that Dutch politicians had been trying to avoid.[12] Nevertheless, his effect was to politicize the very notion of consensus. In doing so, he forced the other political parties to clarify their relations with one another and he set the stage for the emergence or expansion of other anti-consensus populist movements in the future.[13]

Fortuyn was assassinated shortly before the May 2002 elections and his political movement did not last long beyond his death. Support for the eponymous list he started collapsed in the 2003 parliamentary election and all but disappeared by the time Dutch voters went to the polls in 2006. Nevertheless, Dutch discontent with the political system remained acute and so did the desire to find alternatives to the traditional political parties. Jan Marijnissen's Socialist Party and Geert Wilders' PVV have probably benefited the most from this discontent. Although they represent extremes of left and right, the two groups share a distaste for the old way of doing Dutch politics. They also share a suspicion of European integration and a distrust of corporatist arrangements.[14]

If there is a common theme in political evolution of the two countries, it is the growing emphasis on difference—between indigenous and immigrant, north and south, left and right, confessional and secular, and national and European. The Belgians and the Dutch are increasingly divided by their politics, and Belgian and Dutch politicians are increasingly unwilling to overcome these divisions. Liberals will not coalesce with Social Democrats, Christian Democrats will not unite with Socialists, and almost everyone is determined to avoid forming a government with the parties of the extreme right. Within these divisions, the challenge for politicians is to emphasize their distinctiveness. Breaking with the past and considering alternative futures is the easiest way to proceed.

The problem is that radical posturing can move beyond political control. The Dutch veto of the European constitutional treaty is one example. Jan Peter Balkenende's cabinet did not want to call a referendum and it certainly did not intend to lose the referendum once it was scheduled. Nevertheless, the Dutch turned out in record numbers to deal the European constitutional treaty a historic defeat. Now the question is whether such popular insurrection will be repeated.

## Implications

There is nothing new in the fact that Belgium and the Netherlands are internally divided. In the political science literature, the two countries are paradigms for how deeply divided groups of people can learn to live together. What is new is how they are divided and what is surprising is that the lessons of the past no longer seem applicable. Consociational democracy worked much better with one set of divisions than it does with the others. Part of the explanation lies with elites, who no longer seem as willing to cooperate. Part lies with the Belgians and Dutch themselves, who seem all too eager to punish coalescent or consensual elites. But an increasing share of the explanation lies in the institutional framework. The big fights in both countries are over the reform of social services that were created to help cement the consociational system into place. They are also over distributive policies that were intended to cushion the impact of participation in world markets on those groups who have had to adjust to the competition. Finally, the Belgians and the Dutch fight over patterns of decision-making that seem to take too long, to give too much power to minority groups, and to result in more continuity than change. As all of these battles come to the surface, Belgium and the Netherlands suffer more acutely from their domestic fractiousness as a result.

The importance of these cases for our understanding of political systems more generally should not be overestimated.[15] Belgium and the Netherlands are two small countries in a very wealthy part of Western Europe. They have few analogs in the wider world and so offer few easily transportable lessons for other countries to adopt. Nevertheless, the Belgian and Dutch cases suggest three observations: about the importance of behavior as well as institutions, about the limitations of institutionalized consensus building, and about the facility of small-state adjustment.

To begin with, the Belgian and Dutch cases reveal that while institutions matter, it is also important to consider how institutions are used and whether the use of institutions is popularly accepted. Belgian political institutions have become more consensual over time. Belgian politics has not. Meanwhile, the institutionalization of corporatist bargaining has not prevented corporatist institutions from becoming a focal point for popular discontent. Concerted wage bargaining was kept secret in the 1980s; now wage concertation has to be supported by law. A similar line of argument applies in the Netherlands as well. Even when consensus was most effective economically, there were many reasons why it was politically unpopular. Indeed, it is ironic that the international celebration of the Dutch model came just as the model itself began to fall apart.

The point about institutions and their use is generic. The observation about institutionalized consensus building is more case-specific. What the examples of Belgium and the Netherlands suggest is that the success of consociational democracy is historically contingent. The consociational arrangements—with their political parties, social groups, schools, hospitals, and media—were successful at managing one set of cleavages and yet poorly suited to adapting to another. Hence it was almost inevitable, at least with the benefit of hindsight, that any softening of the cleavages between Catholics, Protestants, and nonconfessional groups would cause the consociational order to whither away.

What is less clear is whether the alternative to consociational democracy is pluralism per se. Throughout this book I have used consociational democracy and pluralism as contrasting ideal types, but my focus was always unequal. Consociational democracy received close attention; pluralism got only a broad brush. The Belgian and Dutch cases show the importance of redressing the balance. The "pluralism"—if that is even the right term—that emerges from once consociational democracies contains both institutions and attitudes that are different from those found in countries like the United States. Mapping those differences is important not only to understand how once consociational democracies will develop but also to understand which policies they are likely to implement and which they are likely to reject. National responses to economic change depend to a great extent on the characteristic features of national politics. Therefore, understanding the residual influence of consociational democracy on countries like Belgium and the Netherlands is important to seeing how they adjust.

The Belgian and Dutch cases suggest that small-state adjustment strategies are becoming more difficult to implement over time. Indeed, it is likely that the era of small-state adjustment in the classical consensual sense is over for both countries. Political transformation has exposed Belgium and the Netherlands to the full implications of their domestic diversity. Using the language of Alberto Alesina and Enrico Spolaore, Belgium and the Netherlands have become larger rather than smaller. They are just as open to world markets, but they are more vulnerable to the domestic distributive conflicts that world market forces threaten to unleash. Faced with a shock to their competitiveness, the Belgians and the Dutch may not find the common will to respond. Instead they may find that their only possible avenue for adjustment is through the market. This will not be fatal, but as the experience of the 1970s shows it can be a painful result.

The increasing vulnerability of the Belgians and the Dutch to the influence of world markets is not unique. In some respects

# Conclusion

at least, it is universal. Globalization is making countries more diverse. This is obviously true in the context of migration, but it is possible to make the claim in more subtle ways as well. The deepening of world markets creates powerful new sources of risk and uncertainty which result in deep domestic divisions whether we are aware of them or not. These divisions crystallize only once the shock takes place and the winners and losers are known.[16] Hence while countries may be small in a conventional sense and while they certainly act as price takers in an economic sense, most countries are becoming "large" in the sense that they are no longer so homogenous as they were in the past. The rise of xenophobic or anti-immigrant movements is only one possible manifestation of the problem. A more general increase in populist political mobilization could also result.[17]

As countries become more domestically diverse, the challenge is to make sure that political representation expands to adapt. National politicians must also ensure that this political transformation does not undermine traditional patterns of economic policymaking along the way. When economic strategies become inoperable, politicians have to figure out how they can be replaced. The Belgian and Dutch cases are important because they underscore the difficulty of the task at hand.

# Notes

### Introduction

1. This paragraph places me somewhere in the "varieties of capitalism" literature. For a sample, see Esping-Andersen (1999), Hall and Soskice (2001), Scharpf and Schmidt (2000a, 2000b), Schmidt (2002), and Swank (2002). For a classic treatment of consociational democracy, see Lijphart (1968, 1969) and Steiner and Ertman (2002).
2. Olsson, Rothstein, and Strandberg (2003).
3. Jones (2002) and Mudde (1999).
4. Jones (1999) and Kurzer (1988, 1993).
5. Delsen and de Jong (1998), Hendriks and Toonen (2001), and Visser and Hemerijck (1997).
6. The push came from the Liberal right (Bouveroux 1992) but was soon picked up by the Christian Democratic Center as well (Van Hecke 1994). And, while the center-left continued to hold on to power, the language of "political renewal" came to dominate the mainstream of political discourse.
7. Lijphart (1984a) and Mair (1994).
8. Kurzer (1993).
9. See, e.g., Blyth (2002), Hall (1989), and McNamara (1998).
10. This is a large literature. For a sample, see Cafruny and Ryner (2003) and Moss (2005).
11. I make this argument directly in my contribution to Moss (2005).
12. See the essays by Herbert Kitschelt and Kees van Kersbergen in Kitschelt et al. (1999).
13. Lijphart (1968, 1969, 1975).
14. Cameron (1978).
15. Katzenstein (1984, 1985).

# Notes

16. Katzenstein (2003: 11) refers to this sense of vulnerability as "the first and most important explanatory variable" in his argument.
17. This is another huge literature. See, e.g., Garrett (1998).
18. Katzenstein (2003).
19. This borrows from Schwartz (1994).
20. Katzenstein (2003: 14–19).
21. Kirchheimer (1966) and Lipset (1963: 439–56).
22. Blanchard and Summers (1987), Budd, Levine, and Smith (1987), Drèze (1987), Giersch (1987), Lindbeck (1992), Lindbeck and Snower (1987a, 1987b), and Malinvaud (1987).
23. Three works representative of this majority are de Neubourg (1992), Hartog and Theeuwes (1993), and Mehta and Sneessens (1990).
24. Krugman (1987).
25. Contrast, e.g., the analyses of Malinvaud (1980) and Therborn (1986).
26. Edelman and Fleming (1965: 260).
27. This reasoning follows the insider–outsider argument originally put forward by Olson (1971) and elaborated upon by, *inter alia*, Lindbeck and Snower (1987a, 1987b).
28. This should not be understood to imply that unemployment was (or is) without nonfinancial costs. Rather, it meant that unemployed workers were willing to take longer to look for better-paying jobs in order to re-enter the workforce.
29. For this and the preceding paragraph, see Lindbeck (1991).
30. In economic terms, the "matching function" or "Beveridge curve" shifted. The empirical concern, then, is whether there was one discrete shift, or long and continuous shifting. The first instance can be attributed to a shock to the labor market, and the second to a gradual deterioration of labor market conditions. See Blanchard and Diamond (1989) and Bean (1989).
31. OECD (1970).
32. Here it is important to consider the role of first- and second-order pricing effects. The rise in energy prices is first-order in that it takes place immediately. The rise in labor costs is second-order—taking place over a more gradual time frame and only in reaction to the first-order price increases.
33. Scholten (1987: 120) and Geul, Nobelen, and Slomp (1985).

34. Inglehart (1971) and Inglehart (1977).
35. Indeed, it is possible to argue that the vertical social organization evident in Belgium and the Netherlands was the very essence of "faction" which Madison viewed as inimical to the cause of liberty. *Federalist Papers* (1961: 77–84).
36. In fact, Arend Lijphart coined the term "consociational democracy" to describe "these deviant cases of fragmented but stable democracies...." Lijphart (1969: 211).
37. Strictly speaking, there are only two or three "pillars" involved. In the Netherlands, the pillars are Catholic, Calvinist, and nonconfessional. In Belgium, they are Catholic and nonconfessional.
38. See, e.g., Rokkan (1977).
39. Inglehart (1971: 1011–12). The distinction between elite-challenging and elite-directed forms of participation is made in Inglehart (1977).

## Chapter 1

1. Katzenstein (1985).
2. Katzenstein (1985: 21).
3. Katzenstein (1985: 29).
4. Katzenstein (1985: 36–8).
5. Alesina and Spolaore (2005). The title of this section is taken from their book.
6. Alesina and Spolaore (2005: 219).
7. This is the principal argument in Katzenstein (1984).
8. The story of the Oslo Alliance is taken from van Roon (1989).
9. Davenport (1982).
10. Marquez Mendez (1986). See also Sapir (1992).
11. Sapir (1992: 1500).
12. These averages are estimated "post-Tokyo Round." See Herin (1986, Table 1).
13. Marquez Mendez (1986: 26).
14. Louffir and Reichlin (1993).
15. Wijkman (1990: 19).
16. Lecraw (1984) and Pelkmans and Beuter (1987).
17. Pelkmans (1987).
18. Henderson (1992).

## Notes

19. Treaties Establishing the European Communities: Abridged Edition (1987: 23).
20. Diebold (1959).
21. Dahrendorf (1994).
22. "Officiële sluiting van laatste steenkoolmijn" *De Standaard* (October 1, 1992) 2.
23. Davenport (1982: 245).
24. Swann (1988: 205).
25. Moravcsik (1991).
26. Jones (2004).
27. For an application of this argument to the crisis following the French and Dutch referenda on the European Constitutional Treaty, see Jones (2005).
28. Katzenstein (1997).
29. CEPR (1992: 14).
30. Wijkman (1992: 10).
31. Franck (1983: 85).
32. Wadhwani (1989).
33. Cawson (1985: 8).
34. See Waelbroeck's (1987) comment on Newell and Symons (1987).
35. For a sociological discussion of the differences between organized business and organized labor, see Streeck (1992: ch. 3).
36. Chamberlain and Kuhn (1969).
37. Olson (1971).
38. See the comments by Seppo Jonkapohja on the study by Calmfors and Driffill. Jonkapohja (1988).
39. Calmfors and Driffill (1988: 15). See also Summers (1987) on Newell and Symons (1987).
40. Schmitter (1981).
41. Scholten (1987).
42. Nobelen and Akkermans (1983).
43. Lindblom (1977: 170–88) and Bowler (1987).
44. Schmitter (1982).
45. Schmitter (1989) and van der Ploeg (1987).
46. Flanagan et al. (1983: 115) and Newell and Symons (1987: 579–80). Writing before the defection of the Swedish Metal Employers Association, Karl-Olof Faxén (1982) of the Swedish Employers Confederation argued that the link between real wage restraint and a

closing of the wage gap between skilled and unskilled workers was unclear.
47. For an early survey of the literature, see Cawson (1978).
48. Schmitter (1982: 275).
49. Grant (1985: 7).
50. Van den Brande (1987) and Vanderstraeten (1986).
51. Katzenstein (1985: 95).
52. Gourevitch (1986).
53. In reference to the Social and Economic Council of the Netherlands, J. Pen wrote: "The institutional pattern and ideology is reminiscent of the corporate state, although it is not the done thing to remind people of it." Cited in Edelman and Fleming (1965: 228).
54. Schmitter (1986: 165).
55. Schmitter (1974: 85).
56. Schmitter (1981, 1986).
57. This argument is a recurrent theme in Schmitter's writings, although he is not a proponent. For his critique, see Schmitter (1981). Schmitter argues that the creation of intermediate sovereignties "may provide one element for explaining why the more neo-corporatist polities have proven demonstrably more 'governable' in recent decades than pluralist ones...." Schmitter (1986: 182).
58. Wolfgang Streeck (1992: 64).
59. Schmitter (1981).
60. Cawson (1978: 183).
61. Schmitter (1985). For Schmitter's definition of sovereignty, see p. 33.
62. Schmitter (1986: 167, 181).
63. This is particularly the case in economic policymaking, where "[politicians] face a number of collective action dilemmas in the development and implementation of economic policies that are consistent with the goal of sustainable growth. Delegation of economic policy-making authority helps solve these collective action problems.... By delegating policy-making authority, political actors force themselves to co-operate with each other." Bernhard and Granato (1991: 2).
64. Strayer (1970) and Hinsley (1986). The equation of state sovereignty and state autonomy is nonetheless problematic. Jacques Maritain (1951: ch. 2) argues that the influence of absolutist theories of the state has rendered the term "sovereignty" so overburdened that its use should be abandoned in political philosophy.

# Notes

65. Emphasis and italics are mine. See Weber (1947: 154, 156).
66. Landauer (1983: 3).
67. Lippmann (1961).
68. Keynes (1963: 313–14).
69. As Simon Reich (1990: 53) explains: "Not all fascist regimes become corporatist in liberal democracies; not all corporatist regimes were once fascist. But where corporatist regimes were formerly fascist, a link still exists. Fascism and state corporatism are not the same thing, but they share common characteristics. The three forms of regime are not mutually exclusive. Viewed in this way, state and societal corporatism are ideal types on a continuum of regimes; the primary distinction between them focuses on the legitimate boundaries of state coercion and discrimination."
70. For a review of the early postwar "federalist" movements, see Loth (1990). See also Spinelli (1965: 13–24) and Brugmans (1988: ch. 7).
71. Brugmans (no date).
72. For the argument that the collapse of the EDC marked the end of the European movement, see the introductory and concluding chapters of Aron and Lerner (1956).
73. The importance of intermediate economic objectives was continuously recognized by Monnet and Schuman, but also by the Dutch and Belgians during the early 1950s. Griffiths and Milward (1986).
74. Haas (1968: xii).
75. Silj (1967).
76. Spinelli (1960: 340).
77. Brugmans (1965: 247–61).
78. Bulmer (1985), Brewin (1987), Noel (1989), and Ludlow (1992).
79. Inglehart (1990) and Streeck and Schmitter (1991).
80. This paradox is best described in the writings of Stanley Hoffmann (1968, 1982, 1989) and David Calleo (1965, 2001).
81. Interview with Prince Nikolaus of Liechtenstein, October 22, 1992.
82. Smith (1992).
83. Examples of both of these can be found in the history of France during the 1980s. See McCarthy (1990).
84. Lippmann (1961).
85. Hall (1986: 261).
86. Mosca (1939: 369).
87. Galbraith (1992).

88. This phenomenon is described in Wilson (1981).
89. Von Mises (1983: 105).
90. Weber (1947: 154–5).
91. See the introductory and concluding chapters in Katzenstein (1978).
92. Gourevitch (1986: 230).
93. This should not be taken as a contradiction of the argument put forward by Katzenstein (1984) in his study of Austria and Switzerland. There he argues that corporatism allows for the flexibility necessary for change. That is true. The point here is that change might also include the rejection of corporatist bargaining.
94. See, e.g., Keohane and Hoffmann (1991) and Sbragia (1992).

## Chapter 2

1. Huggett (1971: 166), International Monetary Fund (1950: 66, 132), Messing (1988: 530), and van der Zee (1989).
2. For the influence of Keynes on Lieftinck, see Bakker and van Lent (1989). See also de Wolff and Driehuis (1980: 47–53).
3. Bakker and van Lent (1989).
4. The Foundation of Labour (*Stichting van den Arbeid*) offered an ideal starting point for broad cooperation between the social partners. From its inception, the Foundation brought together employers' associations and trade union federations for the promotion of the working class and the maintenance of industrial peace. In its manifesto, the Foundation declared: "This agreement represents the achievement of a complete consensus on the communal organization of labor. The principal foundations of this consensus were set down in a Foundation of Labour dedicated to the promotion of social peace, order and justice. This agreement anticipates a communal partnership in the social area, at the firm as well as at the regional and national levels. *The Foundation offers its services to the government in the fulfilment of duties to the general good.*" Cited in van Doorn et al. (1976: 28)—translation and emphasis mine.
5. The government's power in this regard was established in the exceptional resolution on labor relations (Buitegewoon Besluit Arbeidsverhoudingen) of October 5, 1945. The Board of Government Conciliators is the *College van Rijksbemiddelaars*.

**Notes**

6. Manning (1986: 419–24) and Heinen (1990).
7. Griffiths (1980a: 278–9), Griffiths (1991: 210–13), Guillen (1986), and Manning (1986).
8. Messing (1988: 531).
9. Fischer (1980: 42–71) and Klein (1980: 5–11).
10. Although the correct technical term is *zuilen*, it is difficult not to agree with Lijphart in his later reflections that subnational political cultures is a more accurate description (Lijphart 1984b). Indeed, Daalder used the term "subnational political cultures" as a synonym for *zuilen* (Daalder 1966).
11. Lipset attributes the original argument to Sigmund Neumund (1963: 74).
12. This point was suggested by Stuurman (1983), who argues that the very existence of pillarized society raises the question why pillars exist in the first place. The answer, he suggests, is that pillars evolved as part of a larger effort to limit the power of women and the working classes in Dutch society.
13. Middendorp (1991).
14. *Nederlandse Volksbeweging* (NVB). Bosmans (1988a: 563) and Daalder (1966: 213).
15. The Catholic Party changed name from the *Rooms-katholieke Staatspartij* (RKSP) to the *Katholieke Volkspartij* (KVP). The socialists and some radicals grouped under the banner of the *Partij van de Arbeid* (PvdA). And, in January of 1948, the liberals coalesced in the *Volkspartij voor Vrijheid en Democratie* (VVD). The two main Calvinist parties, the *Christelijke Historische Unie* (CHU) and the *Anti-Revolutionaire Partij* (ARP), retained their prewar names. Bosmans (1988a: 565–80).
16. Bosmans (1988a: 577–80).
17. The socialist trade union federation is the *Nederlands Verbond van Vakverenigingen* (NVV); the communists ran the *Eenheidsvakcentrale* (EVC); the Catholics had the *Katholieke Arbeidersbeweging* (KAB), which in 1964 changed over to the *Nederlands Katholiek Vakverbond* (NKV); and the Protestants had the *Christelijk Nationaal Vakverbond* (CNV). Van Doorn et al. (1976: 24–42).
18. *Centraal Sociaal Werkgeversverbond* (CSWV) and after 1968 the *Verbond van Nederlandse Ondernemingen* (VNO).
19. Brinkman (1988: 64–5).

20. Bosmans (1988*a*: 579).
21. For the Dutch name of the VVD, see n. 15.
22. Daalder (1966), Duynstee (1966), and Visser (1986).
23. Visser (1986: 44).
24. It is interesting to note that the PvdA vote loss was due at least in part to residual attempts at political reform. The party leadership chose to head its electoral list with several names instead of relying on the popular Willem Drees. Sole reliance on Drees, it was feared, would be regarded as a return to the old socialist pillar. In the event, however, constituencies where Drees headed the list saw fewer vote losses that those headed by political reform candidates like Schermerhorn. Brinkman (1988: 82–5).
25. In fact, the two-thirds majority was even more important for the passage of constitutional reforms related to the Dutch East Indies. Parts of the opposition had voted for the reforms during their first reading by the Beel cabinet, but reserved the right to change their voters during the bill's second reading. Rather than face a vote of no confidence, Beel agreed to unbind the parliament and call for early elections. Formation of a second narrow Red-Rome coalition would have served no purpose, particularly as the PvdA lost seats. The crisis in Indonesia was perhaps the single most important political issue of the Beel administration. Indeed, it also had a definitive impact on the construction of the Drees–Van Schaik cabinet. During the government formation, however, the PvdA was also concerned about the future of economic reform. PvdA party leader M. van der Goes van Naters wrote during the formation of the Drees cabinet that if the VVD and the CHU could not agree on a progressive economic program, then a two-party cabinet would be preferable to any other solution. See, Visser (1986: 42, 44). For an exhaustive treatment of the Dutch Indonesian policy, see de Jong (1988).
26. Duynstee (1966: 16–24) and Visser (1986: 21–56).
27. Brinkman (1988).
28. Bosmans (1988*b*).
29. Fischer (1980: 42–7).
30. The citation is from the First Report on Industrialization. Fischer (1980: 44).
31. Griffiths (1980*b*).
32. *Wet op de Bedrijfsorganisatie*, January 27, 1950.

# Notes

33. The Social and Economic Council is the *Sociaal-Economische Raad*. The representatives of the state are not necessarily representatives of the government. Rather, they are academics or other experts appointed by the Crown to represent the general interest.
34. Lijphart (1982: 30–2).
35. Fischer (1980: 139–47).
36. Bosmans (1988*a*: 583).
37. The injunction on the representatives to the Social and Economic Council that they act in the general interest, rather than in the interest of their particular groups, was a polite fiction. Given the overlap between membership on the council and participation in the Foundation of Labour, there was little reason to believe that the one group could be nonpartisan while the other was not. Abert (1969: 60). See also Bosmans (1988*a*: 563) and Maritain (1951).
38. *Quadragesimo Anno*. Abert (1969: 63–4).
39. The principle that agreements reached in collective bargaining could be applied throughout the economy was established in the December 24, 1927, law on collective labor agreements (*Wet op der Collective Arbeids Overeenkomst*).
40. van Doorn et al. (1976: 41). Note ellipsis in original.
41. The failure of these *Publiekrechtelijk Bedrijfs Organisaties* (PBOs) is a subject of frequent discussion in the literature concerning the Industrial Organization Act. See, in particular, Abert (1969: 61–6).
42. Cox (1990).
43. Here it is important to distinguish between consociationalism as a form of political organization and corporatism as a mechanism for the development and implementation of policies. The two terms, while similar, are not interchangeable. Neither is corporatism necessarily derivative of consociationalism nor vice versa. See Scholten (1987).
44. De Wolff and Driehuis (1980: 37).
45. This argument is a close paraphrase of Griffiths (1980*a*: 277).
46. According to some estimates, the colony in Indonesia accounted for fully one-seventh of Dutch GNP. Huggett (1971: 166) and Bakker and van Lent (1989: 152–3).
47. Bakker and van Lent (1989: 142–4).
48. Again, I am indebted to Griffiths (1980*a*: 278).

49. Manning (1986).
50. See Griffiths and Millward (1986). Stikker was succeeded by two ministers for Foreign Affairs, J. W. Beyen and Josef Luns. Beyen was responsible for international commercial relations.
51. The Dutch National Bank is *De Nederlandische Bank* (DNB). Bakker and van Lent (1989: 160–8).
52. Kennedy (1991) and Marsh (1992).
53. Article 9, paragraph 1 of the Bank Act, 1948. The translation is taken from Eizenga (1983: 10).
54. Den Dunnen (1973: 284).
55. Lieftinck argues that there were no "real" disagreements between the PvdA Finance Ministers and the Bank's President Holtrop because they agreed fundamentally on the primacy of government economic policy over monetary stability. Bakker and van Lent (1989: 162).
56. Den Dunnen (1973: 294).
57. Fase (1992).
58. Abert (1969: 16).
59. Abert (1969: 27).
60. *Centraal Planbureau*, est. 1945.
61. Edelman and Fleming (1965: 242) and Abert (1969: 80–1).
62. Bakker and van Lent (1989: 177).
63. Messing (1988: 531).
64. Edelman and Fleming (1965: 272).
65. Finance Minister Lieftinck strongly advocated protectionist measures against the ultimately successful opposition of Economics Minister J. R. M. van den Brink. Bakker and van Lent (1989: 118–20).
66. Abert (1969: 81).
67. For this and the previous paragraph, see Edelman and Fleming (1965: 244–7).
68. The Drees III cabinet fell and was replaced by the interim center-right Beel II cabinet on December 22, 1958. Elections took place on March 12, 1959, and led to the formation of the De Quay center-right cabinet on May 19. The vote loss for the PvdA in the 1959 election was marginal but important. From 32.7 percent in the election of June 13, 1956, the PvdA fell to 30.4 percent in 1959. The PvdA's withdrawal from the cabinet involved a deep split with the Catholic party over the relationship between church and state. Nevertheless, the 1957 real wage cuts were an important catalyst

# Notes

in the final divorce between the two parties. Bosmans (1988*a*: 586–9).
69. Griffiths (1980*a*).
70. *Centraal Bureau voor de Statistiek* (CBS).
71. Van Doorn et al. (1976: 81–90).
72. Van Doorn et al. (1976: 90–104).
73. Abert (1969: 158–72).
74. European Commission (1993*a*, Tables 30 and 31).
75. This point is made directly by Edelman and Fleming (1965: 251).
76. Flanagan et al. (1983: 113–22).
77. European Commission (1972: 277–8, 298) and den Dunnen (1973: 308–11).
78. Den Dunnen (1973: 322–5).
79. Messing (1988: 547).
80. Lamers (1983: 82). See also Van Ark et al. (1994: 40–2).
81. Den Dunnen (1973: 322–3).
82. Bosmans (1988*a*: 598).
83. Den Dunnen (1979: 40) makes this argument in respect to credit restrictions, saying: "As other policy instruments failed to maintain economic equilibrium, a disproportionately heavy burden came to rest on credit policy." However, given the limitations inherent to credit restrictions on the Dutch commercial banking sector, it is equally reasonable to argue that the poor performance of that policy exacerbated the shortcomings of fiscal and price–incomes policy.
84. Tromp (1989: 85–8) and Wolinetz (1988: 135–7).
85. Wolinetz (1988: 146–9).
86. Tromp (1989: 89).
87. Bakker and van Lent (1989: 224–5).
88. Irwin and Dittrich (1984: 268–96).
89. Wolinetz (1989: 87).
90. Nypels and Tamboer (1985: ch. 1). The failure of the 1972 social pact was a formative moment in the career of socialist Wim Kok.
91. Lipset (1963: 439, 450) opened his essay on the "end of ideology" with the admonition that: "democracy requires institutions which support conflict and disagreement as well as those which sustain legitimacy and consensus. In recent years, however, democracy in the Western world has been undergoing some important changes

as serious intellectual conflicts among groups, representing different values have declined sharply." The result, Lipset argued, is a changeover in the relative influence of elites. Where before elites had the ability to guide social development: "As soon as the masses have access to the society's elite, as soon as they [the elites] must consider mass reaction in determining their own actions, the freedom of the elite (whether political or artistic) is limited."

92. Kindleberger (1987: 167–84).
93. Milward (1992: 50).
94. Meade et al. (1962: 290–1).
95. Huyse (1980: 28–31).
96. The Renardist-syndicalists were the Liège-based *Mouvement syndical unifié*, headed by André Renard.
97. The FGTB-ABVV is the *Fédération générale de travail de Belgique-Algemeen belgisch vakverbond*, the MOC-ACW is the *Mouvement ouvrier chrétien-Algemeen christelijke werknemersverbond*, the CSC-ACV is the *Confédération des syndicats chrétiens-Algemeen christelijke vakverbond*, and the FIB-VBN is the *Fédération des industries de Belgique-Verbond der belgische nijverheid*. See Claeys (1973: chs. 4 and 5).
98. *Comité Central Industriel-Centrale Raad voor het Bedrijfsleven*. Deleeck (1992: 131–41).
99. Brepoels (1988: 150).
100. Witte (1990a: 246) and Vandenbroucke (1981: 105).
101. Vandeputte (1987: ch. 1) and Witte (1990a: 237–40).
102. Kurzer (1993: 83–5); Milward (1992: 52–3); Joye (1964).
103. Meynen (1990: 282–4) and Vandenbroucke (1981: 105–9).
104. Eyskens (1993: 226).
105. Union membership data from Claeys (1973: 133). See also Vandeputte (1987: 35–7).
106. Milward (1992: 50–6, 62–3).
107. The citation is from the maiden speech of Bank's President Maurice Frère in Banque National de Belgique (1949: 7–8).
108. Eyskens (1993: 229).
109. Milward (1992: 58).
110. Kindleberger (1987).
111. This point is emphasized by a later governor of the Belgian National Bank, Robert Vandeputte, in his economic history of postwar Belgium. See Vandeputte (1985: 39).

# Notes

112. See Chapter 7, articles 75 and 76 of the royal decree of September 13, 1948.
113. Studies have shown a statistical relationship between the ideological color of the ruling coalition and the growth of the public sector, the distribution of income, and the inflation–unemployment trade-off. De Grauwe (1985), Capron (1986), and Boone and Willeme (1989).
114. The Belgian currency was the franc in French and the frank in Flemish. My preference is to use the Flemish spelling in order to avoid any confusion with the French currency.
115. The then Finance Minister Eyskens argued that "the percentage of the devaluation was calculated to forestall domestic price inflation." Durant (1983: 73).
116. Eyskens (1993: 269). The list of objections is attributed to Achiel van Acker.
117. The national majority for the King's return was 58 percent, with 72 percent supporting in Flanders, 48 percent in Brussels, and 42 percent in Wallonia.
118. See Mabille (1986: 305, 309–12), Witte (1990*a*: 246–52), and Brepoels (1988: 158–9).
119. Huyse (1980: 26–8) and Brepoels (1988: 159).
120. Lorwin (1966) and Witte (1990*b*: 258–64).
121. Vandeputte (1985: 35).
122. The Catholic CSC-CVP suffered a tremendous 6.6 percentage point loss in this election, falling from 47.7 percent in 1950 to 41.1 percent in 1954.
123. Vandeputte (1987: 53–5).
124. Vandenbroucke (1981: 144–6).
125. Milward (1992: 160–3).
126. Milward (1992: 99–101).
127. Milward (1992).
128. Meynen (1978: 499).
129. Milward (1992: 108).
130. Wayne Snyder estimates that the net impact of general government on the growth of Belgian GDP during the period from 1955 to 1965 was only about +5 percent—much lower than in the United States, France, Germany, Italy, or the UK. Snyder (1969).
131. Vandenbroucke (1981: 146–8) and Milward (1992: 111).
132. Chaput and de Falleur (1961*a*, 1961*b*).

133. *Bureau de programmation économique–Bureau voor economische programmatie*, established October 14, 1959; *Comité national de l'expansion économique–Nationaal comité voor economische expansie*, established November 25, 1960.
134. Mabille (1986: 323, 329).
135. The King pronounced the independence of the Congo on June 30, 1960.
136. Durant (1983: 161–70) and Meynen (1990: 286–8).
137. Meynen (1990: 288), Durant (1983: 168–71), and Vandenbroucke (1981: 149–51).
138. Lorwin (1966: 171–2).
139. Brussels, of course, retained higher incomes per capita than Flanders.
140. Meynen (1978).
141. Vandeputte (1987: 81–91), Mabille (1986: 324), and Claeys (1973: 133).
142. European Commission (1993*a*: Tables 10 and 23).
143. Data from European Commission (1993*a*), various tables. See also Vandeputte (1987: 90–2).
144. Van Rijckeghem (1982: 596) notes that price controls were directed at commodities included in the consumer price index, in order to influence wage growth indirectly through indexation. He also reports results from econometric analysis which reveal that indexation provided a floor, and not a ceiling, for wage settlements. Thus even indirect controls on wage growth had little effect.
145. Lebegue (1969).
146. Data from the National Institute for Statistics (NIS). Note that historians express great skepticism with respect to the accuracy of NIS strike data, suggesting that official figures represent only 50 percent of the true total. Meynen (1978: 497).
147. Vandeputte (1987: 97–9).
148. TALENT (1969: 516).
149. Milward (1992: 156), European Commission (1993*a*: Table 20), and van Rijckeghem (1980: 592–3).
150. Lebegue (1969: 245).
151. Vandeputte (1987: 99–101).
152. European Commission (1993*a*: Table 28).
153. Deschouwer (1989: 36).
154. Covell (1988).

# Notes

155. Vandeputte (1987: 84–9).
156. The different institutional roles played by the ideological pillars in Belgian and Dutch society after the 1960s marks the primary distinction between depillarization in Belgium and the Netherlands during the 1970s. See Huyse (1980).
157. The Flemish regional party was the *Volksunie* (VU), the largest Walloon regional party was the *Rassemblement Wallon* (RW), and the French-speaking Brussels party was the *Front démocratique des Bruxellois francophones* (FDF).
158. Claeys (1973: 171), Mabille (1986: 328), and Meynen (1990: 299).
159. Vandeputte (1985: 109–10).
160. Claeys (1973: 163–5).
161. European Commission (1972: 396).
162. Durant (1983: 237–9).
163. The *Bureau de Plan-Planbureau* replaced the Office for Economic Planning.
164. Vandeputte (1987: 102, 115) and Vandenbroucke (1981: 173–9).

## Chapter 3

1. European Commission (1993*a*: Table 35).
2. McCracken et al. (1977), Corden (1986: 84–95), and Steinherr (1974).
3. Here it should be noted that Belgium benefited from a net inflow of direct investment, but an even greater net outflow of portfolio investment during the period from 1960 to 1973. In the Netherlands, the situation was reversed until 1971—with net portfolio flows coming into the Netherlands, and direct investments going out. After 1971, both net portfolio and net direct investments were leaving the country.
4. Data aggregated from International Monetary Fund (1989: 232, 530).
5. OECD (1970: 9).
6. European Commission (1993*a*: Table 39).
7. These proportions are extrapolated from the "other EEC" column of a table reporting the average import share of internal demand in 1969. France and Germany are reported separately. The disproportionate weight of Italy in the remainder implies that the figures for Belgium

# Notes

and the Netherlands are probably greater than 50 percent. OECD (1970: Table 21).
8. Michels (1973).
9. An important part of the change in Belgian monetary policy was the relaxation of the requirement that all exchange rate changes be approved by act of parliament. This was done on July 3, 1972. See Banque National de Belgique (1973: ix).
10. For the Netherlands, see Zijlstra (1979) and Fase (1987). For Belgium, see Vandeputte (1978: 653–60), de Clerq (1978), and de Strycker (1977).
11. For a useful overview of small country exchange rate experience under the European snake regime, see Thygesen (1979).
12. Data from OECD (1986: Table 2.15).
13. The active population in Belgium and the Netherlands, respectively, grew at an average annual rate of 0.5 percent and 1.2 percent during the period from 1960 to 1968, and at a rate of 0.9 percent during the six years thereafter. OECD (1986).
14. De Neubourg (1992: 215).
15. See, e.g., Driehuis (1986: 310–11).
16. Tollet (1987) and Hartog and Theeuwes (1993).
17. Lindbeck (1992).
18. Hartog and Theeuwes (1993: 86). Note that in their theoretical review of the relationship between unemployment and job vacancies, Blanchard and Diamond (1989) attribute most of the changes in that relationship to structural shifts in the economy, and not to minor frictional adjustments in the functioning of the job market.
19. The highly controversial Den Hartog and Tjan model is an application of earlier Solow growth models to the Dutch situation. See den Hartog and Tjan (1974).
20. While this argument stands to reason, it does not tend itself to precise mathematical estimation. Ilzkovitz (1985: 528–30).
21. Edelman and Fleming (1965: 260).
22. Malinvaud (1980).
23. Bean (1989).
24. More correctly, it requires a change in real unit labor costs relative to the real cost of capital.
25. One of the major assumptions of the vintage models used to diagnose the existence of structural unemployment is that the amount of labor

# Notes

required to use any specific piece of machinery is relatively fixed. Looking at the unemployment data for Belgium and the Netherlands, this assumption appears to have been a fairly close approximation of reality. Den Hartog and Tjan (1976).
26. OECD (1986).
27. Peters (1978). This essay is included in a collection debating the merits of the Den Hartog–Tjan model as adopted by the Central Planning Bureau in the VINTAF series of econometric planning models. The essays were originally printed the Dutch economics weekly, *Economisch Statististische Berichten*. My thanks to Professor Richard Griffiths for pointing out the importance of this debate. There is, however, a side of the debate over the Den Hartog–Tjan analysis which is not included in the volume, and which arose among the ranks of the Dutch labor movement. See de Klerke et al. (1975*a*, 1975*b*, 1977). The first two articles are published with commentaries by Den Hartog and Tjan.
28. Driehuis (1990: 341). For Belgium, see LeRoy (1981) and van Ypersele (1981).
29. European Commission (1993*a*: Table 31).
30. The German authorities revalued by 3 percent on March 19, 1973, and by 5.5 percent on June 29, 1973. The Dutch authorities followed with a 5 percent revaluation on September 17. The Belgians refused to alter their exchange rate. Banque National de Belgique (1974: ix).
31. Constant 1982 dollars. See Olson (1988: 50).
32. Black (1985: 5–6).
33. European Commission (1993*a*: Table 47).
34. The condition for relying on the mid-cycle inflation-adjusted balance as an indicator for economic performance is that economic actors incorporate wealth effects in their consumption patterns: a decline in real (inflation-adjusted) wealth should result in an increase in savings out of current income. Price and Muller (1984).
35. See Wellink (1987) and Quaden (1984).
36. European Commission (1993*a*: Table 29).
37. Van der Laan (1977: 1106–7) and Kervijn (1981: 83).
38. See, e.g., Söderström (1986).
39. Vandeputte (1985: 163–5).
40. Hallerberg (2004).
41. Ellman (1977) and Wellink (1987).

# Notes

42. Data from OECD (1986: Tables 1.13, 2.15, and 6.3).
43. Therborn (1986: 23, 31, 32).
44. Kurzer (1988, 1993).
45. For Belgium, see Covell (1988), Deschouwer (1989), and Rudd (1986). For the Netherlands, see de Jong and Pijnenberg (1986), Tromp (1989), and Wolinetz (1988).
46. Inglehart (1990: ch. 8) and Wolinetz (1989: 86–7).
47. The institutionalization of trade unions was particularly pronounced in Belgium, where the purely public institutions of the welfare state never assumed control over the disbursement of benefits. Indeed, the difference in institutional roles explains why value change resulted in different patterns of depillarization in Belgium and the Netherlands. While Dutch depillarization signaled a straightforward decline in the ideological salience of social cleavages, in Belgium the "erosion of the original philosophical-ethical identity" of the different pillars was compensated for by an expansion of their institutional reach. See Huyse (1984).
48. Bundervoet (1983).
49. Bundervoet (1983) and Wolinetz (1989).
50. As one observer of the Dutch situation noted: "The period after the Den Uyl cabinet appeared for the social democrats to be marked by the lack of a plan (*planloosheid*) as well as the lack of power (*machtloosheid*)." Lehning (1984: 80).
51. Kervijn (1981: 94) attributes the definition of the art of politics as "making possible tomorrow what is impossible today" to Jean Monnet. The remainder of the sentence is a paraphrase of Kervyn's own warning to Belgian politicians at the start of the 1980s. As a contemporary observer, Kervijn placed emphasis on the normative content of his analysis. My paraphrase is to regard it as objectively accurate as well.
52. Wellink (1987).
53. Delpéréere (1983).

## Chapter 4

1. This argument is a variation of the claim made in the context of welfare state reform by Green-Pedersen (2002).

# Notes

2. Keynes (1964: 383).
3. To put this back into the framework expounded by Peter Katzenstein (2003), the role of politicians is not only to explain the vulnerability of small states but also to learn what is best to do about it. See also Blyth (2002).
4. Scholten (1987) and Smits (1983).
5. See, e.g., Akkermans and Nobelen (1983) and Geul et al. (1985).
6. See also Van Zanden (1998: 173).
7. Katzenstein (2003: 15).
8. The share of respondents claiming to be satisfied or fairly satisfied with the functioning of democracy in their country was down to 35 percent in Belgium in Autumn 1981 and 50 percent in the Netherlands in Autumn 1982. Data source: European Commission.
9. Mommen (1987: 28–32).
10. De Ridder (1986: 26–71).
11. De Ridder (1986: 75–108).
12. De Ridder (1986: 124–31).
13. The ACW economic working group was chaired by the head of labor-movement finances, Hubert Detremmerie, and is often referred to as the Detremmerie Group.
14. De Ridder (1991*b*: 129–30). The acronym JET stands for *Jeugd, Ekonomie, Toekomst*—or Youth, Economy, Future.
15. Consider the statement made by Mark Eyskens: "Above all not only the coalition had to be changed, but also the method for governing had to be altered. If I had not made the unfortunate six months in office, it is likely that the next government would not have been in a position to receive the necessary special powers from parliament." De Ridder (1986: 108–9).
16. Martens (1985: 117) admits to this trade-off in a somewhat elliptical passage recorded in his own oral history of the period.
17. De Ridder (1991*b*: 131–8). See also Nothomb (1987: 254).
18. De Ridder (1991*b*: 140–6).
19. Smits (1983: 206–7).
20. Brepoels (1988: 195) and Smits (1983: 197).
21. See also Dewachter (1986: 354).
22. De Jong and Pijnenberg (1986: 167).
23. De Jong and Pijnenberg (1986).
24. Tromp (1989: 92–6).

25. The *informateuren* of the 1981 cabinet had hoped to avoid this conflict by keeping both Van Agt and Den Uyl out of the cabinet; however, they were unsuccessful. See Joustra and van Venetië (1991: 194).
26. Scholten (1987: 144).
27. This personal understanding of Lubbers is derived from the many interviews done by Joustra and van Venetië (1991). For a description of Lubbers' leanings to the left, see the interview with Wil Albeda, pp. 169–84; and for a description of Lubbers' management style, see the interview with Hans Margés, pp. 199–212.
28. Timmermans and Bakkema (1989: 187). The authors conclude (p. 190) that during the "no-nonsense Lubbers cabinet" there was less party-political conflict, and more policymaking by way of compromise. See also Timmermans (2003: 109).
29. De Jong and Pijnenberg (1986: 160).
30. Tromp (1989: 96).
31. Wolinetz (1988: 144–5).
32. Scholten (1987: 144).
33. Lubbers (1997).
34. Visser and Hemerijck (1997: 97).
35. Joustra and van Venetië (1991: 206, 230–1).
36. For a more detailed treatment of the adjustment measures adopted by Martens and Lubbers, see Smits (1983, 1984) and Ellman (1986). See also Visser and Hemerijck (1997) and Hemerijck, Unger, and Visser (2000).
37. Data source: European Commission.
38. Quaden (1987: 145).
39. Data from the European Commission.
40. Data from the European Commission.
41. The calculation of real exchange rates using alternate price indexes distinguishes between the effects of changes in the nominal exchange rate and the effects of changes in the relative prices of goods and labor. Because of the way real exchange rates are calculated, a change in the nominal exchange rate will have the same impact on both real exchange rates, while a change in the relative price of goods versus labor will widen or narrow the gap between the two real exchange rates. For example, the large depreciation witnessed for Belgium in 1982 corresponds with the 8.5 percent devaluation of the Belgian frank within the European monetary system. Thereafter,

### Notes

depreciations in the real exchange rate reflect the decline in Belgian wage costs relative to Germany.
42. OECD (1989a: 14), OECD (1989b: 11), Durez and Escarmelle (1987: 271–4), and Kana and Klene (1987: 221–2).
43. Green-Pedersen (2002).
44. De Neubourg (1992: 219).
45. De Ridder (1991b: 145–63).
46. De Ridder (1991a).
47. Van den Brande (1987: 115).
48. Of course such enabling legislation not only shielded the unions but also silenced the opposition. See Hemerijck, Unger, and Visser (2000: 237).
49. Nypels and Tamboer (1985: 113–30).
50. Wolinetz (1989: 92–3).
51. Wolinetz (1989: 95).
52. Graafland (1992: 596–8).
53. The Netherlands is an outliner in the study by Calmfors and Driffill (1988).
54. Van Waarden (2002: 54), Visser and Hemerijck (1997), Andeweg and Irwin (2002: 144–8).
55. Centraal Planbureau (1983: 71).
56. Here it may be useful to recall that the original snake agreement purported to limit the variability of European currencies in their pegs on the dollar. Hence the agreement that no two European currencies would deviate by more than 2.25 percent became the snake, while the requirement that no country's dollar exchange rate vary by more than 2.25 percent represented the tunnel.
57. This asymmetry derived from the obvious difference between a strong currency country gaining foreign exchange reserves, and a weak currency country losing foreign exchange reserves: the weak currency country would be forced to intervene in the currency markets before the strong currency country.
58. The definitive account of the EMS negotiations is Ludlow (1982).
59. See, e.g., Woolley (1992).
60. In the words of Wolfgang Rieke (1988: 289): "The EMS discipline helped certain partner countries in the task (of disinflation), but it was not the prime force causing them to pursue anti-inflationary adjustment."

61. Of course, this argument holds all other variables constant. In fact, maintaining the parity between the Belgian frank and the Deutschemark was complicated by excessive levels of Belgian public debt—particularly foreign debt, which required servicing from current account revenues. Thus the remarkable stability of the frank–mark exchange rate is even more surprising than simple data inflation convergence would suggest.
62. See Gros and Thygesen (1992: ch. 3).
63. Gros and Thygesen (1992: 73–7). The Belgian 1982 devaluation is an oft-told story for students of the EMS. However, two factors that are often left out are the importance of the IMF to Belgian policymakers, and the conflict between the Liberals, who wanted a deep devaluation, and the Christian-Democratic labor movement economists, who wanted only a limited devaluation. Regarding the first point, it was the IMF that—in October 1981—cautioned Belgium about the need to implement austerity measures or face a devaluation of more than 14 percent. So when Martens sought approval for his February 1982 devaluation, he went first to the IMF and not to the ECOFIN Council of the EC. Regarding the second point, the economists from the Christian-Democratic labor movement originally wanted to devalue the frank by only 10–11 percent—thereby protecting the purchasing power of labor income. Liberal Finance Minister Willy De Clercq, who had been an outspoken proponent of the strong frank in the Tindemans government, either wanted no devaluation at all or a deeper devaluation that would not have to be repeated. De Clercq won in the struggle and insisted on a devaluation of 12 percent. Thus the German decision to limit Belgium's devaluation to 8.5 percent sided then with the Christian-Democratic labor movement and against the Liberals and the IMF. See de Ridder (1986) and Martens (1985).
64. Toirkins (1989: 128). See also Brakman et al. (1991). For those who argue that the EMS unambiguously strengthened Central Bank independence, this rare example of ministerial oversight represents an important anomaly to be explained. See Kurzer (1993: 160–3, 220–6). However, this assertion is not meant to overemphasize the role of the EMS in Kurzer's general argument about economic policymaking in Belgium and the Netherlands. As she pointed out in an earlier paper, "the degree of government control over central bank policy still made

# Notes

some difference after 1982, regardless of membership in the EMS." Kurzer (1988: 29).
65. See, e.g., Rose (1999).
66. Visser and Hemerijck (1997).
67. These trend results are unique among the countries surveyed by Eurobarometer during the 1980s.
68. Smits (1986: 457–68) and Visser and Wijnhoven (1990: 87–90).
69. De Ridder (1991*b*: 167) and Gladdish (1991: 67–8).
70. Brepoels (1988: 199–200) and Wolinetz (1990).
71. Van Waarden (2002: 62).
72. Delsen (2002: 69–70).
73. OECD (1997: 54–5).
74. Hemerijck, Unger, and Visser (2000: 240–1).
75. Jones (1999).
76. Salverda (2005).
77. Gijsels (1992) and Vaes and Demelenne (1995).
78. Bouveroux (1992).
79. See Van Hecke (1994). After resigning as chair of the Flemish Christian Democrats, Van Hecke later defected to the VLD. See De Gucht and Van Hecke (2001).
80. Deschouwer (2002).
81. Huyse (1994).
82. Koole and Daalder (2002: 34).

## Conclusion

1. See, e.g., Delsen (2002), Hendriks (2001), and the foreword to Bouveroux (2003).
2. I should clarify what I mean by "adjustment strategy." My claim is not that the Lubbers and Martens governments of the early 1980s mapped out a precise blueprint for the development of their countries over the decades to follow. On the contrary, I agree with writers like Anton Hemerijck (2001) that the policy process is marked by continuous innovation. Nevertheless, I maintain that Lubbers and Martens played a vital role in breaking the deadlock of the 1970s. This puts me at odds with writers like Jaap Woldendorp (2005), who challenge the notion that the agreement reached at Wassenaar in 1982 was a watershed. On the basis of my analysis in Chapter 4, I believe it

# Notes

is fair to claim that Martens and Lubbers started a process of wage moderation that was accepted either explicitly or implicitly by wage negotiators and particularly by trade unions. And they focused the attentions of macroeconomic policymakers on how to use the opportunities available in the European Community and now European Union. These two prime ministers did not invent the small country adjustment strategy, but they did reinitiate it.
3. SER (1997).
4. Jones (1998*b*: 168).
5. Jones (1998*a*: 48–50).
6. Dehaene (1995).
7. Jones (2003).
8. Jones (1998*a*, 1998*b*).
9. Dehaene (1995: 101–4).
10. See, e.g., Pellikaan et al. (2003, 2007) and De Winter et al. (2006).
11. De Winter et al. (2006) and Deschouwer (2006).
12. Van der Brug (2003, 2004).
13. Jones (2002).
14. See, e.g., the chapter on Social Democracy in Marijnissen (2006).
15. A similar point is made about Norway by Moses (2000).
16. Strange (1997) and Moses (2006).
17. Jones (2007).

# References

Abert, J. G. (1969). *Economic Policy and Planning in the Netherlands: 1950–1960*. New Haven: Yale University Press.

Akkermans, T. and P. W. M. Nobelen, eds. (1983). *Corporatisme en Verzorgingsstaat*. Antwerp: Stenfert Kreuse.

Alesina, A. and E. Spolaore (2005). *The Size of Nations*. Cambridge, MA: MIT Press.

Andeweg, R. B. and G. Irwin (2002). *Governance and Politics of the Netherlands*. London: Palgrave.

Aron, R. and D. Lerner, eds. (1956). *La Querelle de al C.E.D*. Paris: Librarie Armond Colin.

Bakker, A. and M. M. P. van Lent (1989). *Pieter Lieftinck 1902–1989: Een Leven in Vogelvlucht*. Utrecht: Veen uitgevers.

Banque National de Belgique (1949). *Rapport Annuel: 1948*. Brussels: BNB.

—— (1973). *Rapports 1972*. Brussels: BNB.

—— (1974). *Rapports 1973*. Brussels: BNB.

Bean, C. (1989). 'Capital Shortage.' *Economic Policy: A European Forum* 8, pp. 11–53.

Bernhard, W. and J. Granato (1991). 'The Delegation of Economic Policy and Sustainable Economic Growth.' *Papers in International Political Economy* 144. Chapel Hill: Duke University Programme in Political Economy.

Black, S. W. (1985). 'Learning from Adversity: Policy Responses to Two Oil Shocks.' *Essays in International Finance* No. 196. Princeton: Princeton University Press.

Blanchard, O. J. and P. Diamond (1989). 'The Beveridge Curve.' *Brookings Papers on Economic Activity* 1, pp. 1–76.

—— and L. H. Summers (1987). 'Hysteresis in Unemployment.' *European Economic Review* 31:1/2, pp. 288–95.

# References

Blyth, M. (2002). *Great Transformations: Economic Ideas and Institutional Change in the Twentieth Century.* Cambridge: Cambridge University Press.

Boone, C. and P. Willeme (1989). 'Politieke samenstelling van regering en functionele inkomstverdeling in België.' *Cahiers économiques de Bruxelles*, pp. 45–67.

Bosmans, J. (1988*a*). 'Het maatschappelijk-politieke leven in Nederland: 1945–1980.' In J. C. Boogman et al., eds. *Geschiedenis van het Moderne Nederland: Politieke, Economische en Sociale Ontwikkelingen.* The Hague: De Haan, pp. 562–608.

—— (1988*b*). 'Drees en Romme.' In H. Daalder and N. Cramer, eds. *Willem Drees.* Houten: Unieboek, pp. 95–108.

Bouveroux, J. (1992). *De Partij van de Burger: De Verruiming van de Vlaamse Liberalen.* Antwerp: Standaard Uitgenerij.

—— (2003). *Van Zwarte Zondag tot Paars Groen.* Antwerp: Houtekiet.

Bowler, S. (1987). 'Corporatism and the "Privileged Position" of Business.' *West European Politics* 10:2, pp. 157–75.

Brakman, S., J. de Haan, and C. J. Jepma (1991). 'Is de gulden hard genoeg?' *Economisch Statistische Berichten*, pp. 16–20.

Brepoels, J. (1988). *Wat zoudt gij zonder 't werkvolk zijn: Anderhalve eeuw arbeiders-strijd in België.* Leuven: Kritak.

Brewin, C. (1987). 'The European Community: A Union of States without a Unity of Government.' *Journal of Common Market Studies* 26:1, pp. 1–23.

Brinkman, M. (1988). 'Drees en de Partij van de Arbeid.' In H. Daalder and N. Cramer, eds. *Willem Drees.* Houten: Unieboek, pp. 57–94.

Brugmans, H. (no date). *De Europese Idee en haar verwerkelijking.* Kampen: Uitgeverij J.H. Kok.

—— (1965). *L'idée Européenne: 1918–1965.* Bruges: Tempelhof.

—— (1988). *Wij, Europa: Een halve eeuw strijd voor emancipatie en Europees federalisme.* Transcribed by Hanna Kirsten. Leuven: Kritak.

Budd, A., P. Levine, and P. Smith (1987). 'Long-term Unemployment and the Shifting U-V Curve: A Multi-country Study.' *European Economic Review* 31:1/2, pp. 296–305.

Bulmer, S. (1985). 'The European Council's First Decade: Between Interdependence and Domestic Politics.' *Journal of Common Market Studies* 24:2, pp. 89–104.

# References

Bundervoet, J. (1983). 'Vakbond en politiek in crisistijd.' *Res Publica* 25:2–3, pp. 219–36.

Cafruny, A. W. and M. Ryner, eds. (2003). *A Ruined Fortress? Neoliberal Hegemony and Transformation in Europe.* Lanham: Rowman and Littlefield.

Calleo, D. P. (1965). *Europe's Future: The Grand Alternatives.* New York: Norton.

——(2001). *Rethinking Europe's Future.* Princeton: Princeton University Press.

Calmfors, L. and J. Driffill (1988). 'Centralization of Wage Bargaining.' *Economic Policy: A European Forum* 6, pp. 13–47.

Cameron, D. (1978). 'The Expansion of the Public Economy: A Comparative Analysis.' *American Political Science Review* 72:4, pp. 1243–61.

Capron, H. (1986). 'Préférences idéologiques, contrainte électorale et résultats macroéconomiques.' *Cahiers économiques de Bruxelles*, pp. 51–84.

Cawson, A. (1978). 'Pluralism, Corporatism and the Role of the State.' *Government and Opposition* 13:2, pp. 178–98.

——(1985). 'Introduction—Varieties of Corporatism: The Importance of the Meso-level of Interest Intermediation.' In A. Cawson, ed. *Organized Interests and the State: Studies in Meso-corporatism.* London: Sage, pp. 1–22.

Centraal Planbureau (1983). *Centraal Economisch Plan 1983.* 's Gravenhage: Staatsuitgeverij (May).

CEPR (1992). 'Is Bigger Better?: The Economics of EC Enlargement.' *Monitoring European Integration 3: A CEPR Annual Report.* London: Centre for Economic Policy Research.

Chamberlain, N. W. and J. W. Kuhn (1969). 'The Politics of Management.' In A. Flanders, ed. *Collective Bargaining: Selected Readings.* Middlesex: Penguin Books, pp. 369–89.

Chaput, G. and R. de Falleur (1961*a*). 'La production et l'investissement des régions flamande wallone et bruxelloise.' *Cahiers économiques de Bruxelles* 10, pp. 179–208.

————(1961*b*). 'La production et l'investissement des régions flamande, wallone et bruxelloise.' *Cahiers économiques de Bruxelles* 11, pp. 373–91.

Claeys, P. H. (1973). *Groupes de pression en Belgique.* Brussels: Editions du CRISP.

## References

Corden, W. M. (1986). *Inflation, Exchange Rates and the World Economy: Lectures in International Monetary Economics*, Third Edition. Chicago: University of Chicago Press.

Covell, M. (1988). 'Stability and Change in the Belgian Party System.' In S. B. Wolinetz, ed. *Systems in Liberal Democracies*. London: Routledge, pp. 105–29.

Cox, R. H. (1990). 'Alternative Patterns of Welfare State Development: The Case of Public Assistance in the Netherlands.' *West European Politics* 13:4, pp. 85–102.

Daalder, H. (1966). 'The Netherlands: Opposition in a Segmented Society.' In R. A. Dahl, ed. *Political Oppositions in Western Democracies*. New Haven: Yale University Press, pp. 188–236.

Dahrendorf, R. (1994). 'Ein Europa für die Zukunft.' *Der Spiegel* (January) pp. 28–9.

Davenport, M. (1982). 'The Economic Impact of the EEC.' In A. Boltho, ed. *The European Economy: Growth and Crisis*. Oxford: Oxford University Press, pp. 225–58.

De Clerq, W. (1978). 'Le franc belge, monnaie forte.' Speech given before the Belgo-German association, 19 April.

De Grauwe, P. (1985). 'The Growth of the Public Sector in Belgium under Centre-Right and Centre-Left Governments.' *International Economics: Research Paper* 49. Leuven: Katholieke Universiteit Leuven.

De Gucht, K. and J. van Hecke (2001). *Het einde der pilaren: Een Toscaans gesprek (opgetekend door Dirk Achten en Yves Desmet)*. Antwerp: Houtekiet.

De Jong, J. J. P. (1988). *Diplomatie of strijd: Het Nederlands beleid tijdens de Indonesische revolutie 1945–1947*. Amsterdam: Boom Meppel.

—— and B. Pijnenberg (1986). 'The Dutch Christian Democratic Party and Coalitional Behaviour in the Netherlands: A Pivotal Party in the Face of Depillarization.' In G. Pridham, ed. *Coalitional Behaviour in Theory and Practice*. Cambridge: Cambridge University Press, pp. 145–70.

De Klerke, R. A., H. B. M. van der Laan, and K. G. T. Thio (1975a). 'Het CPB en de ontwikkeling van de werkgelegenheid.' *Economisch Statistische Berichten* 60: 3002, pp. 480–4.

—————— (1975b). 'Het CPB en de ontwikkeling van de werkgelegenheid (II).' *Economisch Statistische Berichten* 60:3009, pp. 664–6.

# References

De Klerke, R. A., H. B. M. van der Laan, and K. G. T. Thio (1977). 'Unemployment in the Netherlands: A Criticism of the de Hartog-Tjan Model.' *Cambridge Journal of Economics* 1:3, pp. 291–306.

De Neubourg, C. (1992). 'Arbeidsmarktontwikkelingen in België en Nederland vanuit een internationaal perspectief.' *Maandschrift Economie* 65:3, pp. 209–26.

De Ridder, H. (1986). *Geen winnaars in de Wetstraat*. Leuven: Davidsfonds.

—— (1991*a*). 'De Vier van Poupehan.' *Knack* 21:12, pp. 10–13.

—— (1991*b*). *Omtrent Wilfried Martens*. Tielt: Lannoo.

De Strycker, C. (1977). 'Die belgische Geld- und Währungspolitik.' *Zeitschrift für das gesamte Kreditwesen* 30:23, pp. 1157–61.

De Winter, L., M. Swyngedow, and P. Dumont (2006). 'Party System(s) and Electoral Behavior in Belgium: From Stability to Balkanisation.' *West European Politics* 29:5, pp. 93–6.

De Wolff, P. and W. Driehuis (1980). 'A Description of Post War Economic Developments and Economic Policy in the Netherlands.' In R. T. Griffiths, ed. *The Economy and Politics of the Netherlands since 1945*. The Hague: Martinus Nijhoff.Griffiths, pp. 13–60.

Dehaene, J.-L. (1995). *Sleutels voor morgen*. Hasselt: Esopus.

Deleeck, H. (1992). *De architectuur van de welvaartsstaat*. Leuven: Acco.

Delpéreere, F. (1983). *Chroniques de crise: 1977–1982*. Brussels: CRISP.

Delruelle, N., R. Evalenko, and W. Fraeys (1970). *Le comportement politique des électeurs belges: Enquête de sociologie électorale, La Rupture de 1965, Ses prolongements en 1968*. Brussels: Editions de l'Institut de Sociologie, ULB.

Delsen, L. (2002). *Exit Polder Model? Socioeconomic Change in the Netherlands*. London: Praeger.

—— and E. de Jong, eds. (1998). *The German and Dutch Economies: Who Follows Whom?* Heidelberg: Physica-Verlag.

Den Dunnen, E. (1973). 'Monetary Policy in the Netherlands.' In K. Holbik, ed. *Monetary Policy in Twelve Industrial Countries*. Boston: Federal Reserve Bank of Boston, pp. 282–328.

—— (1979). 'Postwar Monetary Policy.' *De Economist* 127:1, pp. 21–57.

Den Hartog, H. and H. S. Tjan (1974). 'Investeringen, lonen, prijzen en arbeidsplaatsen: Een jaargangenmodel met vaste coëfficiënten voor Nederland.' *Occasional Papers, 2*. The Hague: Centraal Planbureau.

—— —— (1976). 'Investments, Wages, Prices and the Demand for Labour: A Clay-Clay Vintage Model for the Netherlands.' *De Economist* 124:1/2, pp. 32–54.

Deschouwer, K. (1989). 'Patterns of Participation and Competition in Belgium.' *West European Politics* 12:4, pp. 28–41.
—— (2002). 'Falling Apart Together: The Changing Nature of Belgian Consociationalism.' *Acta Politica* 37, pp. 68–85.
—— (2006). 'And the Peace Goes On? Consociational Democracy and Belgian Politics in the Twenty-First Century.' *West European Politics* 29:5, pp. 895–911.
Dewachter, W. (1986). 'Changes in a Particracy: The Belgian Party System from 1944 to 1986.' In H. Daalder, ed. *Party Systems in Denmark, Austria, Switzerland, the Netherlands and Belgium*. London: Francis Pinter, pp. 285–363.
Diebold, W., Jr. (1959). *The Schuman Plan: A Study in Economic Co-operation, 1950–1959*. New York: Frederick A. Praeger for the Council on Foreign Relations.
Drèze, J. H. (1987). 'Underemployment Equilibria: From Theory to Econometrics and Policy.' *European Economic Review* 31:1/2, pp. 9–34.
Driehuis, W. (1986). 'Unemployment in the Netherlands, 1960–1983.' In C. Bean et al., eds. *The Rise in Unemployment*. Oxford: Basil Blackwell, pp. 297–312.
—— (1990). 'A Disequilibrium Analysis of the Dutch Economy.' In J. H. Drèze and C. R. Bean, eds. *Europe's Unemployment Problem*. Cambridge, MA: MIT Press, pp. 329–65.
Durant, G. (1983). *Gaston Eyskens: Minister van Staat*. Zele: Reinaert Uitgeverij.
Durez, M. and J. F. Escarmelle (1987). 'L'investissement.' In G. Quaden, ed. *L'économie belge dans la crise*. Brussels: Editions LABOUR, pp. 239–76.
Duynstee, F. J. F. M. (1966). *De kabinetformaties 1946–1965*. Deventer: Kluwer.
Edelman, M. and R. W. Fleming (1965). *The Politics of Price-Wage Decisions: A Four-country Analysis*. Urbana: University of Illinois Press.
Eizenga, W. (1983). 'The Independence of the Federal Reserve System and of the Netherlands Bank: A Comparative Analysis.' *SUERF Series 41a*. Tilburg: Société Universitaire Européenne de Recherches Financières.
Ellman, M. (1977). 'Report from Holland: The Economics of North Sea Hydrocarbons.' *Cambridge Journal of Economics* 1:3, pp. 281–90.

# References

Ellman, M. (1986). 'Recent Dutch Macroeconomic Experience.' In J. Sargent, ed. *Foreign Macro-economic Experience: A Symposium*. Toronto: University of Toronto Press, pp. 57–69.

Esping-Andersen, G. (1999). *Social Foundations of Postindustrial Economies*. Oxford: Oxford University Press.

European Commission (1972). *Monetary Policy in the Countries of the European Economic Community: Institutions and Instruments*. Luxembourg: European Community.

——(1993a). *European Economy: Annual Economic Report for 1993*. Luxembourg: European Community.

——(1993b). *Growth, Competitiveness, Employment: The Challenges and Ways Forward into the 21st Century (White Paper)*. Luxembourg: European Community, three volumes.

Eyskens, G. (1993). *De Memoires*. Collected and edited by Jozef Smits. Tielt: Lannoo.

Fase, M. M. G. (1987). 'Dutch Monetarism in Retrospect.' *Reprint 228*. Amsterdam: De Nederlandsche Bank.

——(1992). 'A Century of Monetary Thought in the Netherlands.' *Reprint 321*. Amsterdam: De Nederlandsche Bank.

Faxén, K.-O. (1982). 'Incomes Policy and Centralised Wage Formation.' In A. Boltho, ed. *The European Economy: Growth and Crisis*. Oxford: Oxford University Press, pp. 365–89.

*Federalist Papers* (1961). New York: New American Library.

Fischer, A. (1980). *L'industrialization contemporaine des Pays Bas*. Paris: Publications de la Sorbonne.

Flanagan, R. J. et al. (1983). *Unionism, Economic Stabilization and Incomes Policies: European Experience*. Washington, DC: Brookings Institution.

Franck, C. (1983). 'Belgium: Committed Multilateralism.' In C. Hill, ed. *National Foreign Policies and European Political Co-operation*. London: George Allen and Unwin for RIIA, pp. 85–105.

Galbraith, J. K. (1992). *The Culture of Contentment*. Boston: Houghton-Mifflin.

Garrett, G. (1998). *Partisan Politics in the Global Economy*. Cambridge: Cambridge University Press.

Geul, A., P. W. M. Nobelen, and H. Slomp (1985). 'De komende vijf jaar: Overlegeconomie of interventiestaat?' *Social Maandblad Arbeid* 40:7/8, pp. 506–19.

# References

Giersch, H. (1987). 'Economic Policies in the Age of Schumpeter.' *European Economic Review* 31:1/2, pp. 35–52.

Gijsels, H. (1992). *Het Vlaams Blok*. Leuven: Uitgeverij Kritak.

Gladdish, K. (1991). *Governing from the Center: Politics and Policy-Making in the Netherlands*. DeKalb: Northern Illinois University Press.

Gourevitch, P. (1986). *Politics in Hard Times: Comparative Responses to Economic Crises*. Ithaca: Cornell University Press.

Graafland, J. J. (1992). 'Insiders and Outsiders in Wage Formation: The Dutch Case.' *Empirical Economics* 17:4, pp. 583–602.

Grant, W. (1985). 'Introduction.' In W. Grant, ed. *The Political Economy of Corporatism*. London: MacMillan Publishers, pp. 1–31.

Green-Pedersen, C. (2002). *The Politics of Justification: Party Competition and Welfare State Retrenchment in Denmark and the Netherlands from 1982 to 1998*. Amsterdam: Amsterdam University Press.

Griffiths, R. T. (1980a). 'The Netherlands and the EEC.' In R. T. Griffiths, ed. *The Economy and Politics of the Netherlands since 1945*. The Hague: Martinus Nijhoff, pp. 277–301.

—— (1980b). 'The Netherlands Central Planning Bureau.' In R. T. Griffiths, ed. *The Economy and Politics of the Netherlands since 1945*. The Hague: Martinus Nijhoff, pp. 135–61.

—— (1991). 'De economische achtergronden van de Europese integratie 1945–1957.' In W. A. F. Camphuis and C. G. J. Wildeboer Schut, eds. *Europese eenwording in historisch perspectief*. Zaltbommel: Europese Bibliotheek, pp. 206–22.

—— and A. S. Milward (1986). 'The Beyen Plan and the European Political Community.' In W. Maihofer, ed. *Noi si mura: Selected Working Papers of the European University Institute*. Florence: European University Institute, pp. 595–621.

Gros, D. and N. Thygesen (1992). *European Monetary Integration: From the European Monetary System to European Monetary Union*. London: Longmans.

Guillen, P. (1986). 'Le projet d'union économique entre la France, L'Italie et le Benelux.' In R. Poideven, ed. *Histoire des débuts de la construction européenne*. Brussels: Bruylant, pp. 143–64.

Haas, E. B. (1968). *The Uniting of Europe: Political, Social and Economic Forces, 1950–1957*. Stanford: Stanford University Press.

Hall, P. A. (1986). *Governing the Economy: The Politics of State Intervention in Britain and France*. New York: Oxford University Press.

# References

Hall, P. A., ed. (1989). *The Power of Economic Ideas: Keynesianism Across Nations*. Princeton: Princeton University Press.

—— and D. Soskice, eds. (2001). *Varieties of Capitalism: The Institutional Foundations of Comparative Advantage*. Oxford: Oxford University Press.

Hallerberg, M. (2004). *Domestic Budgets in a United Europe: Fiscal Governance from the End of the Bretton Woods System to EMU*. Ithaca: Cornell University Press.

Hartog, J. and J. Theeuwes (1993). 'Postwar Unemployment in the Netherlands.' *European Journal of Political Economy* 9:1, pp. 73–112.

Heinen, A. (1990). 'Die Europa-Diskussion in den Niederlande.' In W. Loth, ed. *Die Anfänge der europäischen Integration 1945–1950*. Bonn: Europa Union Verlag, pp. 87–102.

Henderson, D. (1992). 'International Economic Integration: Progress, Prospects and Implications.' *International Affairs* 68:4, pp. 633–53.

Hendriks, F. (2001). 'Polder Politics in the Netherlands: The "Viscous" State Revisited.' In F. Hendriks and T. A. J. Toonen, eds. *Polder Politics: The Re-invention of Consensus Democracy in the Netherlands*. Aldershot: Ashgate, pp. 21–35.

—— and T. A. J. Toonen, eds. (2001). *Polder Politics: The Re-invention of Consensus Democracy in the Netherlands*. Aldershot: Ashgate.

Herin, J. (1986). 'Rules of Origin and Differences Between Tariff Levels in EFTA and in the EC.' *EFTA Occasional Paper, 13*. Geneva: EFTA.

Hemerijck, A. (2001). 'The Dutch Negotiating Economy: Learning Through Concertation.' In F. Hendriks and T. A. J. Toonen, eds. *Polder Politics: The Re-invention of Consensus Democracy in the Netherlands*. Aldershot: Ashgate, pp. 95–113.

—— B. Unger, and J. Visser (2000). 'How Small Countries Negotiate Change: Twenty-Five Years of Adjustment Policy in Austria, the Netherlands, and Belgium.' In F. W. Scharpf and V. A. Schmidt, eds. *Welfare and Work in the Open Economy, Volume II: Diverse Responses to Common Challenges*. Oxford: Oxford University Press, pp. 163–75.

Hinsley, F. H. (1986). *Sovereignty*, Second Edition. London: Cambridge University Press.

Hoffmann, S. (1968). '"Obstinate or Obsolete?": The Fate of the Nation-State and the Case of Western Europe.' In S. Hoffmann, ed. *Conditions of World Order*. Boston: Houghton Mifflin, pp. 110–63.

—— (1982). 'Reflections on the Nation-State in Western Europe Today.' *Journal of Common Market Studies* 21:1/2, pp. 21–37.

## References

——(1989). 'The European Community and 1992.' *Foreign Affairs* 68:4, pp. 27–47.

Huggett, F. E. (1971). *The Modern Netherlands*. New York: Praeger.

Huyse, L. (1980). *De Gewapende vrede: De Belgische politiek na 1945*. Leuven: Kritak.

——(1984). 'Pillarization Reconsidered.' *Acta Politica* 19, pp. 145–58.

——(1994). *De Politiek voorbij: Een blijk op de jaren negentig*. Leuven: Uitgeverij Kritak.

Ilzkovitz, F. (1985). 'Les déterminants des investissements des entreprises en Belgique.' *Cahiers économiques de Bruxelles* 108, pp. 487–545.

Inglehart, R. (1971). 'The Silent Revolution in Europe: Intergenerational Change in Post-Industrial Societies.' *American Political Science Review* 65, pp. 991–1017.

——(1977). *The Silent Revolution: Changing Values and Political Styles among Western Publics*. Princeton: Princeton University Press.

——(1990). *Culture Shift in Advanced Industrial Society*. Princeton: Princeton University Press.

International Monetary Fund (1950). *International Finance Statistics* 3:2. Washington, DC: International Monetary Fund.

——(1989). *International Finance Statistics Yearbook, 1989*. Washington, DC: International Monetary Fund.

Irwin, G. and K. Dittrich (1984). 'And the Walls Came Tumbling Down: Party Dealignment in the Netherlands.' In R. J. Dalton, S. C. Flanagan, and P. A. Beck, eds. *Electoral Change in Advanced Industrial Democracies: Realignment of Dealignment?* Princeton: Princeton University Press, pp. 267–97.

Jones, E. (1998a). 'Belgium: Keeping Up with the Pack?' In E. Jones, J. Frieden, and F. Torres, eds. *Joining Europe's Monetary Club: The Challenges for Smaller Industrial States*. New York: St Martin's Press, pp. 43–59.

——(1998b). 'The Netherlands: Top of the Class.' In E. Jones, J. Frieden, and F. Torres, eds. *Joining Europe's Monetary Club: The Challenges for Smaller Industrial States*. New York: St. Martin's Press, pp. 149–70.

——(1999). 'Is Competitive Corporatism an Adequate Response to Globalization? Evidence from the Low Countries.' *West European Politics* 22:3, pp. 159–81.

——(2002). 'Politics Beyond Accommodation? The May 2002 Dutch Parliamentary Elections.' *Dutch Crossing* 26:1, pp. 61–78.

## References

Jones, E. (2003). 'Liberalized Capital Markets, State Autonomy, and European Monetary Union.' *European Journal of Political Research* 42:3, pp. 111–36.

——(2004). 'The Politics of Europe 2003: Differences and Disagreements.' *Industrial Relations Journal* 35:6, pp. 483–99.

——(2005). 'The Politics of Europe 2004: Solidarity and Integration.' *Industrial Relations Journal* 36:6, pp. 436–55.

——(2007). 'Populism in Europe.' *SAIS Review* 27:1, pp. 37–47.

Jonkapohja, S. (1988). 'Discussion.' *Economic Policy: A European Forum* 6, pp. 48–9.

Joustra, A. and E. van Venetië (1991). *Ruud Lubbers: Manager in de politiek*. Baarn: Sesam.

Joye, P. (1964). *Les trusts en Belgique: La concentration capitaliste*. Brussels: Société Populaire d'Edition.

Kana, I. and N. Klene (1987). 'Pays Bas: Risques de ralentissement conjuncturel, mais assainissement structurel.' *Chroniques d'actualité de la S.E.D.E.I.S.* 36:6, pp. 221–5.

Katzenstein, P. J., ed. (1978). *Between Power and Plenty: Foreign Economic Policies of Advanced Industrial States*. Madison: University of Wisconsin Press.

——(1984). *Corporatism and Change: Austria, Switzerland, and the Politics of Industry*. Ithaca: Cornell University Press.

——(1985). *Small States in World Markets: Industrial Policy in Europe*. Ithaca: Cornell University Press.

——ed. (1997). *Tamed Power: Germany in Europe*. Ithaca: Cornell University Press.

——(2003). '*Small States* and Small States Revisited.' *New Political Economy* 8:1, pp. 9–30.

Kennedy, E. (1991). *The Bundesbank: Germany's Central Bank in the International Monetary System*. London: Pinter Publishers for the RIIA.

Keohane, R. O. and S. Hoffmann, eds. (1991). *The New European Community: Decision-Making and Institutional Change*. Boulder: Westview.

Kervijn, A. (1981). 'La politique économique face à la crise.' *Recherches économiques de Louvain* 47:1.

Keynes, J. M. (1963). *Essays in Persuasion*. New York: Norton.

——(1964). *The General Theory of Employment, Interest, and Money*. New York: Harcourt, Brace, and World, Inc.

## References

Kindleberger, C. P. (1987). 'Belgium after World War II: An Experiment in Supply-Side Economics.' In A. Steinherr and D. Weiserbs, eds. *Employment and Growth: Issues for the 1980s*. Dordrecht: Martinus Nijhoff, pp. 167–84.

Kirchheimer, O. (1966). 'The Transformation of the Western European Party Systems.' In J. LaPalombara and M. Weiner, eds. *Political Parties and Political Development*. Princeton: Princeton University Press, pp. 177–200.

Kitschelt, H., P. Lange, G. Marks, J. D. Stephens, eds. (1999). *Continuity and Change in Contemporary Capitalism*. Cambridge: Cambridge University Press.

Klein, P. W. (1980). 'The Foundations of Dutch Prosperity.' In R. T. Griffiths, ed. *The Economy and Politics of the Netherlands since 1945*. The Hague: Martinus Nijhoff, pp. 1–12.

Koole, R. and H. Daalder (2002). 'The Consociational Democracy Model and the Netherlands: Ambivalent Allies?' *Acta Politica* 37, pp. 23–43.

Krugman, P. (1987). 'Slow Growth in Europe: Conceptual Issues.' In R. Z. Lawrence and C. L. Schultze, eds. *Barriers to European Growth: A Transatlantic View*. Washington, DC: Brookings Institution, pp. 48–75.

Kurzer, P. (1988). 'The Politics of Central Banks: Austerity and Unemployment in Europe.' *Journal of Public Policy* 8:1, pp. 21–48.

—— (1993). *Business and Banking: Political Change and Economic Integration in Western Europe*. Ithaca: Cornell University Press.

Lamers, L. (1983). 'The Reconstruction of Reality: The Adaptation of the Dutch Social Security System to the Changing Structure of Employment.' In L. Bekemans, ed. *Social Security and Employment*. Maastricht: European Centre for Work and Study, pp. 59–83.

Landauer, C. (1983). 'Corporate State Ideologies: Historical Roots and Philosophical Origins.' *Research Series, 54*. Berkeley: Institute of International Studies.

Lebegue, J. (1969). 'La politique économique belge de 1963 à 1967.' *Cahiers économiques de Bruxelles* 42, pp. 237–73.

Lecraw, D. J. (1984). 'Some Economic Effects of Standards.' *Applied Economics*, August, pp. 507–22.

Lehning, P. B. (1984). 'Socialisten tussen plan en macht.' In J. W. de Beus and J. A. A. van Doorn, eds. *De Interventiestaat:Tradities, ervaringen, reacties*. Amsterdam: Boom Meppel, pp. 52–87.

# References

LeRoy, R. (1981). 'Quelles stratégies d'emploi face á la crise?' *Recherches économiques de Louvain* 47:1, pp. 95–110.

Lijphart, A. (1968). 'Typologies of Democratic Systems.' *Comparative Political Studies* 1:1, pp. 3–44.

—— (1969). 'Consociational Democracy.' *World Politics* 21:2, pp. 207–25.

—— (1975). *The Politics of Accommodation: Pluralism and Democracy in the Netherlands*, Second Edition, Revised. Berkeley: University of California Press.

—— (1982). *Verzuiling, pacificatie en kentering in de nederlandse politiek*. Amsterdam: De Bussy.

—— (1984a). *Democracies: Patterns of Government in Twenty-One Countries*. New Haven: Yale University Press.

—— (1984b). 'The Politics of Accommodation: Reflections Fifteen Years Later.' *Acta Politica* 19, pp. 9–18.

Lindbeck, A. (1991). 'Microfoundations of Unemployment Theory.' *Labour* 5:2, pp. 3–23.

—— (1992). 'Macroeconomic Theory and the Labour Market.' *European Economic Review* 36:2/3, pp. 209–35.

—— and D. Snower (1987a). 'Efficiency Wages versus Insiders and Outsiders.' *European Economic Review* 31:1/2, pp. 407–16.

—— —— (1987b). 'Union Activity, Unemployment Persistence and Wage-Employment Ratchets.' *European Economic Review* 31:1/2, pp. 157–67.

Lindblom, C. E. (1977). *Politics and Markets: The World's Political Economic Systems*. New York: Basic Books.

Lippmann, W. (1961). In W. E. Leuchtenburg and B. Wisky, eds. *Drift and Mastery: An Attempt to Diagnose the Current Unrest*. Englewood Cliffs: Prentice Hall.

Lipset, S. M. (1963). *Political Man: The Social Bases of Politics*. New York: Anchor Books.

Lorwin, V. R. (1966). 'Belgium: Religion, Class, and Language in National Politics.' In R. A. Dahl, ed. *Political Oppositions in Western Democracies*. New Haven: Yale University Press, pp. 147–87.

Loth, W., ed. (1990). *Die Anfänge der europäischen Integration 1945–1950*. Bonn: Europa Union Verlag.

Louffir, R. and L. Reichlin (1993). 'Convergences nominale et réelle parmi les pays de la CE et de L'AELE.' *Observations et diagnostiques économiques* 43, pp. 69–92.

## References

Lubbers, R. (1997). 'Ruud Lubbers en de hete adem van een nooit voorgelezen regeringsverklaring.' *SER Bulletin* 12.

Ludlow, P. (1982). *The Making of the European Monetary System: A Case Study of the Politics of the European Community.* London: Butterworths Scientific.

—— (1992). 'Report on Maastricht: A Major Step Forward.' *International Economic Insights* 3:1, pp. 32–5.

Mabille, X. (1986). *Histoire de la politique belge: Facteurs et acteurs de changement.* Brussels: CRISP.

Mair, P. (1994). 'The Correlates of Consensus Democracy and the Puzzle of Dutch Politics.' *West European Politics* 17:4, pp. 97–123.

Malinvaud, E. (1980). *Profitability and Unemployment.* London: Cambridge University Press.

—— (1987). 'The Legacy of European Stagflation.' *European Economic Review* 31:1/2, pp. 53–65.

Manning, A. (1986). 'Les Pays-Bas face á l'Europe.' In R. Poideven, ed. *Histoire des débuts de la construction européenne.* Brussels: Bruylant, pp. 419–44.

Marijnissen, J. (2006). *Enough! A Socialist Bites Back.* Amsterdam: SP. <http://international.sp.nl/publications/>.

Maritain, J. (1951). *Man and the State.* Chicago: University of Chicago Press.

Marquez Mendez, A. J. (1986). 'The Contribution of the European Community to Economic Growth.' *Journal of Common Market Studies* 24:4, pp. 261–77.

Marsh, D. (1992). *The Bundesbank: The Bank that Controls Europe.* London: Mandarin.

Martens, W. (1985). *Een gegeven woord.* Tielt: Lannoo.

McCarthy, P. (1990). 'France Faces Reality: Rigueur and the Germans.' In D. P. Calleo and C. Morgenstern, eds. *Recasting Europe's Economies: National Strategies in the 1980s.* Lanham: University Press of America, pp. 25–78.

McCracken, P. et al. (1977). *Towards Full Employment and Price Stability: A Report to the OECD by a Group of Independent Experts.* Paris: OECD.

McNamara, K. R. (1998). *The Currency of Ideas: Monetary Politics in the European Union.* Ithaca: Cornell University Press.

# References

Meade, J. E., H. H. Liesner, and S. J. Wells (1962). *Case Studies in European Economic Union: The Mechanics of Integration*. Oxford: Oxford University Press.

Mehta, F. and H. Sneessens (1990). 'Belgian Unemployment: The Story of a Small Open Economy Caught in a Worldwide Recession.' In J. H. Drèze and C. R. Bean, eds. *Europe's Unemployment Problem*. Cambridge: MIT Press, pp. 120–55.

Messing, F. (1988). 'Het economische leven in Nederland: 1945–1980.' In J. C. Boogman et al., eds. *Geschiedenis van het moderne Nederland: Politieke, economische en sociale ontwikkelingen*. The Hague: De Haan, pp. 517–61.

Meynen, A. (1978). 'De grote werkstaking 1960–1961: Een inleidend overzicht van de ekonomische en socio-politieke achtergronden van de grote werkstaking 1960–1961.' *Belgisch tijdschrift voor nieuwste geschiedenis* 9:3/4, pp. 481–515.

——(1990). 'De economische en sociale politiek sinds de jaren 1950.' In E. Witte et al., eds. *Politieke geschiedenis van België: Van 1830 tot heden*. Brussels: VUB Press, pp. 279–324.

Michels, M. (1973). 'L'expérience recente du contrôle des entrées de capitaux dans plusieurs pays européennes.' *Cahiers économiques de Bruxelles* 60, pp. 491–521.

Middendorp, C. P. (1991). *Ideology in Dutch Politics: The Democratic System Reconsidered 1970–1985*. Maastricht: Van Gorcum.

Milward, A. S. (1992). *The European Rescue of the Nation-State*. London: Routledge.

Mommen, A. (1987). *Een tunnel zonder einde: Het neo-liberalisme van Martens V en VI*. Antwerp: M&I.

Moravcsik, A. (1991). 'Negotiating the Single European Act: National Interests and Conventional Statecraft in the European Community.' *International Organisation* 45:1, pp. 19–56.

Mosca, G. (1939). *The Ruling Class (Elementi di Scienza Politica)*. Translated by Hannah D. Kahn. Edited by Arthur Livingston. New York: McGraw-Hill.

Moses, J. W. (2000). *OPEN States in the Global Economy: The Political Economy of Small-State Macroeconomic Management*. New York: St Martin's Press.

——(2006). *International Migration: Globalization's Last Frontier*. London: Zed Books.

## References

Moss, B. H., ed. (2005). *Monetary Union in Crisis: The European Union as a Neo-Liberal Construct.* Basingstoke: Palgrave.

Mudde, C. (1999). 'The Single-Issue Party Thesis: Extreme Right Parties and the Immigration Issue.' *West European Politics* 22:3, pp. 182–97.

Newell, A. and J. S. V. Symons (1987). 'Corporatism, Laissez-faire and the Rise of Unemployment.' *European Economic Review* 31:3, pp. 567–601.

Nobelen, P. W. M. and T. Akkermans (1983). 'Kan corporatisme de verzorgingsstaat redden?' In T. Akkermans and P. W. M. Nobelen, eds. *Corporatisme en verzorgingsstaat.* Antwerp: Stenfert Kreuse, pp. 5–15.

Noël, E. (1989). 'The Single European Act.' *Government and Opposition* 24:1, pp. 3–14.

Nothomb, C.-F. (1987). *De waarheid mag gezegd worden.* Brussels: Elsevier.

Nypels, F. and K. Tamboer (1985). *Wim Kok: Vijftien jaar vakbeweging.* Raamgracht: Stichting FNV Pers.

OECD (1970). *Inflation: The Present Problem.* Paris: Organisation for Economic Co-operation and Development.

—— (1986). *Economic Outlook: Historical Statistics, 1960–1984.* Paris: Organisation for Economic Co-operation and Development.

—— (1989a). *Economic Surveys: Belgium-Luxembourg 1988/1989.* Paris: Organisation for Economic Co-operation and Development.

—— (1989b). *Economic Surveys: Netherlands 1988/1989.* Paris: Organisation for Economic Co-operation and Development.

—— (1997). *OECD Economic Outlook No. 62.* Paris: Organisation for Economic Co-operation and Development.

Olson, M. (1971). *The Logic of Collective Action: Public Goods and the Theory of Groups.* Cambridge, MA: Harvard University Press.

—— (1988). 'The Productivity Slowdown, the Oil Shocks, and the Real Cycle.' *Journal of Economic Perspectives* 2:4, pp. 43–69.

Olsson, U., B. Rothstein, and U. Strandberg (2003). 'Special Section: Small States in the World of Markets.' *New Political Economy* 8:1, pp. 3–7.

Pelkmans, J. (1987). 'The New Approach to Technical Harmonisation and Standardisation.' *Journal of Common Market Studies* 25:3, pp. 249–69.

—— and R. Beuter (1987). 'Standardization and Competitiveness: Private and Public Strategies in the EC Color TV Industry.' In H. Landis Gabel, ed. *Product Standardisation and Competitive Strategy.* North-Holland: Elsevier Science Publishers, pp. 171–215.

# References

Pellikaan, H., T. van der Meer, and S. L. de Lange (2003). 'The Road from a Depoliticized to a Centrifugal Democracy.' *Acta Politica* 38:1, pp. 23–49.

—— S. L. de Lange, and T. van der Meer (2007). 'Fortuyn's Legacy: Party System Change in the Netherlands.' *Comparative European Politics* 5:3, pp. 282–302.

Peters, P. J. L. M. (1978). 'De kernvraag blijft: in welke mate neo-keynsiaans, in welke mate neo-klassiek?' In W. Driehuis and A. van der Zwan, eds. *De voorbereiding van het economische beleid kritisch bezien*. Leiden: H. E. Stenfert Kroese, pp. 74–82.

Price, R. W. R. and P. Muller (1984). 'Structural Budget Indicators and the Interpretation of Fiscal Policy Stance in OECD Economies.' *OECD Economic Studies* 3, pp. 27–72.

Quaden, G. (1984). *La crise des finances publiques*. Liége: Ciriec.

—— ed. (1987). *L'économie belge dans la crise*. Brussels: Editions LABOUR.

Reich, S. (1990). *The Fruits of Fascism: Postwar Posterity in Historical Perspective*. Ithaca: Cornell University Press.

Rieke, W. (1988). 'Comment.' In F. Giavazzi, S. Micossi, and M. Miller, eds. *The European Monetary System*. Cambridge: Cambridge University Press, pp. 288–91.

Rokkan, S. (1977). 'Towards a Generalized Concept of Verzuiling: A Preliminary Note.' *World Politics* 25:4, pp. 563–70.

Rose, A. (1999). 'Extraordinary Politics in the Polish Transition.' *Communist and Post-Communist Studies* 25:4, pp. 41–67.

Rudd, C. (1986). 'Coalition Formation and Maintenance in Belgium: A Case Study of Elite Behaviour and Changing Cleavage Structure, 1965–1981.' In G. Pridham, ed. *Coalitional Behaviour in Theory and Practice*. Cambridge: Cambridge University Press, pp. 117–44.

Salverda, W. (2005). 'The Dutch Model: Magic in a Flat Landscape?' In U. Becker and H. Schwartz, eds. *Employment 'Miracles': A Critical Comparison of the Dutch, Scandinavian, Swiss, Australian and Irish Cases versus Germany and the U.S*. Amsterdam: Amsterdam University Press, pp. 39–63.

Sapir, A. (1992). 'Regional Integration in Europe.' *The Economic Journal* 102:45, pp. 1491–506.

Sbragia, A., ed. (1992). *Europolitics: Institutions and Policymaking in the 'New' European Community*. Washington, DC: Brookings Institution.

# References

Scharpf, F. W. and V. A. Schmidt, eds. (2000a). *Welfare and Work in an Open Economy, Volume 1: From Vulnerability to Competitiveness*. Oxford: Oxford University Press.

—— (2000b). *Welfare and Work in an Open Economy, Volume 2: Diverse Responses to Common Challenges*. Oxford: Oxford University Press.

Schmidt, V. A. (2002). *The Futures of European Capitalism*. Oxford: Oxford University Press.

Schmitter, P. C. (1974). 'Still the Century of Corporatism?' In F. B. Pike and T. Stritch, eds. *The New Corporatism: Socio-Political Structures in the Iberian World*. Notre Dame: University of Notre Dame Press, pp. 85–131.

—— (1981). 'Interest Intermediation and Regime Governability in Contemporary Western Europe and North America.' In S. Berger, ed. *Organising Interests in Western Europe: Pluralism, Corporatism and the Transformation of Politics*. Cambridge: Cambridge University Press, pp. 237–85.

—— (1982). 'Reflections on Where the Theory of Neo-Corporatism Has Gone and Where the Praxis of Neo-Corporatism May Be Going.' In G. Lehmbruch and P. C. Schmitter, eds. *Patterns of Corporatist Policy-making*. London: Sage, pp. 259–79.

—— (1985). 'Neo-Corporatism and the State.' In W. Grant, ed. *The Political Economy of Corporatism*. London: MacMillan, pp. 32–62.

—— (1986). 'Democratic Theory and Neo-Corporatist Practice.' In W. Maihofer, ed. *Noi si mura: Selected Working Papers of the European University Institute*. Florence: European University Institute, pp. 158–88.

—— (1989). 'Corporatism is Dead! Long Live Corporatism.' *Government and Opposition* 24:1, pp. 54–73.

Scholten, I. (1987). 'Introduction: Corporatist and Consociational Arrangements.' In I. Scholten, ed. *Political Stability and Neo-Corporatism: Corporatist Integration and Societal Cleavages in Western Europe*. London: Sage, pp. 120–52.

Schwartz, H. (1994). 'Small States in Big Trouble: State Reorganization in Australia, Denmark, New Zealand, and Sweden in the 1980s.' *World Politics* 46:4, pp. 527–55.

SER (1997). 'Ruud Lubbers en de hete adem van een nooit voorgelezen regeringsverklaring.' *SER Bulletin* 12 (December).

Silj, A. (1967). 'Europe's Political Puzzle: A Study of the Fouchet Negotiations and the 1963 Veto.' *Occasional Papers in International Affairs no. 17*. Cambridge: Harvard Centre for International Affairs.

# References

Smith, A. D. (1992). 'National Identity and the Idea of European Unity.' *International Affairs* 68:1, pp. 55–76.

Smits, J. (1983). 'Belgian Politics in 1982: Less Democracy for a Better Economy.' *Res Publica* 25:2–3, pp. 181–217.

—— (1984). 'Belgian Politics in 1983: Communitarian Struggles Despite the Economic Crisis.' *Res Publica* 26:4, pp. 473–5.

—— (1986). 'Belgian Politics in 1985: "No Turning Back".' *Res Publica* 28:3, pp. 441–74.

Snyder, W. (1969). 'Measuring the Effects of Belgian Budget Policies.' *Cahiers économiques de Bruxelles* 44, pp. 527–48.

Söderström, H. T. (1986). 'Exchange Rate Strategies and Real Adjustment after 1970: The Experience of Smaller European Economies.' *SNS Occasional Paper*. Stockholm: Centre for Business and Policy Studies.

Spinelli, A. (1960). *Europa non cade dal cielo*. Bologna: Il Mulino.

—— (1965). *Rapporto sull'Europa*. Milano: Edizioni di Communità.

Steiner, J. and T. Ertman, eds. (2002). 'Consociationalism and Corporatism in Western Europe: Still the Politics of Accommodation?' *Acta Politica* 37:1/2.

Steinherr, A. (1974). 'Is There an Explanation for the Current Inflation.' *Recherches économiques de Louvain* 40:2, pp. 117–38.

Strange, S. (1997). *Casino Capitalism*. Manchester: Manchester University Press.

Strayer, J. R. (1970). *On the Medieval Origins of the Modern State*. Princeton: Princeton University Press.

Streeck, W. (1992). *Social Institutions and Economic Performance: Studies of Industrial Relations in Advanced Capitalist Economies*. London: Sage.

—— and P. C. Schmitter (1991). 'From National Corporatism to Transnational Pluralism: Organized Interests in the Single European Market.' *Politics and Society* 19:2, pp. 133–65.

Stuurman, S. (1983). *Verzuiling, kapitalisme en patriarchaat: Aspecten van de ontwikkeling van de moderne staat in Nederland*. Nijmegen: Socialistische Uitgeverij Nijmegen.

Summers, L. H. (1987). 'Comments.' *European Economic Review* 31:3, pp. 606–14.

Swank, D. (2002). *Global Capital, Political Institutions, and Policy Change in Developed Welfare States*. Cambridge: Cambridge University Press.

Swann, D. (1988). *The Economics of the Common Market*, Sixth Edition. London: Penguin Books.

## References

TALENT (1969). 'La crise des paiements dans le marché commun.' *Cahiers économiques de Bruxelles* 44, pp. 457–525.

Therborn, G. (1986). *Why Some Peoples Are More Unemployed Than Others.* London: Verso.

Thygesen, N. (1979). 'Exchange Rate Experiences and Policies of Small Countries: Some European Examples of the 1970s.' *Essays in International Finance No. 136.* Princeton: Princeton University Press.

Timmermans, A. (2003). *High Politics in the Low Countries: An Empirical Study of Coalition Agreements in Belgium and the Netherlands.* Ashgate: Aldershot.

—— and W. E. Bakkema (1989). 'Conflicten in Nederlandse kabinetten.' In R. B. Andeweg, ed. *Ministers en Ministerraad.* s' Gravenhage: Velotekst, pp. 175–92.

Toirkins, S. J. (1989). 'De Minister van Financiën: In het spanningsveld van financiële wensen en mogelijkheden.' In R. B. Andeweg, ed. *Ministers en Ministerraad.* s' Gravenhage: Velotekst, pp. 127–45.

Tollet, R. (1987). 'Travail et chômage.' In G. Quaden, ed. *L'économie belge dans la crise.* Brussels: Editions LABOUR, pp. 79–130.

*Treaties Establishing the European Communities: Abridged Edition* (1987). Luxembourg: European Community.

Tromp, B. (1989). 'Party Strategies and System Change in the Netherlands.' *West European Politics* 12:4, pp. 82–97.

Vaes, B. and C. Demelenne (1995). *Le cas Happart: La tentation nationaliste.* Brussels: Editions Luc Pire.

Van Ark, B. et al. (1994). 'Characteristics of Economic Growth in the Netherlands During the Post-War Period.' *CEPR Discussion Papers No. 932.* London: Centre for Economic Policy Research.

Van den Brande, A. (1987). 'Neo-Corporatism and Functional-Integral Power in Belgium.' In I. Scholten, ed. *Political Stability and Neo-Corporatism: Corporatist Integration and Societal Cleavages in Western Europe.* London: Sage, pp. 95–119.

Van der Brug, W. (2003). 'How the LPF Fuelled Discontent: Empirical Tests of Explanations of LPF Support.' *Acta Politica* 38:1, pp. 89–106.

—— (2004). 'Voting for the LPF: Some Clarifications.' *Acta Politica* 39:1, pp. 84–91.

Van der Laan, H. (1977). 'Over de sectorale differentiatie van de reële arbeidskostenontwikkelingen.' *Economisch Statistische Berichten* 62:3129, pp. 1105–10.

# References

Van der Ploeg, F. (1987). 'Trade Unions, Investment and Employment: A Non-Co-operative Approach.' *European Economic Review* 31:7, pp. 1465–72.

Van der Zee, H. (1989). *De Hongerwinter: Van Dolle Dinsdag tot Bevrijding.* The Hague: Uitgeverij BZZTÔH.

Van Doorn, K. et al. (1976). *De beheerste vakbeweging: Het NVV tussen loonpolitiek en loonstrijd, 1959–1973.* Amsterdam: Van Gennep.

Van Hecke, J. (1994). *De Slogans Voorbij: Appèl aan de Verantwoordlijke Vlaming.* Tielt: Lannoo.

Van Rijckeghem, W. (1982). 'Benelux.' In A. Boltho, ed. *The European Economy: Growth and Crisis.* Oxford: Oxford University Press, pp. 581–609.

Van Roon, G. (1989). *Small States in Years of Depression: The Oslo Alliance 1930–1940.* Maastricht: Van Gorcum.

Van Waarden, F. (2002). 'Dutch Consociationalism and Corporatism: A Case of Institutional Persistence.' *Acta Politica* 37, pp. 44–67.

Van Ypersele, J. (1981). 'La politique économique belge.' *Recherches économiques de Louvain* 47:1, pp. 39–54.

Van Zanden, J. L. (1998). *The Economic History of the Netherlands, 1914–1995: A Small Open Economy in the 'Long' Twentieth Century.* London: Routledge.

Vandenbroucke, F. (1981). *Van crisis tot crisis: Een socialistisch alternatief.* Leuven: Kritak.

Vandeputte, R. (1978). 'België in het internationaal monetaire stelsel.' In O. de Raeymaeker, ed. *Belgische buitenlandse en internationale betrekkingen.* Leuven: Leuven University Press, pp. 653–60.

—— (1985). *Economische geschiedenis van België 1944–1984.* Tielt: Lannoo.

—— (1987). *Sociale gescheidenis van België 1944–1985.* Tielt: Lannoo.

Vanderstraeten, A. (1986). 'Neo-corporatisme en het Belgische sociaal-economisch overlegsysteem.' *Res Publica* 18:4, pp. 671–88.

Visser, A. (1986). *Alleen bij uiterste noodzaak?: De rooms-rode samenwerking en het einde van de brede basis 1948–1958.* Amsterdam: Uitgeverij Bert Bakker.

Visser, J. and A. Hemerijck (1997). *'A Dutch Miracle': Job Growth, Welfare Reform and Corporatism in the Netherlands.* Amsterdam: Amsterdam University Press.

Visser, W. and R. Wijnhoven (1990). 'Politics Do Matter, But Does Unemployment?' *European Journal of Political Research* 18, pp. 71–96.

# References

Von Mises, L. (1983). *Nation, State and Economy: Contributions to the Politics and History of Our Time*. Translated by Leland B. Yeager. New York: New York University Press.

Wadhwani, S. (1989). 'Incomes Policies: The British Experience.' In V. L. Urquidi, ed. *Incomes Policies*. New York: St Martin's Press, pp. 111–35.

Waelbroeck, J. (1987). 'Comments.' *European Economic Review* 31:3, pp. 602–5.

Weber, M. (1947). *The Theory of Social and Economic Organization*. Translated by A. M. Henderson and Talcott Parsons. Edited by Talcott Parsons. New York: Oxford University Press.

Wellink, A. H. E. M. (1987). 'De ontwikkelingen in de jaren zeventig en tachtig en enkele daaruit te trekken lessen.' *Reprint 201*. Amsterdam: De Nederlandische Bank.

Wijkman, P. M. (1990). 'Patterns of Trade and Production in Western Europe: Looking Forward After Thirty Years.' *EFTA Occasional Papers, 32*. Geneva: EFTA.

——(1992). 'The European Free Trade Area Expanded?: The European Community, EFTA and Eastern Europe.' *EFTA Occasional Papers, 43*. Geneva: EFTA.

Wilson, W. (1981). *Congressional Government: A Study in American Politics*. Baltimore: Johns Hopkins University Press.

Witte, E. (1990a). 'Tussen restauratie en vernieuwing (1944–1950).' In E. Witte et al., eds. *Politieke geschiedenis van België: Van 1830 tot heden*. Brussels: VUB Press, pp. 227–56.

——(1990b). 'Conflicten en conflictbeheersing in de levensbeschouwelijke sfeer.' In E. Witte et al., eds. *Politieke geschiedenis van België: Van 1830 tot heden*. Brussels: VUB Press, pp. 257–78.

Woldendorp, J. (2005). *The Polder Model: From Disease to Miracle? Dutch Neo-Corporatism, 1965–2000*. Amsterdam: Thela Thesis.

Wolinetz, S. B. (1988). 'The Netherlands: Continuity and Change in a Fragmented Party System.' In S. B. Wolinetz, ed. *Systems in Liberal Democracies*. London: Routledge, pp. 130–58.

——(1989). 'Socio-Economic Bargaining in the Netherlands: Redefining the Post-War Policy Coalition.' *West European Politics* 12:1, pp. 79–98.

——(1990). 'The Dutch Elections of 1989: Return to the Centre-Left.' *West European Politics* 13:2, pp. 280–6.

# References

Wolinetz, S.B. (1990). 'The Dutch Elections of 1989: Return to the Centre-Left.' *West European Politics* 13:2, pp. 280–6.

Woolley, J. T. (1992). 'Policy Credibility and European Monetary Institutions.' In A. Sbragia, ed. *Europolitics: Institutions and Policymaking in the 'New' European Community*. Washington, DC: Brookings Institution, pp. 157–90.

Zijlstra, J. (1979). 'Monetary Theory and Monetary Policy: A Central Banker's View.' *De Economist* 127:1, pp. 3–20.

# Index

Albania 33
Austria 29–30, 37
Alesina, Alberto 31–32, 223
Andriessen, Frans 175
Ansiaux, Hubert 136
Austria 156

Balkenende, Jan Peter 221
Baudouin 121
Beel, L. J. M. 88, 90
Belgian National Bank 117–119, 130, 135–136, 187
 attitude toward inflation 118–119, 135, 150
 nationalization 117
Benelux 39, 43, 83–84, 95
Beveridge curve 226 n. 30, 241 n. 18
Beyen, J. W. 96, 235 n. 50
Board of Government Mediators (NL) 83–84, 98, 103, 231 n. 5
Bretton Woods System 12, 16, 23, 106, 119, 134, 139–142, 144–145, 157, 167
Brugmans, Hendrik (Henri) 70
Bundesbank 96, 106, 144–145, 150
Byatt, Dominic xvi

Calleo, David P. xvi
Cals, J. M. L. T. 107, 109
Cameron, David 7–8
capital controls 17, 240 n. 3
Cawson, Alan 63
Central Planning Bureau (NL) 98, 147–148, 191
Central Statistics Bureau (NL) 102
Christian Democrats 22, 87, 108
 fusion (NL) 173, 175
 de-confessionalization 108, 159
 loss of power 25, 218–219
 regional division (B) 135, 219–220

Churchill, Winston 68
Communism 27–28
 collapse in 1989 27
Communists 22, 92
competitiveness 11, 84, 181–183, 202, 207, 211
consociational democracy 1, 6, 21–22, 30, 74, 221–223
 Belgium 116–118, 133–134, 172
 breakdown 79, 135, 138, 167
 Netherlands 85–87, 93, 108
 political renewal 108, 158–159, 207, 225 n. 6
 populist challengers 204–206, 224
 relationship with corporatism 94
corporatism 29–30, 33, 36, 77, 167, 185
 Belgium 115, 130–132, 187–188
 defection 56, 103
 definition 50, 62
 historical association with fascism 61, 67, 86, 230 n. 69
 Netherlands 87, 189–190
 political representation 62–63
 typical example 54–55
 willingness to cooperate 51, 153, 186
Cool, August 137
Cools, André 136

Daalder, Hans 232 n. 10
Debunne, Georges 137
De Clerq, Willy 172, 247 n. 63
Dedecker, Jean-Marie 219
de Gaulle, Charles 69, 103, 125
Dehaene, Jean-Luc 205, 210–211, 218
Delcoigne, Georges xvi
delegation 65–66
 *see also,* legitimacy, sovereignty
De Neubourg, C. 186
De Ridder, Hugo 188

273

# Index

Den Uyl, Joop 154, 159, 173, 243 n. 50
Den Dunnen, Emile 97, 236 n. 83
Den Hartog, H. 147–149
Denmark 29–30, 145, 194
  Maastricht Treaty veto 47
depillarization xiv, 167
Detremmerie, Hubert 187, 244 n. 13
Dewinter, Filip 204
Drees, Willem 88–90, 93, 109–110, 141, 233 n. 24
Duisenberg, Wim 189
Dutch National Bank 96–98, 189
  attitude toward inflation 96, 150
  credit restrictions 105–106
  liquidity ratio 97, 105
Dutch Peoples Party 87
Duvieusart, Jean 121

EC 37, 39, 102, 127
  1992 program 40, 42, 45
  empty chair 46, 104
  Luxembourg compromise 70
  Rome Treaty 39, 46, 102, 125–126
  Single European Act 44
ECSC 44, 68–69, 96, 112–113, 123–124
  Paris Treaty 44, 46, 125–126
  Schuman Plan 118
economies of scale 31
ECU 193
EDC 46, 68–69, 96, 230 n. 72
EEA 39, 46, 71
EEC, *see* EC
EFTA 37, 40, 43
  enlargement of EU to include 38, 46, 71
elections 204–206
  Belgium 122, 133–134, 154, 199, 210, 238 n. 122
  Netherlands 9, 89, 108, 173–174, 199, 220, 235–236 n. 68
EMS 34, 163, 191–198, 247–248 n. 64
  support for fiscal austerity 197
  *see also*, exchange rates
employers' associations 53, 189
  defection from centralized bargaining 56
end of ideology *see* value change
EPC 96
ERM, *see* EMS
EU 38
  Constitutional Treaty 45, 47, 221, 228 n. 27
  Maastricht Treaty 44, 47

Eurobarometer 169, 199
exchange rates 195
  floating 106
  hard currency policy 17, 33–34, 141, 145, 194–195
  pegging 17, 34, 140–145, 157, 167
  real exchange rates 245–246 n. 41
  realignments 106, 135–136, 151, 170, 194, 196–197, 242 n. 30, 247 n. 63
  'snake' mechanism 141, 145, 151, 192, 241 n. 11, 246 n. 56
export-led growth 19, 184
Eyskens, Gaston 118, 120–121, 125, 128–129, 148, 170, 238 n. 115
Eyskens, Mark 170–171, 187, 244 n. 15

Faxèn, Karl-Olaf 228 n. 46
federalists 69
fiscal policy 35, 151–152, 176, 211, 238 n. 130
  EMS support 197
  Netherlands 154, 162, 175
Flemish Bloc/Flemish Interest 2, 204–205
Fortuyn, Pim 2, 9–10, 220
  anti-consensus rhetoric 10
Foundation of Labour (NL) 83–84, 91, 93, 98–99, 231 n. 4, 234 n. 37
Fouchet Plan 47, 69, 102–103
France 21, 29, 31, 39, 45, 145, 194
free trade 33–35, 191
  difference with regional integration 36–37
  preferential trading relations 39, 46
  protectionism 95
Frère, Maurice 237 n. 107
full employment 99, 104, 144, 153

Galbraith, John Kenneth 75
GATT 44
Germany 17–18, 20–21, 29, 37, 39, 45, 47, 201
  corporatism 6, 86
  fiscal policy 152
  interest rate differentials with 18, 151, 211, 216
  *see also*, Bundesbank
globalization 30–32, 224
Gol, Jean 172
Gourevitch, Peter 77
Grant, Wyn 58
Great Britain, *see* United Kingdom
Griffiths, Richard 242 n. 27

274

# Index

Grootjans, Frans 171
Gros, Daniel xvi

Haas, Ernst 69
Hall, Peter 74
Happart, José 204
Heywood, Paul xvi
Hemerijck, Anton 8, 248 n. 2
Hofstra, Hendrick 97
holding companies (B) 113, 115
Holtrop, Marius 97, 235 n. 55
Houthuys, Jef 137, 187–188
Hume, David 75
Huyse, Luc 205

ideology 23
income distribution 92, 105, 116, 198–204
  convergence/divergence 126
  regional balance (B) 128–129, 138, 203
inflation 142–143, 194
interdependence 76
Ireland 47, 194
Inglehart, Ronald 20
  *The Silent Revolution* 20, 23
Italy 39, 194

Japan 41–42
JET 170, 187

Katzenstein, Peter J. xvi, 7–10, 26, 28–29, 32, 226 n. 16, 231 n. 93
  meaning of small 29
  *Small States and World Markets* 8–9, 12, 28
Kervijn, Albert 162, 243 n. 51
Keynes, John Maynard 67, 83, 166
  Keynesian economics 24, 100, 119, 125
  neo-Keynesianism 149–150
Kindleberger, Charles 111
Kleinknecht, Alfred 210
Korean War 122
Kok, Wim 188, 190, 198, 236 n. 90
Kurzer, Paulette xvi, 4, 156–157, 161

Lefèvre, Theo 128
Leopold III 118, 120–121
  referendum on return 120, 238 n. 117
legitimacy 66–68, 72–73
  EU membership 71
  perceptions 72
Leysen, Vaast 171

Liberals 22
  Belgium 132–133, 205
  Netherlands 89
Lieftinck, Pieter 83, 96–97, 99, 109, 235 n. 55, 235 n. 65
Lijphart, Arend 3, 6–8, 227 n. 36, 232 n. 10
Lippmann, Walter 67, 74
Lipset, Seymour Martin 86, 236–237 n. 91
Lubbers, Ruud 19, 24–25, 78–79, 164, 166–167, 174–175, 190, 198–201, 205, 210
Luns, Joseph 102, 235 n. 50

macroeconomic policy, *see* fiscal policy, monetary policy
Madison, James 21, 227 n. 35
Mair, Peter 3
Major, Louis 115, 128–129, 137
Marijnissen, Jan 220
Maritain, Jacques 92, 229 n. 64
Martens, Wilfried 19, 24–25, 78–79, 164, 166–167, 169, 198–201, 205, 210, 244 n. 16
  coalition formation 170–171
McCarthy, Patrick xvi
Milward, Alan 111, 125
monetary policy 35
  *see also*, Belgian National Bank, Bundesbank, Dutch National Bank
Monnet, Jean 43, 230 n. 73, 243 n. 51
Moses, Jonathon xvi
Myrdal, Gunnar xiv

NAFTA 43
neofunctionalism 69–70
neoliberalism 5, 157
new left 108–109, 159
Nixon, Richard 144
Nothomb, Charles-Ferdinand 171–172

OECD 16–17, 143
oil price shock 16, 18, 23, 139, 143
*ontzuiling*, *see* "depillarization"
Oslo Alliance 37, 47, 227 n. 8

Pen, J. 229 n. 53
Philips 147
pillarization xiv, 22–23, 227 n. 37, 232 n. 10, 232 n. 12
pluralism 1–2, 21, 74, 139, 223
Poland 45
postmaterialism, *see* value change

275

# Index

price-incomes policy 1, 4, 49, 62, 176, 183–184, 186
   Belgium 114, 127
   employment effects 203–204
   indexation 17, 147, 169
   Netherlands 98, 100, 102–103, 110
   price-wage spiral 18, 143–145
   statutory 49–50
   wage explosions 13
   *see also*, corporatism, inflation

Reagan, Ronald 2, 5, 164
regional integration 33, 36, 77, 167
   benefits 38–41
   costs 41–45
   Dutch approach 84, 95, 102
   influence 45–47
   steps 38
   supranational 44
Reich, Simon 230 n. 69
Renard, André 114–115, 121, 123, 126–129, 237 n. 96
right-wing extremism 2
Romme, C. P. M. 87, 90
Ruding, Onno 197
rules of origin 40

Scandinavia 30–33, 37
Schmelzer, W. K. N. 107–109
Schermerhorn, Willem 87, 233 n. 24
Schmitter, Philippe 58, 62–63, 67, 229 n. 57
Scholten, Ilja 174
School Conflict (B) 121–122, 126, 132
Schuman, Robert 43, 230 n. 73
Schwartz, Herman 8
Segers, P. W. 171
small state model 29–32, 223
   homogeneity 30–32
   *see also* Katzenstein, Peter
Snoy et d'Oppeurs, Jean-Charles 136
Social and Economic Council (NL) 91, 99–100, 103, 110, 147, 210, 229 n. 53, 234 n. 33, 234 n. 37
Socialists 22
   PvdA (NL) 87–89, 101
sovereignty 70–71
   autonomy 64
   definition 65, 229 n. 61, 229 n. 64
   delegation 65
   intermediate 63
Soviet Union 27
Spaak, Paul Henri 128–129

Spain 45
Spinelli, Altiero 69
Spolaore, Enrico 31, 223
Steiner, Jurg xvi
Stikker, D. U. 95, 235 n. 50
Stuurman, Siep 232 n. 12
Sweden 2, 29, 156
   defection from centralized bargaining 56, 228 n. 46
   snuff debate 41
Switzerland 30, 33, 37

Thatcher, Margaret 5, 164
Therborn, Göran 156–157, 161
Tindemans, Leo 154, 159, 171–172
Tjan, H. S. 147–149
trade unions 14
   Belgium 114, 116, 123, 129–131, 136, 169
   centralization 52, 136
   conflict with government 145, 159–160
   insiders and outsiders 52, 157–158, 161, 190, 226 n. 27
   membership 160–161
   Netherlands 88, 101, 110
   peak bargaining 52, 187–188
   strikes 84, 88, 100, 103, 126–128, 131, 136–137
   unemployment 12
Tromp, Bart 108
Turkey 30

unemployment 12, 91, 146–150, 184–185
   structural 15, 149
   technical 18
   *see also*, corporatism, price-incomes policy
United Kingdom 21, 29, 45, 47, 50, 145, 201
   application to join the EC 103
   Commonwealth 37
United States 1–2, 17, 21, 37, 41–42, 47, 50, 68, 111, 223

value change 11, 20, 23, 133, 155, 236 n. 91
   postmaterialism 20, 158
   *see also*, new left
van Acker, Achille 123, 238 n. 116
van Agt, Dries 162, 173–174
van den Brande, A. 188
van den Brink, J. R. M. 235 n. 65
Vandeputte, Robert 237 n. 111
van der Goes van Naters, M. 233 n. 25
van Houte, Jean 123
van Mierlo, Hans 204

# Index

van Schaik, J. R. H. 90
van Veen, Chris 189–190, 198
varieties of capitalism 225
Verhofstadt, Guy 204–205
Verplaetse, Fons 187
*verzuiling,* see pillarization
*Vlaams Blok/Vlaams Belang, see* Flemish Block/Flemish Interest
voluntary industrial standards 40, 42
von Mises, Ludwig 75

Wassenaar Accords 189, 248–249 n. 2
Weber, Max 65, 75

welfare states 7, 15
  competitiveness 11, 154–155
  consociational structure 94, 133, 160, 243 n. 47
  Netherlands 93, 106–107
  unemployment 12
welfare chauvinism 2
Wellink, Nout 162
Wilder, Geert 219
Woldendorp, Jaap 248–249 n. 2
Wolinetz, Steven xvi, 110, 189

Yugoslavia 27